THE LOST INDICTMENT
OF ROBERT E. LEE

THE LOST INDICTMENT OF ROBERT E. LEE

The Forgotten Case against an American Icon

John Reeves

ROWMAN & LITTLEFIELD
Lanham • Boulder • New York • London

Published by Rowman & Littlefield
An imprint of The Rowman & Littlefield Publishing Group, Inc.
4501 Forbes Boulevard, Suite 200, Lanham, Maryland 20706
www.rowman.com

Unit A, Whitacre Mews, 26–34 Stannary Street, London SE11 4AB

Distributed by NATIONAL BOOK NETWORK

British Library Cataloguing in Publication Information Available

Library of Congress Cataloging-in-Publication Data Available

ISBN: 978-1-5381-1039-3 (cloth : alk. paper)
ISBN: 978-1-5381-1040-9 (electronic)

♾ ™ The paper used in this publication meets the minimum requirements of American National Standard for Information Sciences—Permanence of Paper for Printed Library Materials, ANSI/NISO Z39.48-1992.

Printed in the United States of America

Shall we permit the indictment to go forth to the world and to posterity without vindication of our motives and our conduct? Are we willing that our enemies shall be historians of our cause and our struggle? No! A thousand times no! —Jubal Early

I am not disposed to speak of General Lee. It is enough to say that he stands high on the catalogue of those who have imbrued their hands in their country's blood. I hand him over to the avenging pen of History. —Charles Sumner

The gentleman does not needlessly and unnecessarily remind an offender of a wrong he may have committed against him. He can not only forgive, he can forget; and he strives for that nobleness of self and mildness of character which imparts sufficient strength to let the past be but the past. —Robert E. Lee

CONTENTS

ACKNOWLEDGMENTS

Winston Churchill reportedly said of the Labour Party leader Clement Attlee, "Mr. Attlee is a very modest man. Indeed he has a lot to be modest about." Similarly, writing this book has made me extremely aware of my own modest abilities.

Fortunately, I've been able to benefit from some truly outstanding historians who have written on the Civil War. I am especially indebted to: David Blight, John Fabian Witt, Elizabeth Varon, Martha Hodes, Jonathan White, Brooks Simpson, William Blair, and Richard Lowe. I've been inspired by their high standards of excellence in my own writing.

I'm also very grateful for the exceptional work of the various Lee biographers. In particular, I found the insights of Thomas Connelly, Emory Thomas, Alan Nolan, Elizabeth Brown Pryor, and Douglas Southall Freeman to be invaluable.

Some of my happiest moments have been spent poring over old documents in a wide variety of libraries. I'd like to thank the librarians and archivists from the Library of Congress, Library of Virginia, National Archives, and Washington and Lee University. I'm in awe of their dedication to the historical craft. I'm especially thankful to Matthew Penrod of the National Park Service. His thoughts on Lee were tremendously helpful.

I got the idea for this book while working as an editor for *The Motley Fool*. I'm forever grateful to my former employer for providing me with a sabbatical that allowed me to devote precious time to this project—one that was completely unrelated to my day-to-day work responsibilities at the time, I should add—while it was still in its nascent stages. Those crucial eight weeks gave me the confidence to eventually devote myself completely to the book.

I also received early encouragement from John Wright of the John W. Wright Literary Agency. His belief in the project strengthened my determination to pursue it further. I'm very thankful for his wise advice along the way.

I've been extremely lucky to have several thoughtful readers of the manuscript. My former colleague, Abbie Redmon, provided essential editorial guidance on the early chapters. And my good friend—and English teacher—Andy Leddy provided thoughtful feedback throughout the entire writing process. Finally, Chris Solimine has generously devoted countless hours to helping me improve the narrative. As a successful screenwriter, he's an accomplished storyteller who offered a fresh perspective on the subject. Over the course of numerous conversations, he patiently tried to explain what worked and what didn't.

My two children, Maxim and Sophie, provided the necessary moral support for completing the book. They cheerfully listened to my accounts of the latest discoveries and never complained about dad always being upstairs in his office. I look forward to reading their own books someday. I should also acknowledge our dog, Ozzy, who has literally been at my feet during the entire writing process. Like Emily Dickinson's dog, Ozzy may know, but doesn't tell.

Finally, I'd like to thank my wife, Justine Kalas Reeves. There is no way this book could have ever been written without her love and encouragement. It mustn't have been easy when I floated the idea of leaving a well-paying job to write a book about the legal issues facing Robert E. Lee. Yet, Justine believed in the idea all along and has done everything in her power to support me throughout the writing of this book. In the Pixar movie *Ratatouille*, the food critic said, "The world is often unkind to new talent, new creations. The new needs friends." Justine has been this project's best friend.

INTRODUCTION

Reevaluating Robert E. Lee

A nation that does not know its history and heed its history has lost itself. Unless you know where you came from you do not know where you are going to.

—Woodrow Wilson

Until recently, history had been kind to Robert E. Lee. Woodrow Wilson believed General Lee was a "model to men who would be morally great."[1] Douglas Southall Freeman, who won a Pulitzer Prize for his four-volume biography of Lee, described his subject as "one of a small company of great men in whom there is no inconsistency to be explained, no enigma to be solved."[2] Winston Churchill called him "one of the noblest Americans who ever lived."[3] For well over a century, we celebrated Lee's memory across America. Monuments were raised in his honor, and schools were named after him. There was even a stained-glass window devoted to Lee's life at the National Cathedral in Washington, DC, though it was removed shortly after the protests in Charlottesville, Virginia, in 2017.

Immediately after the Civil War, however, many northerners believed Lee should be hanged for treason and war crimes. Americans might be surprised to learn that in June 1865 a Norfolk, Virginia, grand jury indicted Robert E. Lee for treason. In his instructions to the grand jury, Judge John C. Underwood described treason as "wholesale murder," and declared that the instigators of the rebellion had "hands dripping with the blood of slaughtered innocents."[4]

In early 1866, Lee decided against visiting friends while in Washington, DC, for a congressional hearing, because he was conscious of being perceived as a "monster" by citizens of the nation's capital. Yet inexplicably, roughly fifty years after that trip to Washington, Lee had been transformed into a venerable American hero, who was highly regarded by southerners *and* northerners alike. Almost a century after Appomattox, Dwight D. Eisenhower had Lee's portrait on the wall of his White House office. By 1975, President Gerald Ford eagerly pardoned General Lee, thereby correcting what was believed to be a "110-year oversight of American history."[5]

Blessed with good looks and noble forebears, Robert E. Lee graduated second in his class at West Point and later earned laurels during the Mexican War. On the eve of the Civil War, he was offered the command of the Union Army. Famously, he turned it down and chose to serve the cause of the Confederate States of America. During his inspirational leadership of the Army of Northern Virginia from June 1862 to April 1865, Lee gained the everlasting devotion of his fellow southerners. His favorite lieutenant, General "Stonewall" Jackson, said of him, "General Lee is a phenomenon. I would follow him blindfold."[6] In the decades after his death in 1870, a Lee cult emerged, which eventually took hold in the North by the early twentieth century. Lee remained an extremely popular figure until a few years ago. After the Charleston church shooting in 2015, critics began challenging the Lee myth.

This book tells the story of the forgotten legal and moral case that was made against the Confederate general in the days after the Civil War. The actual treason indictment of Lee went missing for seventy-two years, and many scholars remain unaware it has been found. For 150 years, the indictment against Lee after the war had also figuratively "disappeared" from our national consciousness. By examining the evolving case against him from 1865 to 1870 and beyond, we will better understand the history Americans tried to forget.

★   ★   ★

Pardoning Robert E. Lee for treason in 1975, 110 years after his surrender at Appomattox, proved to be extremely easy. The Lee cult was in full blossom by that time. Most Americans would have found it difficult to believe he hadn't been forgiven already. In April 1975, the US Senate unanimously passed a resolution posthumously restoring full rights of citizenship to General Lee. In July, the House of Representatives approved the legislation by an overwhelming vote of 407 to 10. President Ford then gladly signed the bill in August at a ceremony on the grounds of Lee's former estate at Arlington,

Virginia. The press seemed universally supportive of the move as well. Capturing the positive mood at the time, Lee's great-grandson, Robert E. Lee IV, said "it's an excellent thing for Congress to do, particularly at this time of our Bicentennial."[7]

The chain of events leading to the pardon of Lee resulted from an unexpected discovery of a lost amnesty oath in 1970 at the National Archives. This oath, which had been required to accompany Lee's amnesty application from June 1865, had been misfiled by the State Department at a later date, according to the archivist Elmer Oris Parker.[8] Lee had applied for a pardon to President Andrew Johnson in June 1865, but hadn't initially included the required oath with his application. Many historians subsequently assumed that President Johnson refused to pardon Lee because his amnesty application was incomplete.

Johnson did eventually offer a general amnesty on Christmas Day 1868 that covered Lee and other Confederate leaders who had been under indictment, but he never personally responded to the general's application. When Lee died in 1870, the only remaining disability he faced was a prohibition from holding public office under section 3 of the Fourteenth Amendment. That disability was later struck down by Congress in 1898, but Lee wasn't covered by that legislation since he was deceased.

In 1970, Elmer Parker announced what appeared to be a major breakthrough. He had "discovered" Lee's missing oath, which may have been pigeonholed in 1865. Secretary of State William Seward may have also given away Lee's original application to a friend as a souvenir. Parker believed his discovery proved Lee's amnesty oath had been "duly executed, signed, and notarized" in October 1865. For over a century, the oath had "remained buried in a file in the nation's archives."[9]

Upon detection of the lost oath, Senator Harry Byrd, from Lee's home state of Virginia, requested a pardon for Lee with the restoration of full rights of citizenship. Byrd concluded we could "safely assume that had this oath reached the hands of the President, that General Lee's citizenship would have been restored in full."[10] Only a bureaucratic snafu, it seems, could have prevented a great man like Lee from receiving a full pardon. Almost every congressman agreed Lee was an American hero who had followed his conscience during the war and had then attempted to reconcile North and South after the conflict. A member from Virginia quoted a constituent who asked "if Robert E. Lee is not worthy to be a U.S. citizen, then who is?"[11]

Americans seemed receptive to the belated action on General Lee. It had been only one year since Richard Nixon's traumatic departure from office and the nation remained bitterly divided in the immediate aftermath of the Vietnam War. Pardoning Lee was intended as a unifying gesture that might bring the country together again as it prepared to celebrate its two-hundredth birthday.

There was just one problem. Congress based its decision to pardon Lee in 1975 on inaccurate information. Andrew Johnson didn't overlook Lee's pardon application because a required oath had gone missing. He deliberately chose not to pardon Lee because the southern commander was under indictment for *treason*. In late 1865 and early 1866, Andrew Johnson, famous at the time for his vow to make treason odious, fully intended to have Lee prosecuted and punished under Article III, section 3 of the US Constitution, which stated,

> Treason against the United States, shall consist only in levying war against them, or in adhering to their enemies, giving them aid and comfort. No person shall be convicted of treason unless on the testimony of two witnesses to the same overt act, or on confession in open court.
>
> The Congress shall have power to declare the punishment of treason, but no attainder of treason shall work corruption of blood, or forfeiture except during the life of the person attainted.

Lee faced the possibility of death by hanging if convicted. Surprisingly, it was Lee's indictment for treason that went missing from American history. The story of the legal and moral case against Lee immediately after the war has mysteriously disappeared from our historical memory. The amnesty oath, on the other hand, remained—despite Parker's claim—secure and in possession of the federal government from October 1865 all the way up until the present.

★   ★   ★

During the debate on the Lee pardon resolution in 1975, Congressman John Conyers—an African American member from Michigan—challenged the validity of the "missing oath theory" as an explanation of why Lee wasn't pardoned in 1865. Believing the resolution was merely "bicentennial fluff," Conyers decided nonetheless to investigate the issue further. One of his staff members visited the National Archives and learned that the oath had actually been identified by a clerk named Donald King in 1965, who later brought it to the attention of Mr. Elmer Parker in 1970. Two archivists also told Conyers's staff member that the Lee oath had been on public display since the 1930s and that "it is the position of the Archives that the oath has always been in the

Government's custody, had never been lost, was first stored with the other amnesty documents in the State department and during World War II transferred to the National Archives where it presently resides." As a result of Conyers's investigation, the romantic missing oath theory is untenable. He tried to make this point clear during the debates, but his colleagues were so intent on eulogizing Lee they refused to listen. For the overwhelming majority of Congressmen, the "story" was far more attractive than the truth.[12]

The notion that President Andrew Johnson would have been unaware of Lee's amnesty oath is extremely unlikely, regardless of whether or not it was lost at some point. The national press published Lee's oath in October 1865 and one newspaper reported it had been successfully filed at the State Department.[13] Overall, the evidence suggests the missing oath explanation was a fanciful tale that helped Congress in 1975 "remove the last tarnish of the memory of Robert E. Lee." The reality was far more troublesome for those individuals dedicated to promoting the legacy of Lee. There was absolutely no chance at all that Andrew Johnson would have pardoned the former Confederate general in chief in 1865.

During the closing days of the war, Johnson had solemnly vowed to punish traitors, and believed General Ulysses S. Grant's terms with Lee at Appomattox were too lenient. On one occasion, Johnson told an audience that death would be "too easy a punishment" for traitors like Lee and the other Confederate leaders.[14] The *New York Times*, which led the way back then in making the case against Lee, argued that he had levied war against the United States "more strenuously than any other man in the land, and therefore has been specially guilty of the crime of treason, as defined by the Constitution of the United States."[15] The newspaper *Ohio Farmer* harshly declared, "Robert E. Lee is now so poor that he has not the wherewith to clothe himself. If this be true, let the government relieve him at once—give him ten feet of rope, and six feet of soil. If every traitor earned this reward, Lee surely is the one."[16] The *Cleveland Morning Leader* wrote that Lee had been "Judas-like" in betraying his country.[17]

Around that time, Lee's views on race and slavery were also criticized by many of his contemporaries, who objected to his attempt at portraying himself as a kind and humane slaveholder. Soon after an appearance before a committee of the US Congress in early 1866, Lee was accused in the press of ordering the whipping of several of his slaves after they had tried to run away. According to the testimony of a former slave named Wesley Norris, Lee had frequently told the overseer to "lay it on well" during a brutal assault. After the whippings, Lee allegedly ordered the overseer to wash the slaves' backs with brine.[18]

Upon the publication of this account, Lee bitterly complained to friends in private, but never defended himself publicly against the accusations. As for the treason charges, Lee believed, "Virginia, in withdrawing herself from the United States, carried me along as a citizen of Virginia, and her laws and her acts were binding on me."[19]

President Johnson saw things differently. In the immediate aftermath of the war and Lincoln's assassination, he fully intended to keep his promise of making treason odious. By late May 1865, Johnson had discussed the need for treason trials with Judge John C. Underwood, a federal judge and notorious abolitionist from Virginia, who agreed to call a grand jury for considering indictments. On Wednesday, May 31, 1865, a federal grand jury gathered in Norfolk, Virginia, to contemplate whether or not to indict prominent political and military leaders of the Confederate States of America for treason. After several days of deliberations, the Norfolk grand jury indicted thirty-seven leaders of the Confederacy for treason on June 7, 1865. Robert E. Lee, the former general in chief of the Confederate armies, was the most prominent leader of the group. Among the others were Lieutenant Generals James Longstreet and Jubal Early along with two of Lee's sons and his nephew, Fitzhugh Lee.[20]

Americans are unfamiliar with the attempt to prosecute Lee and other Confederate leaders for treason after the war. How did we forget such an important chapter in our history? The story of the actual physical record of Lee's indictment is curious and symbolic of our memory of that event. According to Bradley T. Johnson, a former Confederate general who was compiling judicial rulings in the 1870s for a book about Chief Justice Salmon Chase, the indictment was lost from the records of the court during the summer of 1865.[21] Over the next seventy-two years, Lee's indictment would remain missing, despite the best efforts of historians and historical societies to find it. As late as 1935, Lee's biographer, Douglas Southall Freeman, would say that the record of the indictment had "disappeared."[22] Today—even though the original document was actually rediscovered in a wooden box in the basement of a Richmond courthouse in 1937—many writers and scholars continue to believe the indictment is still missing.

Over the past 150 years, we've unconsciously blotted out from our collective memory that divisive and painful period immediately following the war and Lincoln's assassination. In David Blight's outstanding book *Race and Reunion*, he quotes Robert Penn Warren who wrote, "When one is happy in forgetfulness, facts get forgotten."[23] Blight believes that post–Civil War Americans struggled with the tension between healing and justice. Over the years, our natural desire for the former often meant forgetting the difficult questions relating to justice. It is important for Americans to *rediscover* this forgotten episode of vital importance to understanding both the life of Robert E. Lee and the history of the United States.

★   ★   ★

The symbolic meaning of the lost indictment helps us better understand the legacy of the Civil War that continues to divide us today. The Confederate General Jubal Early, Lee's foremost defender after the war, underlined the metaphorical meaning of the word "indictment" in a speech to the Southern Historical Society in 1873. After describing how northern journalists and historians had been trying to portray southerners as rebels and traitors, he asked,

> Shall we permit the indictment to go forth to the world and to posterity without vindication of our motives and our conduct? Are we willing that our enemies shall be historians of our cause and our struggle?

Early then answered those questions: "No! A thousand times no!" He would go on to devote tremendous energy in the coming years upholding that vow.[24]

The Norfolk grand jury also indicted Jubal Early in June 1865. Unlike Lee, Early fled to Mexico, perhaps fearing punishment for his role in burning the town of Chambersburg, Pennsylvania, in the Valley campaign of 1864. Early became *the* premier defense counsel for Lee before the bar of history. One historian described Early as "perhaps the most influential figure in nineteenth-century Civil War writing, North or South."[25] His role in elevating Lee's reputation was a critical element in how we remember Lee today.

The renowned abolitionist Frederick Douglass warned future generations of Americans about the danger of forgetting history in a speech titled "Address at the Graves of the Unknown Dead" on Decoration Day, May 30, 1871. Just like Gerald Ford, Douglass delivered the speech at Arlington National Cemetery, the former location of Lee's family estate. Unlike Ford, Douglass boldly raised unpleasant questions:

> If we ought to forget a war which has filled our land with widows and orphans; which has made stumps of men of the very flower of our youth; which has sent them on the journey of life armless, legless, maimed and mutilated; which has piled up a debt heavier than a mountain of gold, swept uncounted thousands of men into bloody graves and planted agony at a million hearthstones—I say, if

this war is to be forgotten, I ask, in the name of all things sacred, what shall men remember?

He urged his audience to never forget that "victory to the rebellion meant death to the Republic." He also reminded them that it was *loyal* Union soldiers that ensured America would be a "united country no longer cursed by the hell-black system of human bondage."[26]

Douglass fought hard, though perhaps unsuccessfully, to ensure the memory of the Confederate cause would never be dissociated from slavery. It angered him to see the "bombastic laudation" of Lee, who Douglass believed was no different than John Wilkes Booth, after the general's death in the autumn of 1870. In one essay, Douglass wrote, "We can scarcely take up a paper that come to us from the South that is not filled with nauseating flatteries of the late Robert E. Lee."[27] In a highly sarcastic voice, Douglass incredulously stated, "It would seem from this that the soldier who kills the most men in battle, even in a bad cause, is the greatest Christian, and entitled to the highest place in heaven." After learning that a journal had declared Lee had died while being depressed about the condition of the country, Douglass replied, "From which we are to infer, that the liberation of four millions of slaves and their elevation to manhood and to the enjoyment of their civil and political rights was more than he could stand, and so he died!"

Despite Douglass's impressive rhetorical ability, the "defense" of Lee proved to be more successful than the "indictment" of the Confederate hero in the decades after the war. In the powerful essay *Between the World and Me*, Ta-Nehisi Coates writes, "American reunion was built on a comfortable narrative that made enslavement into benevolence, white knights of body snatchers, and the mass slaughter of the war into a kind of sport in which one could conclude that both sides conducted their affairs with courage, honor, and élan."[28] Shortly after the war, topics such as "treason" and "slavery" literally became history—not worth the attention of a dynamic nation focused on economic growth and westward expansion.

Views toward Lee seem to be changing, however. After the Charleston church shooting in 2015, many Americans became interested in the debate over how we should consider the memory of Confederate leaders and soldiers. In May 2017, after an acrimonious public discussion, the city of New Orleans removed a statue of Robert E. Lee—133 years after it was unveiled. In August 2017, in the wake of protests in Charlottesville, Virginia, more and more Americans began questioning our veneration of Robert E. Lee and other Confederate figures.

Soon after the Charleston tragedy, Wynton Marsalis, the famous trumpeter and New Orleans native, wondered why his city continued to commemorate the legacy of Robert E. Lee. Marsalis's piece, written during a painful time of national soul-searching, appeared to echo many of the ideas of Frederick Douglass. Marsalis found it difficult to understand why his beloved city would honor someone who "fought for the enslavement of a people against our national army fighting for their freedom."[29] Like Douglass, Marsalis clearly connected the Confederate cause with slavery, writing, "In a nation founded on the credo of freedom struggling to overcome its inhumane legacy of chattel slavery, only profound hubris would lead one people to conclude that the enslavement of another should be THE SUPREME law of the land." Finally, in words that sound as if they were written by Douglass himself, Marsalis declares, "Lee's monument was erected to proclaim this arrogance across the ages, and reclaim as a victory what was lost on the battlefield. It's time for this age to speak back in clear opposition to this hubris."

★ ★ ★

For "this age to speak back," we will have to revisit the history we've been trying so hard to forget over the past century and a half. In 1905 the novelist Henry James traveled to Richmond, Virginia, for a travel book he was writing titled *This American Scene*. After walking around the city for a short while, he sensed there was something missing in Richmond. There appeared, he wrote, "no discernible consciousness, registered or unregistered, of anything."[30] It was only after pausing before Richmond's famous Robert E. Lee monument that he was able to figure out the mystery. The lost cause Lee had fought for was in reality "a cause that could never have been gained."[31] The creation of a "vast Slave State," he believed, was "extravagant, fantastic, and to-day pathetic in its folly."[32]

This book, by providing the missing context surrounding the lost indictment of Robert E. Lee, will clarify these insights. From our current perspective, it's hard to imagine how a rebel chieftain, who had been indicted for treason against his country, could eventually be transformed into a national hero. Only by returning to that bitterly divided period immediately after the Civil War can we begin to solve this historical riddle.

1

"I AM AWARE OF HAVING DONE NOTHING WRONG & CANNOT FLEE."

The end came quickly for Robert E. Lee's Army of Northern Virginia after it abandoned its trenches in front of Richmond and Petersburg, Virginia, on April 2, 1865. Exhausted and starving, many of the soldiers began deserting in even greater numbers. Just one short week prior to its ultimate surrender on April 9, the army would disintegrate, losing half of its total man-power.[1]

General Lee's army had been under siege for ten months as it engaged in demoralizing trench warfare with northern soldiers under General Ulysses S. Grant. The unceasing pressure by Union troops resulted in shortages of men, food, and horses for the Confederates. The horses had become so weak, Lee noted in a report, that they could no longer haul the wagon trains over muddy roads.[2] With additional Federal troops under General William Tecumseh Sherman heading north to link up with Grant, Lee could wait no longer, and he decided to leave his fortifications. Lee's plan was to head south to combine with the Army of Tennessee under Major General Joseph Johnston in North Carolina. Hopefully, he'd be able to outrun the pursuit of Grant's army.

Today, historians estimate that Lee had about sixty thousand troops when he left his trenches. He would be opposed during that final week by about eighty thousand soldiers under Grant. On the day he surrendered, Lee believed he had only around ten thousand soldiers who were actually fit for duty—and he guessed he was outnumbered by five to one. The belief that Lee was only defeated by an enemy possessing far more men and resources would become an article of faith for southerners after the war. Lee ultimately surrendered approximately twenty-eight thousand total troops, many of them having rejoined the ranks after the fighting stopped.[3]

In the days leading up to the surrender, it became abundantly clear to almost everyone that the end had finally arrived. Even General Lee's leading corps commanders knew the days of the "grand old army" were numbered. With the situation becoming more and more desperate, they boldly held a somewhat mutinous private conference on the evening of April 7.[4] There, they commissioned General William N. Pendleton, an Episcopal priest and chief of artillery for the Army of Northern Virginia, to inform Lee that the time had come for negotiations with General Grant.

Pendleton eventually caught up with Lee, who was taking a much needed rest on the morning of April 8 outside his headquarters north of Appomattox Court House. After Pendleton mentioned that the officers felt it was time to surrender, Lee replied, "Oh, no! I trust it has not come to that."[5] He then added,

> General, we have yet too many bold men to think of laying down our arms. The enemy do not fight with spirit, while our boys still do. Besides, if I were to say a word to the Federal commander, he would regard it as such a confession of weakness as to make it the occasion of demanding unconditional surrender—a proposal to which I will never listen.

Lee was emphatic in his conversation with Pendleton that he didn't intend to comply with the wishes of his corps commanders at that particular time. He'd rather die than accept "unconditional surrender" from Grant.[6]

Lee's remarks to Pendleton are revealing about his thinking and strategy at this crucial juncture for his army. When he said "our boys" still fight with spirit, he was most likely trying to pacify his officers, at least for a little while. Several weeks after the surrender, when Lee could be more candid, he told President Jefferson Davis that his soldiers had become "feeble" during the final days, "and a want of confidence seemed to possess officers and men."[7] The "boys" of the Army of Northern Virginia may have possessed greater fighting spirit at earlier stages of the war, but that was no longer true in those trying days leading up to their surrender at Appomattox Court House. Lee, one of the finest military minds in American history, clearly knew this.

Lee's strident unwillingness to accept an unconditional surrender that wouldn't provide any guarantees to his soldiers seems like the real reason he wasn't quite ready to give in to the wishes of his officers at that moment.

General "U. S." Grant actually had a reputation as "Unconditional Surrender" Grant as a result of his actions at Fort Donelson in 1862.[8] When the Confederate defenders of the fort tried to engage in negotiations, Grant responded, "No terms except unconditional and immediate surrender can be accepted. I propose to move immediately upon your works."

Lee, we can assume, felt his army had fought too hard and too well to accept such humiliating terms from an army whose only advantage, he believed, was sheer numbers. Surely, the victors of Fredericksburg and Chancellorsville deserved better than such an ignoble end. What Lee didn't reveal to General Pendleton in their brief conversation is that he was *already* in communication with General Grant about possible terms.[9] And Lee—who was highly regarded by his men for his audacity on the battlefield—was aiming to get a better deal for his army than unconditional surrender. Perhaps he wished to avoid the possibility of his soldiers being shipped to ghastly prison camps up north. He most certainly hoped to secure protections for his officers from future treason trials.

Grant contacted Lee first about surrendering on the evening of April 7. A Virginia doctor had told Grant of a recent conversation he'd had with captured prisoner General Richard Ewell, one of Lee's senior commanders. Ewell had told the doctor that the "cause was lost" and that "for every man killed after this in the war somebody is responsible, and that it would be little better than murder."[10] Ewell went on to say he wasn't sure Lee could surrender without consulting President Davis, but "he hoped he would."

That piece of intelligence from Ewell provides the background to the initiation of a series of letters between Grant and Lee beginning on the 7th and concluding on April 9. Grant knew from recent engagements that Lee's army was "crumbling and deserting."[11] In his initial note, Grant wrote, "The result of the last week must convince you of the hopelessness of further resistance on the part of the Army of Northern Virginia in this struggle."[12] Things had gone from bad to worse for Lee after abandoning his fortifications, and Grant was well aware of that fact.

In Lee's response later that night, it's evident that he was angling for generous terms for his army. Without committing himself to surrender, Lee politely wished to know what Grant was offering.

Grant replied on April 8 by stating that "there is but one condition that I would insist upon, viz, that the men and officers surrendered shall be disqualified for taking up arms again against the Government of the United States until properly exchanged."[13] Surprisingly, "Unconditional Surrender" Grant offered far more liberal terms than had been feared. Instead of insisting on a surrender without any guarantees, Grant proposed a deal based on the system of parole and exchange of prisoners that was quite common at that time. Confederate soldiers might possibly be allowed to return to their homes as long as they gave their word they wouldn't return to the fight. They would be bound by their "paroles"—a word derived from French meaning "on one's honor"—until either the war ended, or they were exchanged for northern prisoners of equal rank. Grant also implied he'd be flexible about secondary matters.

Encouraged, Lee then tried to get even *more* favorable terms, despite his extremely weak bargaining position. To Grant's generous offer, Lee responded that he'd merely been interested in learning Grant's proposals for peace. He then moved the discussion in another direction by saying, "I cannot, therefore, meet you with a view to surrender the Army of Northern Virginia; but as far as your proposal may affect C.S. [Confederate States] forces under my command, and tend to the restoration of peace, I should be pleased to meet you at 10 a.m. tomorrow."[14] Grant believed Lee's delaying tactics were irresponsible under the circumstances. He would later say, "Lee does not appear well in the correspondence." Grant did add, however, that subsequent interviews revealed him to be a "patriotic and gallant soldier."[15]

With his army disintegrating by the hour, Lee tried to shelve any talk of surrender and instead arrange for a more general discussion of peace between the Union and the Confederate States—by this time in the war, it should be noted, Lee was the general in chief of *all* Confederate armies. Attempts at general peace talks had broken down before in the recent past, however, so the probability of this outcome was extremely low.

In late February 1865, Union Major General Edward Ord had met with Confederate Lieutenant General James Longstreet to discuss prisoner exchanges. They both agreed that a possible summit between Grant and Lee might bring an end to the disastrous war. Lee thought the idea worth pursuing and wrote Grant on March 2, "desiring to leave nothing untried which may put an end to the calamities of war."[16] He also advised Grant that he had the authority to act on whatever they agreed upon.

Grant sought guidance from Secretary of War Edwin Stanton, who then talked it over with the president. Stanton forwarded the following response to Grant that had been dictated by President Abraham Lincoln:

> The President directs me to say to you that he wishes you to have no conference with Gen. Lee unless it be for the capitulation of Lee's army, or on solely minor and purely military matters. He instructs me to say that you are not to decide, discuss, or confer upon any political question; such questions the President

holds in his own hands; and will submit them to no military conferences or conventions—mean time you are to press to the utmost, your military advantages.

Grant wrote back to Lee on March 4 advising him that he did not have the authority to meet Lee "for a conference on the subject proposed. Such authority is vested in the President of the United States alone."[17]

The attempt at "general" peace discussion among the military leaders revealed that the president believed Grant had authority to only discuss military matters and that point had been communicated directly to Lee. Attorney General James Speed would later state that a president performs two functions, "one civil, the other military."[18] Civil actions such as pardoning could not be delegated to a battlefield commander. Any powers that might be delegated to General Grant, therefore, could have been solely of a military nature. This distinction would later become critical.

With the likelihood of a humiliating surrender increasing by the hour, Lee decided on one more audacious gamble during the early hours of Sunday, April 9. At 2:00 a.m., Major General John B. Gordon's infantry attempted to break out of the Union encirclement in the vicinity of Appomattox Court House. John Brown Gordon had risen up through the ranks without any military training prior to the war and had become one of Lee's most tenacious commanders. Unfortunately for the Army of Northern Virginia, Gordon's men eventually ran into a much stronger Union force. Lee's aide-de camp, Colonel Charles Marshall, wrote, "it became evident that the end was at hand."[19]

Around 3:00 a.m., Gordon sent a note back through the lines that said, "Tell General Lee, I have fought my corps to a frazzle, and I fear I can do nothing else unless I am heavily supported by Longstreet's corps."[20] Alas, Longstreet's men were already engaged against superior numbers and could offer no assistance. Upon hearing Gordon's message, Lee responded aloud to no one in particular, "Then there is nothing left me to do but to go and see General Grant, and I would rather die a thousand deaths."[21]

Lee's life, up until this point, had consisted of a series of triumphs over formidable obstacles.[22] Abandoned by his profligate father, "Light Horse Harry" Lee, young Robert looked after his mother and eventually secured admission to West Point. As a young adult with relatively few resources, he married the daughter of George Washington's adopted son, and gradually built up an impressive investment portfolio that allowed him to support his growing family. Later, during the Civil War, Lee overcame early struggles to emerge as one of the most successful military leaders of all time. For many southerners, Lee's military exploits surpassed those of George Washington.

Lee's youth could not have been easy. Light Horse Harry, a renowned cavalry commander during the Revolutionary War, piled up debts and was unable to provide a stable environment for his wife and children. After having been beaten by a mob in Baltimore, Harry Lee headed to the West Indies to recover, leaving his family behind. Six-year-old Robert would never see his father again.

Growing up, Lee became quite close to his mother, Ann Carter Lee. By age thirteen, he was already assuming numerous responsibilities in the household, and was frequently looking after Ann Lee who suffered from poor health. Without money for college, Robert decided upon West Point, which was free to attend. Cadet Lee graduated second in his class at the Academy, without having incurred a single demerit. Among his classmates, he was known as the "Marble Model" because of his attractive looks and good behavior.

After graduation, Lee began his adult life with relatively few financial resources. At age twenty-four, he married Mary Custis—the daughter of George Washington Parke Custis. Mary grew up at Arlington House amidst a 1,100-acre estate. Lieutenant Lee had married well. In his twenties and thirties, he invested in banks and railroads and increased his net worth considerably. By age forty, he could comfortably support his wife and seven children.

Lee's most dramatic triumphs were on the battlefield, of course. In one particular engagement during the Mexican War, General Winfield Scott described Lee's actions as "the greatest feat of physical and moral courage performed by any individual in my knowledge."[23] During the Civil War, Lee, who was nicknamed "Granny Lee" for his caution early on, became better known later for his audacity in battle. The Chancellorsville campaign may have marked the pinnacle of his success. With an army only half the size of the enemy, Lee divided his troops and then methodically defeated the Union army. After this stunning victory, Colonel Marshall wrote that Lee "sat in the full realization of all that soldiers dream of—triumph."[24]

Lee almost couldn't bear the thought of surrender at Appomattox, despite his stoic resignation to do his duty. Earlier in the war, he had told a close relative that he preferred "annihilation to submission."[25] As he reflected on what now lay ahead, he looked off into the distance and said, "How easily I could be rid of this, and be at rest! I have only to ride along the line and all will be over!"[26] Recovering, he added, "But it is our duty to live. What will become of the women and children of the South if we are not here to protect them?"[27]

Lee then sent Grant a note requesting "an interview" so they could discuss the surrender in accordance with the terms Grant had laid out in their correspondence.[28] Grant, who had been suffering from a migraine, had spent the previous night bathing his feet in hot water and mustard, and putting mustard plasters on his wrists and neck "hoping to be cured by morning." The instant Grant saw the contents of Lee's note, however, his headache miraculously disappeared.

Lee and Grant agreed to meet at the property of Wilmer McLean at Appomattox Court House, Virginia. The gathering at McLean's property would become one of the most iconic scenes in American history. Two old warriors—both graduates of West Point who vaguely knew of each other during the Mexican War—would shake hands in the living room of a Virginia farmhouse to reunite a suffering nation. For many, Appomattox would symbolize for all time America coming together again, finally heeding Abraham Lincoln's declaration from his First Inaugural: "We are not enemies, but friends."

It should be remembered, however, that the Appomattox agreement didn't end the war—Lee only surrendered the Army of Northern Virginia that day. General Johnston's army would remain in the field for another two weeks before surrendering to Sherman on April 26. And the last Confederate force would finally give up in Texas on June 2, 1865. The war wouldn't be considered officially over until President Andrew Johnson's proclamation on August 20, 1866. This date was significant to prisoners of war whose status would change once the war was declared legally ended.[29]

Grant greeted Lee very cordially, and they engaged in some light conversation for a short time.[30] Eventually, Lee gently terminated the small talk by saying he wanted to discuss the terms of the surrender of his army. Grant then simply stated that he wanted Lee's army to "lay down their arms" and not "take them up again during the continuance of the war unless duly and properly exchanged." Lee said he understood and accepted those terms, and Grant wrote them out in pencil.

After reading the first draft, Lee said that allowing his officers to keep their side arms and horses would have "a very happy effect on his men." He then noted that his cavalrymen and artillerymen owned their own horses, unlike the Union army.

At this time, either Lee or Grant—the sources differ on this point—mentioned that those men would need to have their horses to put in a spring crop, so it was agreed they could keep them. Regardless of whether it was Lee or Grant who actually said it, that particular anecdote has symbolized the transition from war to peace for many Americans. Grant also agreed to provide Lee's starving army with enough food for twenty-five thousand men.

The final terms were then written out by Grant's adjutant Ely S. Parker—a Native American from the Seneca Tribe—as follows:

Appomattox Court-House, Virginia April 9, 1865
General R. E. Lee
Commanding C.S. Army
GENERAL: In accordance with the substance of my letter to you of the 8th instant, I propose to receive the surrender of the army of Northern Virginia on the following terms, to wit: Rolls of all the officers and men to be made in duplicate, one copy to be given to an officer to be designated by me, the other to be retained by such officer or officers as you may designate. The officers to give their individual paroles not to take up arms against the government of the United States until properly exchanged; and each company or regimental commander to sign a like parole for the men of their commands. The arms, artillery, and public property to be parked and stacked, and turned over to the officers appointed by me to receive them. This will not embrace the side-arms of the officers nor their private horses or baggage. This done, each officer and man will be allowed to return to his home, not to be disturbed by United States authority so long as they observe their paroles and the laws in force where they may reside.
Very respectfully,
U. S. Grant, Lieutenant-General.[31]

So, instead of being rounded up and taken off to prisoner-of-war camps, the Confederate soldiers were free to return to their homes for the remainder of the war. The last line—which has been described by the historian Bruce Catton as one of the greatest sentences in American history—was remarkably lenient given the violence and intensity of the fighting over the previous four years.[32] The soldiers could return home "not to be disturbed by United States authority" as long as they obeyed the law. Both Lee and Grant took this agreement to mean there wouldn't be treason trials and prison terms for the Confederate soldiers in the future.[33] Indeed, Grant would later point out that Lee wouldn't have surrendered if he "supposed that after the surrender he was going to be tried for treason and hanged."[34] General E. Porter Alexander, one of Lee's most trusted officers, believed Grant's liberal terms could only be "ascribed to a policy of conciliation deliberately entered upon."[35]

Alexander was mostly correct in his belief. Grant had talked with Lincoln, along with General Sherman and Admiral David D. Porter, about how to treat the rebel soldiers while aboard the *River Queen*, anchored off City Point, Virginia, in March 1865. Lincoln said he wanted to be lenient with the rebels feeling they should "let 'em up easy."[36] He told his commanding officers, "Let them once surrender and reach their homes, they won't take up their arms again. . . . Let them have their horses to plow with. . . . Give them the most liberal and honorable terms." As the historian Brooks D. Simpson has remarked, Grant—who didn't say much during the conversation—was always a very good listener.[37]

Yet, Grant had received mixed signals from his commander in chief. In early March 1865, Lincoln had told him "you are not to decide, discuss, or confer upon any political question." Then in late March, Lincoln appeared to give his general broad leeway for making "honorable terms." The gray area between purely military matters and political questions would pose problems in the future.

Both Lee and Grant attended West Point, where they learned to resist imposing harsh punishments on their defeated enemies.[38] Some soldiers and political leaders throughout history, however, viewed civil wars much differently, as historian John Fabian Witt has shown. Such men as Lord Charles Cornwallis (who surrendered to the Colonial Army at Yorktown) and Napoleon had delivered horrific punishments to rebels in civil wars. That "brave, bad man" Oliver Cromwell was another leader who believed treason and rebellion must be punished severely—ironically, his body would be dug up and hanged when the Stuarts returned to power three years *after* his death.

How would Confederate soldiers and politicians be treated once the remaining Confederate armies in the field were defeated and the war was finally over? As honorable opponents who should be forgiven or traitorous rebels who must be tried and hanged? As we'll see, there were many differences of opinion on these questions. After the assassination of Lincoln, quite a few prominent and influential legal minds would argue that the military agreement at Appomattox would not remain binding on the government once the fighting stopped. Treason trials, especially for leading rebels like Jefferson Davis and Robert E. Lee, might become a reality after all.

When the meeting with Grant was all over, Lee returned to his men around 3 p.m.[39] He told them, "I have done for you all that it was in my power to do." He then concluded his brief remarks by saying, "Go to your homes and resume your occupations. Obey the laws and become as good citizens as you were soldiers." Meanwhile, Grant telegraphed Secretary of War

Edwin Stanton that "General Lee surrendered the Army of Northern Virginia this afternoon on terms proposed by myself."[40]

After surrendering his army, Robert E. Lee told Colonel Marshall to prepare a farewell note to the troops.[41] Lee made a few changes to Marshall's draft, which eventually was titled "General Order No. 9." Lee then signed it, and distributed it to his men. This document would become a central text for southerners in the decades after the war.

Lee began by telling his devoted soldiers why he decided to surrender. The Army of Northern Virginia had been "compelled to yield to overwhelming numbers and resources" and it had become clear that further resistance would have resulted in a "useless sacrifice" of men. Lee decided to make the best deal possible for the army. He commended the men for their "consciousness of duty faithfully performed" and concluded his note by expressing his admiration for their "constancy and devotion" to their country. By using the word "country," he meant the Confederate States of America. That country's relatively brief existence would soon be extinguished, however, as the armies of Generals Grant and Sherman began the final push against General Johnston.

With his farewell complete, Lee declined to attend the formal surrender ceremony.[42] He left his quarters in the field on April 12, and headed home to Richmond as a prisoner on parole. His legal status was just like the rest of his soldiers. Accompanied by his son Custis and several colleagues, he took his time making the journey home of approximately eighty miles. On April 14, the small band arrived at Lee's brother's house on the outskirts of town. There—on the grounds of the property—Lee slept in a tent for the last time in his life. That very same evening, America's political situation would be turned upside down, threatening all of the progress made at Appomattox.

The famous actor John Wilkes Booth had shot President Abraham Lincoln that night at Ford's Theatre. Secretary of State William Seward had also been gravely injured at his home in a related attack. The nation's beloved president, who had steadfastly led the nation through its most harrowing struggle, would die in the early hours of the next morning. With the extent of the conspiracy still unknown, Americans experienced tremendous fear and grief.

On Saturday, April 15, around 3 o'clock in the afternoon, Lee's party finally arrived at Richmond, a city that now resembled a smoking ruin. Countless factories, warehouses, and family homes had been destroyed. As a driving rain soaked him to the bone that day, Lee possibly reflected on all that had been lost as a result of the war.

Personally, it had been an enormous tragedy for the professional soldier, who had served the US Army for thirty-four years prior to the outbreak of hostilities in 1861. The Lees lost numerous family members—among them their twenty-three-year-old daughter Anne Carter Lee—along with their ancestral home "Arlington House" in Arlington, Virginia. The home, which had been bequeathed to Lee's wife Mary Anna Custis—the daughter of George Washington's adopted son—had been seized by the federal troops shortly after the fall of Fort Sumter. Later, the US government took legal title to the property due to unpaid taxes by the Lees. In 1864, the estate was converted into a national cemetery for the Union. Today, we can still see Arlington House on a hill overlooking the Potomac River and Washington, DC. It's now a national landmark on the grounds of Arlington National Cemetery. Lee and his wife never got over the loss of this magnificent property.

The country—both North and South—had experienced tremendous losses as well. Roughly 750,000 soldiers lost their lives during the conflict. Additionally, there were approximately 1.5 million casualties. Among just southerners, around one in three households lost at least one family member, and the South's overall wealth decreased by 60 percent.[43]

As Lee approached his new home on 707 East Franklin Street in Richmond, onlookers began to cheer.[44] He responded to them by raising his hat. And then, moving slowly and with great emotion, he dismounted from his horse, Traveller, made his way through the crowd, and quietly entered his house.

Over the next several weeks, while the rest of the nation was fixated on the dramatic events surrounding Lincoln's assassination, Lee spent most of his time at home, catching up on his sleep. On occasion, he'd slip out late at night for walks around the city. Friends noticed his sadness during that painful time. One of them asked him, "Why will you look so heartbroken?" Lee responded, "Why shouldn't I? My cause is dead! I am homeless—I have nothing on earth."

Just one day after Lee arrived home in Richmond, the famous photographer Mathew Brady took photographs of Lee on his back porch in "several situations."[45] Brady later said, "It was supposed that after his defeat it would be preposterous to ask him to sit, but I thought that to be the time for the historical picture."

Brady was assisted in arranging the session by Lee's wife and Colonel Robert Ould, who was the Confederate agent for the exchange of prisoners during the war. Brady was given just one hour to photograph Lee on Easter Sunday, April 16, which was also, we should remember, one day after the death of Lincoln.

There were six photos in all. First, Lee was photographed while seated.

Figure 1.1. Arlington House (between 1980 and 2006). *Source*: Highsmith, Carol M. Carol M. Highsmith Archive. Library of Congress.

Then he appeared with his son Custis and his aide Colonel Walter Taylor. And then finally, there was a shot of Lee standing in the doorway.

Brady remembered, "There was little conversation during the sitting, but the General changed his position as often as I wished him to."[46] Lee wore his finest uniform along with well-shined black shoes. He didn't, however, wear his sword, sash, and boots.[47] The photographs became hugely popular. Brady remembered selling them by the thousands.[48] And devotees of Lee often asked Mary for signed photos of the general. Brady clearly succeeded in preserving the great man for history.

Lee's biographers have attempted to extract meaning from the photos to help better understand that tragic moment in American history. Douglas Southall Freeman, Lee's leading biographer, sees a "shadow of anguish and defiance lingering on his face."[49] Another historian perceives "the light of battle in his eyes"—Lee is "surrendered but not defeated."[50]

It's probably not all that helpful to project one's own beliefs onto images from 150 years ago. Trying to interpret the meaning behind Lee's various poses seems like a hopeless exercise. It's much more promising to view the photos within the context of what we now know. On that Easter Sunday, just one day after the death of Abraham Lincoln, Robert E. Lee decided to pose for posterity in a clean military uniform with polished shoes. He could have firmly said no, but he didn't. He also could have posed in civilian clothing. What we see *appears* to be a proud, dignified soldier who felt he had nothing to apologize for. And by posing in his own home, instead of on the battlefield or in a jail cell, it feels like the war is over and Lee is a free man.[51]

There's one interesting fact about the photos that is often overlooked by writers on this subject. Lincoln was assassinated by Booth on Friday, April 14, and died on Saturday morning, April 15. Information traveled more slowly back then. One newspaper account notes that Lee was told of Lincoln's death by Robert Ould on Sunday afternoon, April 16—more than twenty-four hours after the event. Since we know Ould is the exact same person who arranged the Brady photo session, there's a real possibility that Lee had *just* heard the news of Lincoln's death prior to sitting for the photos. Lee would later say the South lost a friend in Lincoln, and that Lincoln was likely to be more lenient than his successor, Andrew Johnson.[52] One wonders if he was preoccupied with such thoughts during his time with Brady.

While Lee is held in high esteem by many Americans nowadays, the same could not be said in April 1865. Politicians, soldiers, and ordinary people were much more divided in their opinion of his role in the bloody Civil War. A

Figure 1.2.   Robert E. Lee, April 1865. *Source:* Library of Congress.

perfect symbol of this divided outlook can be seen in Brady's photo of Lee standing alone on his back porch.[53]

Despite being a paroled prisoner, Lee appeared dignified in his uniform in front of the back door to his family home. Here we are meant to see a great leader who fought gallantly for a cause he passionately believed in. Unbeknownst to Lee and Brady, however, someone had preemptively spoiled the picture by writing the word "Devil" on the brick to the left of the door. Brady erased the graffiti once he noticed it and took that photo again.[54] Lee would have a harder time in the coming months "erasing" the beliefs of those who felt he had betrayed his country.

One northern newspaper had a particularly negative reaction to the Brady photos.[55] Just two weeks after the shoot, *The Providence Journal* wrote that it had learned the news that "General Lee has had his photograph taken in six different attitudes, all very life-like." The piece then snidely lists the various moods. The first one is the "meditative mood" where Lee, prior to his resignation, listens to his commanding officer's plans for "the first campaign against the rebels." The second one is the "sneaking mood," where Lee "having determined to become a traitor to his country, is sneaking away from Washington." Provocatively, the fourth mood is labeled the chivalric mood— "permitting the Union prisoners to be starved." The concluding mood, according to the newspaper, is the current one of Lee in Richmond. As the crowd cheers, Lee directs "the United States officers to remove the colored sentinels from his private mansion, as they were quite offensive to him and his wife."

Lee didn't enjoy being in the spotlight, but he couldn't avoid it in the weeks after Appomattox. Despite his love of seclusion, he actually agreed to an interview with Thomas Cook of the *New York Herald* just a week after the sitting for Brady.[56] As a general rule, Lee didn't talk with journalists, so this was an unusual event. The interview appeared in print on Saturday, April 29 and provides us with a fascinating glimpse into the mind of Lee at that pivotal time in our nation's history—its richness as a source makes it worth considering in detail (see appendix A for the complete transcript). Lee's remarks to Cook provoked spirited reactions in both the North and the South. For southerners, Lee personified their noble but failed cause. Indeed, many of his remarks would provide the intellectual underpinnings for the southern outlook that would prevail over the subsequent decades after Appomattox.

For many northerners, however, he appeared disdainful and unapologetic. Worst of all, perhaps, his apparent defiance came at a time when most Americans were still mourning the loss of President Lincoln. Lee, who was almost always careful not to roil the waters of public opinion, most certainly would have been aware of the dangers of being interviewed at such a sensitive time. Remarkably, he agreed to do it anyway. Lee may have been audacious on the battlefield, but he was usually quite circumspect when it came to making public statements.

Cook's interview was surprisingly wide-ranging and intimate. Even though he wrote for a publication that had been very critical of the Lincoln administration, Cook is viewed by most historians as fair and accurate. While Lee told Cook he had no desire to talk politics, he nevertheless shared his views on secession, slavery, the death of Lincoln, and what must be done to restore harmony to the nation. On a personal note, he revealed that he just wanted to "retire to private life and end his days in seclusion." Sadly, he also confessed that he'd have "been pleased had his life been taken in any of the numerous battle fields on which he had fought during the war."

At times, Lee was conciliatory. He said he found notoriety distasteful, "but was ready to make any sacrifice or perform any honorable act that would tend to the restoration of peace and tranquility to the country." Cook also told his readers that General Lee, "strange as it may appear, talked throughout as a citizen of the United States." In the three weeks since Appomattox, Lee had gone from talking about two countries to just one country—even though the war wasn't officially over yet.

Lee's views on the assassination of Lincoln would have been appreciated by northerners. He believed the event was "one of the most deplorable that could have occurred," and he was adamant that no one in a leadership position in the South would have sanctioned such a crime.

Alongside this spirit of reconciliation, Lee also exhibited moments of proud defiance. He warned that if the US government insisted on "arbitrary or vindictive or revengeful policies," then "the end was not yet." The South still had resources and would be able to continue the struggle, if necessary. Offering some cautionary guidance, Lee said, "if a people are to be destroyed they will sell their lives as dearly as possible."

Lee vigorously defended Jefferson Davis when Cook suggested that soldiers might receive amnesty, while politicians would be "held to a strict accountability." Lee believed Davis was no different than any other southerner. Davis, according to Lee, shouldn't suffer more than anyone else—"his acts were that of the whole people, and the acts of the whole people were his acts."

This incredible interview feels raw and authentic to the modern reader—it's as if Lee was caught momentarily without his usual defenses when making public remarks. At times, Lee calmly and benevolently tries to make amends with his former enemies. At other times, however, he implies that the South's return to the Union was *conditional*. A lenient policy might possibly lead to a "restoration of peace and tranquility to the country." Hard measures—like treason trials and prison sentences—could result in an even bloodier conflict down the road, however. The word "restoration" was carefully chosen by Lee, too. He liked the idea of returning to a Union that looked more like the one in 1860 than some other future possibility.

On one crucial level, this interview can be viewed as the opening argument for Lee's defense against any future prosecution or condemnation—by either government lawyers or by the bar of history. Surprisingly, Lee told Cook he was an opponent of secession at the outset of the conflict, but he firmly believed in the doctrine of "States rights." So when Virginia withdrew from the Union, Lee felt "he had no recourse, in his view of honor and patriotism, but to abide her fortunes."

For Lee, there was a legitimate debate surrounding the relative powers of the various states versus the federal government. Ultimately, it required war to settle the disagreement—such a war, according to Lee, "cannot be considered treason." He then made a general remark that obviously applied to him personally: "A man should not be judged harshly for contending for that which he honestly believes to be right."

At this point, in what must have been a pretty shocking perspective for Cook and his readers, Lee argued that slavery, from the southern viewpoint, hadn't been an obstacle at all for securing peace. He added, "The best men of the South have long been anxious to do away with this institution, and were quite willing today to see it abolished." The real challenge in the future, for Lee, was "what will you do with the freed people?" Lee doesn't offer an answer to that question beyond saying, "the negroes must be disposed of" and a humane course would be needed before setting them free.

Lee's thoughts about slavery and freedmen in this interview are curious, if somewhat implausible. He told Cook the South had been ready for peace over the past two years, and that the "best men wanted to do away with the institution." Yet, two years earlier, immediately after the issuance of Lincoln's Emancipation Proclamation that freed the slaves, President Jefferson Davis had declared before the Confederate Congress that "a restoration of the Union has been rendered forever impossible by the adoption of a measure which from its very nature neither admits of retraction nor can coexist with union."[57] And in May 1863, the Confederate Congress, meeting in secret session, passed legislation enabling capital punishments for any white officers and black soldiers who tried to implement emancipation. As the commander of the Army of Northern Virginia, Lee's job was to help enforce that legislation. Finally, at the very beginning of the Confederacy in March 1861, its vice president, Alexander Stephens, said:

> Our new Government is founded upon exactly the opposite idea; its foundations are laid, its corner-stone rests upon the great truth, that the negro is not the equal of the white man; that slavery—subordination to the superior race—is his natural and moral condition.
>
> This, our new Government is first, in the history of the world, based upon this great physical, philosophical and moral truth.[58]

One wonders who Lee was referring to when he said the "best men" wanted to end slavery.

The major tenets of Lee's defense that emerge from the *New York Herald* interview—that his primary loyalty lay with Virginia and that the war wasn't about slavery—soon became central to the Lost Cause tradition—a set of beliefs that were extremely popular in the South in the decades after the war. In his interview with Cook, the combative Confederate general in chief had fired off the first salvo and would now await the return volley. The response would be considerably harsher than Americans might think today. Instead of a president who wanted to "let 'em up easy," there was now a new commander in chief from the border state of Tennessee who vowed to make "treason odious." Ever the stoic, Lee would be ready for whatever came next. Later that spring, he'd tell his adored cousin "Markie," "I am aware of having done nothing wrong & cannot flee."[59] Lee's critics saw things much differently. They would now make *their* case.

2

"THEY SHALL SUFFER FOR THIS, THEY SHALL SUFFER FOR THIS."

A handsome, smartly dressed gentleman arrived at the Kirkwood House in Washington, DC, early in the afternoon on Friday, April 14, 1865. The man asked for a card and a sheet of notepaper, and then wrote down the following message:

> For Mr. Andrew Johnson:
> I don't wish to disturb you; are you at home?
> J. Wilkes Booth[1]

★   ★   ★

The famous actor John Wilkes Booth shot Abraham Lincoln in the back of the head around 9:30 p.m. on the night of April 14 while the president sat in a private box with his wife at Ford's Theatre.[2] At roughly the same time, another assassin viciously attacked Secretary of State William Seward at his home, stabbing him numerous times in the face and throat. Investigators would later discover that the small band of conspirators had also intended to kill Vice President Andrew Johnson, General Ulysses S. Grant, and Secretary of War Edwin Stanton. In the immediate aftermath of the attacks, there was little hope that either Lincoln or Seward would survive. Throughout the early morning hours of April 15, Lincoln's cabinet members understandably assumed there was a broader conspiracy afoot.

Vice President Johnson had gone to bed early in his two-room suite on the second floor of the Kirkwood House on that Friday evening.³ He had been staying at the hotel, which was a few blocks from Ford's Theatre, since assuming his duties as Lincoln's vice president a month earlier. Much later, during the trial of Booth's gang of conspirators, it would be disclosed that Johnson had also been targeted for assassination. A German immigrant named George Atzerodt, who had rented a room on the same floor as Johnson in the Kirkwood House, had been chosen for the deed by Booth. But Atzerodt, having drunk too much on the night of the crimes, lost his nerve and never fulfilled his part of the plan. Booth's note to the vice president earlier that day may have been an attempt to somehow implicate Johnson in the conspiracy. Mary Todd Lincoln, the president's distraught and emotionally unsteady wife, suspected the note indicated Johnson knew of the monstrous plot.⁴

Awakened shortly after the attacks on Lincoln and Seward, Johnson broke down in tears upon hearing the news. Eventually, he buttoned up his coat and headed over to the house of Mr. Petersen, where the mortally wounded Lincoln lay resting. Directly across the street from Ford's Theatre, the house provided more space for the six surgeons who attended the president. Alas, all agreed there was little that could be done for Lincoln, who would not survive the bullet wound to his head. Miraculously, Seward would eventually survive his attack, though the scars on his face never fully healed.

By midnight, the medical personnel at Lincoln's bedside had been joined by members of the cabinet and other leading officials. Secretary of the Navy Gideon Welles noted in his diary, "the giant sufferer lay extended diagonally across the bed, which was not long enough for him. . . . His features were calm and striking."⁵ Outside of Petersen's house, crowds gathered, despite the damp and darkness of the early spring evening in the nation's capital. The city's freedmen were especially overwhelmed by grief. Several hundred African Americans congregated on the avenue outside the White House and remained there weeping throughout the following day. Johnson didn't stay long at the Petersen location, and soon returned to the Kirkwood House, where he spent the next several hours pacing up and down his room, wringing his hands, and muttering, "They shall suffer for this, they shall suffer for this."⁶

Andrew Johnson, a man of medium height with black eyes and a dark complexion, immediately viewed these attacks as the bloody work of traitors who had spent the previous four years trying to destroy the Union. A southerner himself from Tennessee, who had been threatened and harassed by secessionists for his support of the Union, Johnson would passionately exclaim to anyone who would listen that traitors and treason needed to be punished. After the fall of Richmond in early April, he had declared, "treason is the highest

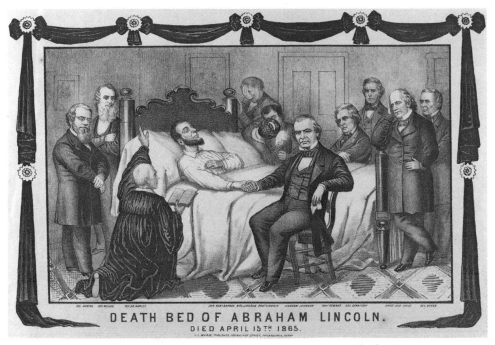

Figure 2.1.   Death Bed of Abraham Lincoln, 1865. *Source:* **The Alfred Whital Stern Collection of Lincolniana. Library of Congress.**

crime known in the catalogue of crimes" and "treason must be made odious and traitors must be punished."[7] For Johnson, death would be "too easy a punishment" for the traitors.

Johnson's desire for retribution represented a stark contrast with the seemingly lenient, benevolent attitude of Abraham Lincoln. On the morning of April 10, the day after the surrender of Robert E. Lee at Appomattox Court House, Johnson had hurried over to the White House so he could protest directly with the president against the indulgent terms given to Lee by Grant. According to one firsthand account, very few people knew at the time that Johnson believed Grant should have held Lee in prison until the administration figured out what to do with him.[8] During the late afternoon on April 14, just hours prior to the attack at Ford's Theatre, Johnson had met privately with the president, telling Lincoln he was going too easy on the rebels.[9] Johnson noted that he'd be much, much tougher on traitors if he were president.

Over at Petersen's house, it became clear that the end was near for Lincoln around 7 a.m. on April 15. With Secretary of War Stanton, Attorney

Figure 2.2.   Andrew Johnson. *Source:* Library of Congress.

General James Speed, and several others still in attendance, the president died at 7:22 a.m. Minutes later, church bells tolled throughout the city, announcing the terrible news. A short prayer was offered by Reverend Phineas Gurley amidst weeping in the parlor. With tears streaming down his face, Stanton said, "Now, he belongs to the ages."[10] Lincoln's funeral, described by the *New York*

Times as "the greatest pageant ever tendered to the honored dead on this continent," would be held four days later.[11]

Despite his intense grief, the energetic Secretary of War had taken control on the evening of the assassination, while Lincoln lay dying and Johnson paced in his room. Upon first hearing of the tragedy, Stanton began an investigation into the crimes, while also organizing Washington's defenses against a possibly larger conspiracy. All the while, he sent updates to the press and government officials about the events of the evening and early morning. The Secretary of War, who had a reputation for political infighting and opportunism, served his country heroically in those hours before Johnson became the next commander-in-chief. Ironically, he'd become one of Johnson's bitterest enemies in the coming years.[12]

General Grant was one of the first persons notified by Stanton after the terrible event. The general and his wife had actually been invited by the Lincolns to attend the play that evening, but Grant declined the invitation, instead taking a train to Burlington, New Jersey. Upon hearing the news, Grant returned to Washington, DC, to assist Stanton with the defense of the nation's capital. When Grant's wife Julia noted Andrew Johnson would now become president, he remarked "for some reason, I dread the change."[13]

After Lincoln was pronounced dead, James Speed—who was the brother of a close friend of Lincoln's in addition to being attorney general—prepared a quick note for the vice president, telling him his inauguration should take place as soon as possible.[14] Johnson replied immediately asking that the ceremony take place at Kirkwood House. Speed and Salmon Chase, Chief Justice of the Supreme Court, then began looking into the former cases of Vice Presidents Tyler and Filmore in order to "examine the Constitution and laws."[15]

The inauguration ceremony was brief.[16] Chase administered the oath at 11:00 a.m. with a handful of cabinet members and politicians in attendance. Johnson kissed the Bible and then made a short speech, saying, "The duties of office are mine. I will perform them. The consequences are with God. Gentlemen, I shall lean upon you. I feel that I need your support. I am deeply impressed with the solemnity of the occasion and the responsibility of the duties of the office I am assuming." Chase concluded the ceremony by saying, "May God guide, support, and bless you in your arduous duties." Everyone then offered Johnson their "sad congratulations." According to newspaper accounts, Johnson appeared in good health and "produced a most gratifying impression" upon everyone there.

Many Americans would have required reassurance that the new president was in "good health" and ready for the daunting task ahead of him. Johnson had only been vice president for less than six weeks, and his first public act had been a complete disaster. In the hours before his inauguration ceremony, Johnson drank several glasses of whiskey with the outgoing vice president, Hannibal Hamlin.[17] He then delivered a drunken inauguration speech in which he pointed to each of the cabinet members and told them one by one that they derived their power from the people. When it came time for his oath, he loudly proclaimed, "I kiss this Book in the face of my nation of the United States." This disgraceful performance was embarrassing for everyone to watch and Johnson was skewered in the press in the days that followed. When a few cabinet members later expressed concerns, Lincoln calmed their fears by saying, "I have known Andy Johnson for many years; he made a bad slip the other day, but you need not be scared; Andy ain't a drunkard." Johnson most likely wasn't an alcoholic, though his sons suffered from the disease.

Just like Lincoln, Andrew Johnson had been born in a log cabin to working-class parents. Few contemporaries would have imagined that young Andy, who left his native North Carolina at age seventeen to become a tailor in Tennessee, could eventually become president of the United States of America.[18] He never attended a single day of school in his life, though he did read a tremendous amount of books on his own as a young man. Johnson did possess, however, an abundance of energy and grit—and a considerable amount of stubbornness, too—which served him well as he climbed up through the ranks from alderman to mayor to state representative and senator, then on to governor and US representative and senator, and then finally to vice president and president. Early in Johnson's career, a journalist described him as a "self-made man—a man for the people and of the people."[19]

A proud Jacksonian Democrat, Johnson vigorously defended the working man against what he believed was a predatory aristocracy in the South. It's not surprising that Johnson clashed frequently with Jefferson Davis, a wealthy planter and slave owner from Mississippi, during their time together in Congress before the war. In the midst of a particularly acrimonious exchange between the two congressmen, Johnson remarked that Davis was part of an "illegitimate, swaggering, bastard, scrub aristocracy, who assumed to know a good deal," yet was lacking in talents and information.[20] A reporter on the scene noted that neither Johnson nor Davis would forget the bitterness of that particular debate.

Johnson fought hard on behalf of white working people, but he was never a champion of laboring slaves and freedmen. Like many southerners prior to the war, Johnson owned slaves. And he defended the peculiar institution all the way up until 1863, the year the Emancipation Proclamation went into effect. The first slave Johnson bought was a fourteen-year-old girl named Dolly. He'd eventually own eight or nine slaves in total and was proud of the fact that he never sold even one of them. The great African American abolitionist Frederick Douglass observed upon meeting Johnson for the first time that, "whatever Andrew Johnson may be, he is no friend of our race."[21]

Johnson's racism is shocking to the modern observer, and yet, sadly, it would help explain his policies while in the White House. During his first term in Congress, Johnson reacted with horror to one bill that he feared "would place every splay-footed, bandy-shanked, hump-backed, thick-lipped, flat-nosed, wooly headed, ebon-colored negro in the country upon an equality with the poor white man."[22] For Johnson, equality between the races was unthinkable, and he never deviated from that position. As president, he wrote Governor Thomas Fletcher of Missouri, "This is a country for white men, and by God, as long as I'm President, it shall be a government for white men."[23]

A colleague once said of Johnson that he "had no confidants and sought none."[24] While his racism was shared by many southerners before the war, his steadfast commitment to the Union was not. As a senator from Tennessee, Johnson became the only member from a Confederate state to remain in the Senate. Northerners welcomed his vigorous defense of the Union, particularly in the dark days of 1860 and 1861.

In one of his greatest speeches, delivered in the Senate in December 1860, he said South Carolina had put itself "in an attitude of levying war against the United States."[25] He added, "it is treason, nothing but treason." A few months later, Johnson declared on the Senate floor that if he were president and was faced with traitors, he would "have them arrested and if convicted, within the meaning and scope of the Constitution, by Eternal God," he'd have them executed.[26] Throughout the war, Johnson exhibited defiance and bravery in the face of relentless attacks by secessionists. His commendable performance during the initial phases of the war made him an attractive choice for vice president in 1864. Facing a tough reelection campaign, Lincoln had felt a War Democrat would strengthen the ticket considerably, so Vice President Hamlin was replaced with Johnson. The party appreciated Johnson's pugnacity, and the choice was well received. Just hours after Lincoln died, Henry Ward Beecher—the abolitionist and brother of Harriet Beecher Stowe—spoke for many northerners when he said, "Johnson's little finger was stronger than Lincoln's loins."[27] That line echoed the thoughts of a leading advisor to England's Charles I, who had said, "the little finger of the prerogative was heavier than the loins of the law."[28] Ominously perhaps for Johnson, Charles's clash with Parliament ended with his beheading.

Gideon Welles arranged for Johnson's first cabinet meeting to be held at noon on Saturday, April 15.[29] The cabinet had met a day earlier, with Lincoln presiding. On that occasion, Lincoln had said he wanted to "avoid the shedding of blood, or any vindictiveness of punishment."[30] He made it clear to his colleagues that he didn't want to hang even the worst of the rebels. Throwing up his hands as if scaring sheep, he said, "Frighten them out of the country, open the gates, let down the bars, scare them off." Stanton even noted that Lincoln spoke very kindly of General Lee and others of the Confederacy.[31] At the new president's first meeting on April 15, Johnson promised that his policy, in all of the essentials, would be the same as Lincoln's. And he asked the members of the cabinet to continue in their jobs without any change.

The next day, Sunday, April 16, Johnson indicated his policy toward the rebel leadership wouldn't be *quite* the same as Lincoln's. At a cabinet meeting in the morning, Johnson announced that he was "not disposed to treat treason lightly," and he'd punish the leading rebels "with exemplary severity."[32] He provided more detail when he met with his former colleagues from the Joint Committee on the Conduct of the War at his temporary headquarters at the Treasury Department later that day. The committee's chairman, Senator Benjamin Wade, greeted Johnson by saying, "Johnson, we have faith in you. By the Gods, there will be no trouble now in running the government."[33] Johnson then replied, "I am very much obliged to you gentlemen, and I can only say you can judge of my policy by my past. Everybody knows what that is. I hold this: Robbery is a crime; rape is a crime; murder is a crime; *treason* is a crime; and *crime* must be punished. The law provides for it and the courts are open. Treason must be made infamous and traitors must be impoverished."[34]

The Joint Committee for the Conduct of the War had been created in 1861 to oversee what appeared to be an increasingly lackluster war effort. Johnson had been an initial member of the group, which consisted of four senators and four representatives. Another original member was George Washington Julian, a radical Republican congressmen from Indiana. He had helped lead the fight to free the slaves and now called for stern punishments for traitors. Even though he and Johnson shared a desire for harsh punishments of the rebels, Julian had been disappointed when Johnson was first nominated to be vice president. According to Julian, Johnson "always scouted the idea that slavery was the cause of our trouble, or that emancipation could ever be tolerated without immediate colonization."[35] Indeed, Julian believed Johnson was "at heart, as decided a hater of the negro and of everything savoring of abolitionism, as the rebels from whom he had separated."

Julian spent much of the weekend after Lincoln's assassination with the

Radical Republican leadership. Surprisingly, he noted in his diary that the hostility and contempt for Lincoln's lenient policies were undisguised, and he reported, "the universal feeling among radical men here is that his death is a godsend."[36] That's why Senator Ben Wade said there "will be no trouble running the government now." Lincoln and Seward had been "the great leaders in the policy of mercy," and Grant's terms with Lee had been too easy. With Lincoln gone and Seward gravely wounded, Julian believed "justice shall be done and the righteous ends of the war made sure." Another member of the committee, Republican senator from Michigan Zachariah Chandler, wrote to his wife, "I believe that the Almighty God continued Mr. Lincoln in office as long as he was useful, and then substituted a better man to finish the work."[37] Chandler ultimately concluded that Lincoln's "heart was too good—too full of the milk of human kindness."

Both Julian and Chandler alluded to a theme that would appear time and again in the various eulogies, speeches, and letters in the days and weeks after Lincoln's death. Many northerners, freedmen, and even southern Unionists believed Lincoln was too *kind* to provide the justice the traitors deserved.[38] Because God had a plan for America, he had mysteriously taken Lincoln's life at the conclusion of the war, leaving the stern and unforgiving Andrew Johnson to finish the job. The fact that Lincoln was assassinated on Good Friday somehow gave it all even more religious significance. Two days later, on Easter Sunday, Reverend C. Parker from the First Dutch Reformed Church spoke of the "great leniency of the late President toward the rebels."[39] Parker floated the idea that "it might have been the purpose of the Almighty that this leniency should not continue, and that the task of punishing traitors should be accomplished with a sterner purpose."

Literary giant Ralph Waldo Emerson, in his eulogy for Lincoln in Concord, Massachusetts, eloquently developed the theme of the kindly Lincoln, who was ill-suited to the harsh work of justice.[40] He began by saying that he doubted "if any death has caused so much pain to mankind as this has caused, or will cause, on its announcement." But Emerson later declared that, despite the pain, the awful event was already "burning into glory around the victim." Lincoln had lived long enough "to keep the greatest promise that ever man made to his fellow men—the practical abolition of slavery." Though he had died tragically, Lincoln had accomplished more than any other American except for George Washington.

Emerson further wondered if Lincoln had "reached the term" and perhaps "could no longer serve us." It might even be possible that "what remained to be done required new and uncommitted hands—a new spirit born out of the ashes of the war; and that Heaven, wishing to show the world a completed benefactor, shall make him serve his country even more by death than his life." He then concluded by declaring, "The kindness of kings consists in justice and strength." The rebels had outraged our easy good nature, and had driven loyal Americans "to an unwonted firmness, to secure the salvation of this country in the next ages."

Herman Melville—poet, lecturer, and author of *Moby Dick*—addressed these themes in verse. In his poem "The Martyr," he begins,

> Good Friday was the day
> of the prodigy and crime,
> When they killed him in his pity,
> When they killed him in his prime
> Of clemency and calm—
> When the yearning he was filled
> To redeem the evil-willed,
> And, though conqueror, be kind;
> But they killed him in his kindness,
> In their madness and their blindness,
> And they killed him from behind.

Here, the saintly Lincoln is killed from behind—John Wilkes Booth, everyone knew, shot Lincoln in the back of the head—despite the president's benevolent intentions toward the rebels. And Melville writes "*they* killed him"— apparently *all* of the Confederacy bore responsibility for the murder.[41]

Melville, like Emerson, hints that God may have felt a sterner leader might be needed for the work ahead:

> He lieth in blood—
> The father in his face;
> They have killed him, the Forgiver—
> The Avenger takes his place,
> The Avenger wisely stern,
> Who in righteousness shall do
> What the heavens call him to,
> And the parricides remand;
> For they killed him in his kindness,
> In their madness and their blindness,
> And his blood is on their hand.

The "Avenger," of course, is Andrew Johnson, who was widely known among Americans to have a tougher stance on traitors than Lincoln. The American people, according to Melville, would support Johnson in stern measures. He concludes with,

> There is sobbing of the strong
> And a pall upon the land;
> But the People in their weeping
> Bare the iron hand;
> Beware the People weeping
> When they bare the iron hand.

The murder of Lincoln promised to usher in a harsher environment for the likes of Robert E. Lee, Jefferson Davis, and other Confederate leaders.

If Emerson and Melville provided especially eloquent expressions of the mysteries of Providence, the Pastor Alonzo Quint delivered a much more earthly appeal for justice in his Easter Sunday sermon following the assassination. Where Emerson cryptically spoke of a new age, and Melville talked of baring the iron hand, Quint clearly laid out a detailed case for the destruction of Southern chivalry, "root and branch, twig and leaf."[42]

At the beginning of his Easter sermon at the North Congregational Church in New Bedford, Massachusetts, Quint remembered Lincoln had spoken kindly of Lee and his army and was planning on a wide amnesty. "Then he was murdered," Quint reminded his parishioners.[43] He then chastised the Confederates for violating their oaths and sense of honor. And he singled out General Lee for his "fiendish treatment of prisoners."[44] Even though Booth shot the president, Quint believed Southern chivalry was responsible for the crime. Other sermons that day boldly stated that Davis and Lee were no different than Booth. As we see in Melville's poem, this was another theme that emerged in the aftermath of the assassination. Regardless of whether or not the Confederate leadership actually planned the assassination directly, it bore responsibility for the act, which was a natural result of treason, according to many northerners and freedmen. Quint believed generals like Lee were "murderers all" and that prison should be their home until the "halter should say that treason is a crime."[45] In addition to the generals, rebel statesmen and judges should be severely punished, too.

At another memorial service in the New York Custom House, a speaker believed Lincoln's death was the work of God, so that punishment could be meted out to the Confederate leaders. Midway through the speech, attendees were yelling, "Hang Lee!" and "The rebels deserve damnation!"[46] In general, the Easter sermons were consistent in their demand for punishing rebels— whether by hanging, exile, or the confiscation of property.

The question of which and how many rebels must be punished was on the minds of many northerners in the days immediately after Lincoln's murder. An early meeting between the new president and radical Republican leader Ben Wade illustrated Johnson's thinking early on. The president asked, "Well, Mr. Wade, what would you do were you in my place and charged with my responsibilities?"[47] Wade replied, "I think I should either force into exile or hang about ten or twelve of the worst fellows: perhaps by way of full measure, I should make it thirteen, just a baker's dozen." Johnson then asked, "But how are you going to pick out so small a number and show them to be guiltier than the rest?" Wade confidently answered, "It won't do to hang a very large number, and I think if you would give me time, I could name thirteen that stand at the head in the work of the rebellion. I think we could all agree on Jeff Davis, Toombs, Benjamin Slidell, Mason, and Howell Cobb. If we did no more than drive these half-dozen out of the country, we should accomplish a good deal." Johnson concluded the meeting by expressing surprise that Wade was prepared to "let the traitors escape so easily." He indicated that he intended a much more thorough policy of punishment toward the rebel leadership and hoped Wade would provide his "heartiest support."

Andrew Johnson would have been well aware that a large number of ordinary citizens supported his desire to make treason odious. In the weeks after taking office, Johnson received hundreds of letters from all across America.[48] Many of the letters—from veterans, widows, and others deeply affected by the war—expressed enthusiasm for Johnson's tougher approach toward the rebels, especially Robert E. Lee and Jefferson Davis. Those two leaders topped everyone's list of those who should be punished to the fullest extent of the law.

Many of the citizen correspondents were in no mood for leniency. A former soldier named Apollos Comstock urged that Lee be arrested "with the other leading military and civil acknowledged heads of Treason," and then killed "by poison or pistol or knife." George Cothman of Buffalo wrote that "Lee prolonged the war two years let him hang and die a traitor's death," and added, "Therefore don't talk to me of mercy or sympathy for Lee any more than for Jeff Davis. There's no difference between traitors." Elisha Chick also zeroed in on the leadership, writing, "The leaders and the forward men of this rebellion ought to be hung or driven from the country, their property confiscated, their lands divided up." Encouragingly, she told Johnson, "The people will sustain you in any measures however stringent you may think it proper to adopt." Another writer said simply, "The whole of the North says hang those culprits."

The citizens who wrote Johnson addressed a number of common themes. They loved Lincoln, but thought he would have been too lenient in pursuing justice. Mary Caldwell wondered if "perhaps God saw that Mr. Lincoln never having experienced what treason is, would be too lenient than he [Andrew Johnson] who had lived in the midst of traitors during this great strife, who has suffered everything but death at their hands." The writers also believed that the Confederate leadership—Jefferson Davis and Robert E. Lee, at the very least—should face punishment. As Samuel Snyder wrote, the ordinary and ignorant rebels should be forgiven, "but certainly all well informed and designing rascals should be severely punished." And finally, the writers felt the assassination of Lincoln was somehow a natural result of treason against the Union. One citizen described John Wilkes Booth as having graduated from the "university of treason" that had Jefferson Davis and Robert E. Lee as teachers.

One of the most heartfelt letters to Johnson, written by a former veteran from Wilkes-Barre, Pennsylvania, is representative of the mass of correspondence, but its simple emotional power makes it stand out, too.[49]

To: Andrew Johnson, President of the Greatest Republic on Earth
I congratulate you on your having arisen to this high and responsible and very useful position.
When the terrible news came of the assassination of President Lincoln I was for one disheartened. Not knowing much of your previous history I feared that the consequences would be exceedingly disastrous. But I am thankful to see the Presidential seat so well filled. (comparatively I might say more than filled). My fears are dispelled and my hopes are realized.
In your case we see that virtue has received its well merited reward. You were from a slave holding state. You stood by your Country and its Constitution. You opposed secession and Rebels. We now see your exaltation. Forming a wonderful contrast to the degradation of Jeff Davis.
We were pleased to hear of the speedy retribution visited upon Booth the assassin and the capture of Davis too. From this point the cry is hang him! hang him! As a Christian I cannot conscientiously ask for vengeance. But I shall not weep if justice is meted out to him as i know it will be when all is known to you.
I have been in the army as a volunteer. And I have or did have three brothers two of whom have been drafted. One my eldest Brother (a healthy and stout

good looking young man) volunteered in the summer of 1862. In the year 1863 he was made a prisoner by the Rebels at Gettysburg and carried to Belle Island near Richmond where he died before the close of the year. Literally starved to death in his own country for which he was fighting. O, God! it drives me almost frantic when I think of these barbarities. Why common and speedy murder looks like mercy compared to such cruelty. The Black Hole of Calcutta has been out done in our own free Country.

It is just that those who caused such terrible suffering should lose their lives. The world should not be troubled with them longer. How can we live in the same country with men of such principles? I hope those principles will be something more than smothered.

Excuse me I have written too much perhaps more than you will have time to read.

God help and strengthen you to do your great work.

I would like to see you and take you by the hand but I do not expect to be in Washington for years yet. I have been reading what you said to the Sunday school children of your City. It did me good (I am superintending a little Sunday school). I intend to read your speech to my Scholars on Sunday.

Of course you will not have time to answer such an unimportant letter. But I would feel highly complimented if you could but send me your autograph. God be with you.

From Your very Humble Servant

Chas. Linskill

Wilkes Barre, PA

Lincoln's death became a touchstone for the grief of so many citizens.[50] Not only did the writer lose a president, he lost his eldest brother, a "healthy and stout looking young man," who cruelly died of starvation in a prison camp. The pain of the loss is still raw: "O, God! It drives me almost frantic when I think of these barbarities." And the requirements of justice were clear: "those who caused such terrible suffering should lose their lives. The world should not be troubled with them longer. How can we live in the same country with men of such principles?"

Americans mourned Lincoln intensely and keenly sought out justice because they were *also* mourning their fathers and brothers who had died in the war. Overall, roughly 750,000 Americans from both sides were killed, with many more wounded and missing. Historian Drew Gilpin Faust reminds us that all of this death "marked a sharp and alarming departure from existing preconceptions about who should die."[51] It was a very sad time in America in the aftermath of the war and Lincoln's violent death.

Walt Whitman captured this sadness beautifully in "When Lilacs Last in the Dooryard Bloom'd."[52] Whitman loved Lincoln and would even wait for him in the mornings, so he could see the president ride by when he was returning from the Soldier's Home, Lincoln's summer lodgings during much of the war.[53] Whitman also had a strong connection with ordinary soldiers from his volunteering at DC military hospitals. This poem was for both Lincoln and the ordinary soldiers. He begins his elegy by referring to Lincoln—the great star in the western sky:

> When lilacs last in the dooryard bloom'd,
> And the great star early droop'd in the western sky in the night,
> I mourn'd, and yet shall mourn with ever-returning spring.

Later, he mentions the even greater loss of all those soldiers:

> I saw battle-corpses, myriads of them,
> And the white skeletons of young men, I saw them,
> I saw the debris and debris of all the slain soldiers of the war . . .

In a powerful image, Whitman talks of breaking copious sprigs of lilac for all of the coffins:

> . . . now the lilac that blooms the first,
> Copious I break, I break the sprigs from the bushes,
> With loaded arms I come, pouring for you,
> For you and the coffins all of you, O death.

In the days after Lincoln's death, Americans were looking to heal their "republic of suffering," and many were hoping to punish those who they believed *caused* that suffering.

In addition to all of the letters flowing in, the new president had thirty-two formal appointments in the two weeks after April 16.[54] He frequently met with state delegations in his temporary workspace at the treasury building. On April 16, he met with the Illinois delegation. On the twenty-first, he met with delegations from Ohio, Maine, and Indiana. Three days later, he welcomed a delegation from every single southern state. The president spent a tremendous amount of time listening to the American people and their representatives during the first days of his administration.

In a typical meeting, Johnson would say a few words to each of the delegations, being sure to include his standard declaration that treason and traitors should be made odious. His talk to the Indiana delegation provided an especially clear statement of his policy toward the rebels and was described by one reporter as "his most definite committal to the line of policy he proposes to pursue." Another reporter believed the Indiana address was "more important than any he has yet delivered."

In his remarks to the Hoosier delegation led by Governor Oliver P. Morton, Johnson began, as he often did, by reminding his listeners that "in reference to what my Administration will be, while I occupy my present position, I must refer you to the past."[55] Then he moved on to the main theme of the address: treason and traitors. As usual, he emphasized that treason was a crime that must be punished. He also noted that most people would, of course, prefer to be kind and lenient, but sometimes the effect of such a policy is to "produce misery and woe to the mass of mankind." He then concluded his remarks on treason by making a distinction between the rebel leadership and the majority of southern working people:

> . . . while I say that the penalties of the law, in a stern and inflexible manner should be executed upon conscious, intelligent, and influential traitors—the leaders, who have deceived thousands upon thousands of laboring men who have been drawn into this rebellion—and while I say, as to the leaders, punishment, I also say leniency, conciliation, and amnesty to the thousands whom they have misled and deceived.

Johnson clearly envisioned punishing Confederate leaders like Jefferson Davis and Robert E. Lee, while also providing a path to amnesty for the vast majority of southerners had who supported the Confederacy.

This common-sense notion of singling out the leadership for punishment while forgiving everyone else was widely held by northerners after the war. One of the most eloquent presentations of that argument had been made by Reverend Henry Ward Beecher, arguably the most famous orator in America at that time, at the flag-raising ceremony at Fort Sumter, South Carolina, on Friday, April 14. The ceremony marked the fourth anniversary of the fall of Fort Sumter and was just hours before the assassination of Lincoln.

Midway through his powerful address, Reverend Beecher said, "I charge the whole guilt of this war upon the ambitious, educated, plotting political leaders of the South."[56] He believed the southern ruling class had tricked the common people "with lies, with sophistries, with cruel deceits and slanders." The result was the desolation and destruction of the South. For their sins, Beecher argued, "God will reveal judgment and arraign at his bar these mighty miscreants," and then these "most-accursed and detested of all criminals" will be tormented for all eternity by God. Sternly, the Reverend added, "thus shall it be with all who betray their country, and all in heaven and upon earth will say, amen." As for the common people who were misled, Beecher urged forgiveness, and hoped that the resources of the nation would be applied to rebuilding their prosperity.

The idea of concentrating on punishing the top Confederate leaders had been formally presented to President Lincoln right before the close of the war. After Lincoln returned from his visit to recently liberated Richmond in early April, Massachusetts Senator Charles Sumner gave him a letter from legal expert Francis Lieber proposing a general prosecution of the leading rebels. Lieber, a legal authority who had written for the administration *General Orders No. 100*—an authoritative compilation of legal guidelines for the armies in the field—desired the trial and execution of roughly a dozen to twenty of the most prominent leaders. He created two lists for Lincoln.[57] The first list consisted of those who *must* be included: Davis, Beauregard, Wilder, Stephens, and Breckinridge. The second list was made up of those who could *not* be excluded: "General Lee &c, &c." Sumner told Lieber that Lincoln "read it with much interest."

The first move against the Confederate leadership came rather quickly after the assassination.[58] On May 2, 1865, Secretary of War Stanton wrote Brigadier General Joseph Holt, the top lawyer for the army, saying the president wanted a list of persons from Canada and Richmond who may have been complicit in the murder of Lincoln and the attempted assassination of Seward. Wasting no time, Holt replied later that day with some names. He advised Stanton that he had heard testimony indicating that Jefferson Davis, George Sanders, Beverley Tucker, Jacob Thompson, William Cleary, and Clement Clay were all behind the assassination plot. Stanton then prepared a proclamation offering rewards for the capture of the men on the list, which was promptly approved by President Johnson and published that same day. The proclamation offered a reward of $100,000 for the capture of Davis, with smaller rewards for the other alleged conspirators.[59] Stanton and Holt were even more intent on punishing rebels than the unforgiving Johnson—the hardliners had clearly seized the reins of the new administration.

In the weeks after offering rewards for the capture of Davis and the others, the Johnson administration slowly and methodically began apprehending the leading members of the Confederate States of America.[60] On May 10, Union cavalrymen finally discovered and arrested Jefferson Davis in southern Georgia, after a widely publicized manhunt. In a last-ditch effort to escape capture, Davis had put on a waterproof coat that looked very much like a woman's dress, thereby providing northern cartoonists, among others, with rich fodder for unflattering depictions of the proud southerner.

Figure 2.3.   Jefferson Davis's attempted escape, 1865. *Source:* **The Alfred Whital Stern Collection of Lincolniana. Library of Congress.**

The diminutive Alexander Stephens, the Confederacy's vice president and former ally of Lincoln, was arrested at his home in Georgia. His captors transported him north on the same steamer as Jefferson Davis. They eventually took him further north, however, and imprisoned him at Fort Warren in Boston Harbor. Clement Clay, one of the alleged conspirators in the Lincoln assassination, voluntarily gave himself up to Union troops, who transported him to Fort Monroe, where he became Davis's neighbor. James Seddon, a former Secretary of War for the Confederacy, was arrested in Virginia and jailed at Fort Pulaski in Georgia.

Many Confederate leaders successfully eluded their northern captors. Robert Toombs, a former Secretary of State for the Confederate States of America, escaped by sailing from New Orleans to Havana. He eventually ended up in Europe, where he remained until 1867. John C. Breckinridge, who ran for president against Lincoln in 1860 and succeeded Seddon as the Confederacy's Secretary of War, also made his way to Cuba. He, too, ended up in Europe, returning to the United States in 1868. The uncompromising Judah Benjamin, who filled multiple roles for the Confederacy, fled to England, where he stayed for the rest of his life.

One of the Confederacy's top two leaders remained in limbo, however. In April and May of 1865, the Johnson administration wasn't quite ready to proceed against Robert E. Lee, who, along with Davis, was at the very top of the Confederate hierarchy. Still a prisoner on parole, Lee chose not to flee, remaining—at least temporarily—in his new home in Richmond, Virginia. Many northerners believed Lee should be on the short list of those Confederates deserving of punishment. A strong case was made against him in the press and other public forums.

Indeed, one of the most constant demands that emerged from the national discussion on treason and traitors was that Lee was foremost among those deserving of punishment. Fiery abolitionist Wendell Phillips referred to Lee as the "bloodiest and guiltiest" of all the rebels and believed there would be "little fitness in hanging any lesser wretch."[61] Frederick Douglass went further, saying John Wilkes Booth was "was not one whit guiltier" than General Lee—a sentiment shared by many.[62] An editorial in the *New York Tribune* offered a similar view of Lee, arguing that "such a man is more guilty than any other."[63] The *Cleveland Morning Leader* declared that compared to Jefferson Davis, who was often referred to as the "arch-traitor," Lee was "the wickeder and baser of the two" because it was "a selfish ambition that led him, Judas-like to betray his country."[64] The *Ohio Farmer*'s stance was equally harsh: "Robert E. Lee is now so poor that he has not the wherewith to clothe himself. If this be true, let the government relieve him at once—give him ten feet of rope, and six feet of soil. If every *traitor* earned this reward, Lee surely is the one."[65]

Many observers couldn't bear the thought that Lee remained unpunished and was free to go about his business in Richmond. Abolitionist Lydia Maria Child spoke of the arrogance of former rebels like Lee. In the journal *Harper's Weekly*, a writer lamented the fact that Lee remained unapologetic for his actions during the war.[66] Especially provocative was Lee's farewell to his troops, where the general offered his admiration to those soldiers who—the columnist adds—"would have destroyed this nation." As long as unbowed

Figure 2.4. *Freedom's immortal triumph! Finale of the Jeff Davis Die-nasty*, 1865.
Source: American cartoon filing series. Library of Congress.

traitors such as Lee remained unpunished, they were thought to be "ready at any favorable moment to open fire again upon the national life and honor." An editorial in *The Liberator*, abolitionist William Lloyd Garrison's publication, believed the farewell order was a "slap in the face" to loyal soldiers.[67] The *New York Times* concurred, viewing the "farewell order" to the troops as a sign of defiance and an offense against propriety. The same editorial felt Lee's decision to be photographed by Mathew Brady in "the toggery of the bastard Confederacy" had troubling political undertones.[68]

Lee's critics often accused him of complicity in the abuse of Union prisoners of war, an extremely emotional topic for Americans at that time. Many believed Lee, as the Confederacy's leading general during the final years of the war, should have protested the atrocious conditions in the southern prisons. Phillips said Americans shouldn't have to "tolerate in our streets the presence of such a wretch whose hand upheld Libby Prison and Andersonville, and whose soul is black with sixty-four thousand deaths of prisoners by starvation and torture." One editorial writer wrote that Lee, "in his tent, might have almost heard the groans of the starving, rotting soldiers of the Union upon Belle Isle and in Libby prison, yet who spoke never a word nor lifted a finger for their relief." The fact that Lee could have done something but didn't was a sign of his poor character, according to several publications. An editorial in *The Liberator* argued, "Lee had the power to prevent or mitigate the sufferings of our prisoners, the worst tyrant and tormenter, from the remotest ages of Paganism down to the cruelest instrument of the French Reign of terror, was not so wicked as he." Critics of Lee found it impossible to believe that he was unable to alleviate the suffering of northern prisoners.

The *New York Times* and *Chicago Tribune* led the way among the nation's newspapers in making the case that Lee be tried and punished for treason. In "The Paroled Rebel Soldiers and the General Amnesty," a lengthy editorial published on June 4, 1865, the *New York Times* argued that Grant's agreement with Lee was a military arrangement only that did not protect the Confederate general from prosecution for treason once the war was over.[69] For the *Times*, Lee levied war against the United States "more strenuously than any other man in the land, and therefore has been specially guilty of the crime of treason, as defined by the Constitution of the United States." Consequently, the government *must* bring a case against the rebel general in chief. The *Chicago Tribune* was possibly even more critical of Lee, and devoted considerable space to challenging his reputation for having Christian values.

In the heated atmosphere after the Lincoln assassination, quite a few northerners compared Lee to the infamous John Brown, the abolitionist who was captured, tried, and hanged for the Harper's Ferry raid in 1859. Brown had been found guilty of treason against the state of Virginia after a jury deliberated for only forty-five minutes. In a letter to the lieutenant governor of Maryland, which was made public in May 1865, the abolitionist Dr. J. E. Snodgrass argued that Lee should be indicted for treason against the state of Maryland, just like Brown had been indicted on charges against Virginia.[70] Lee, of course, had invaded Maryland in 1862, which culminated in the battle of Antietam. Snodgrass noted that far more lives were lost and more property was destroyed by Lee's treason than by Brown's. Yet, Brown had fought for a cause he believed to be just, while Lee was now saying he didn't support slavery, and had thought secession was a bad idea all along. Coincidentally, it had been Colonel Robert E. Lee of the US Army that eventually put down John Brown's short-lived rebellion at Harper's Ferry.

Andrew Johnson, now famous for his vow to make treason odious, surely heard the growing drumbeat for bringing Lee to justice. While the former Confederate general remained free at his home in Richmond, Johnson—working with Attorney General James Speed and a zealous federal judge for Virginia named John C. Underwood—set in motion a process for bringing formal charges against him. America's southern president, who had steadfastly supported the Union throughout the war, would soon confront the southern hero who had tried to destroy it.

3

"HANDS DRIPPING WITH THE BLOOD OF SLAUGHTERED INNOCENTS."

The Johnson administration moved immediately toward prosecuting Lee and the other Confederate leaders for treason. Just ten days after the assassination of Abraham Lincoln, Judge John C. Underwood traveled to Washington, DC, to meet Andrew Johnson at his temporary rooms at the Treasury Department—the president had graciously allowed the distraught Mary Lincoln to remain in the White House until late May.[1] Underwood led a delegation of loyal southerners made up of a "large number of southern gentlemen, refugees from the wrath of the rebellion." Johnson, who warmly greeted each member of the delegation, was profoundly moved by meeting men who had "undergone, for the truth's sake, sufferings similar to his own." At 11:00 a.m., Judge Underwood offered a few remarks on behalf of his delegation. Southern Unionists, who represented a small percentage of the overall population of the Confederate states, had risked their lives and fortunes in order to remain loyal to the US government.

Underwood began by thanking Johnson for his recent speeches promising to punish the Confederate leaders for treason. Southern Unionists, the judge noted, had nothing but kindness for the common people, and would not say, like Joshua of old, that "everyone who rebels shall be put to death." No, Underwood believed punishment should be reserved for the "wicked leaders" who are "neither humbled nor subdued." Emphasizing the continued defiance of the former Confederate leadership, Underwood declared that it is "folly to give sugar plums to tigers and hyenas." As a judge and a southern resident, he underlined why it was important to pursue justice. Clemency and mercy for traitors would be "cruelty and murder to the innocent and unborn." Only by punishing the traitors severely, Underwood argued, could the United States hope to avoid another revolt in the future. He reinforced this point by saying, "If General Jackson [President Andrew Jackson, 1829–1837] had punished the treason of Calhoun, we should not have witnessed this rebellion." Underwood then concluded his address with the belief that Johnson's administration would prove "a terror to evil doers and a protection to all who pursued the paths of peace."

Johnson thanked Underwood for his remarks that had enunciated and expressed his own feelings "to the truest extent." Happy to be among his countrymen, Johnson—who had served as military governor of the liberated portions of Tennessee from 1862 to 1864—wondered if loyal southerners perhaps had a better sense of the "true policy which should be pursued." After his opening pleasantries, Johnson delivered his usual thoughts on the need to punish treason. On the importance of justice, he fully supported Underwood's belief, arguing that "mercy without justice is a crime." Johnson finished his brief talk by vowing to discharge his duty toward the rebel leadership.

★ ★ ★

The life of John Curtis Underwood, who led the delegation of loyal southerners that day, seems highly implausible in retrospect.[2] Raised in central New York, he moved to Virginia as a young man, where he married Maria Gloria Jackson, a cousin of Stonewall Jackson. Later, as the sole federal district judge for Virginia from 1864 to 1871, Underwood would play a central role in Reconstruction. During that time, he'd oversee the indictment of Lee and thirty-eight other Confederate leaders in addition to presiding, alongside Chief Justice Salmon Chase, at the trial of Jefferson Davis. As a champion of Radical Republicanism in what had been *the* leading state of the Confederacy, Underwood would become the most hated man in Virginia in the nineteenth century.

Though largely forgotten today, Underwood's story is one of drama, bravery, and idealism. In his commitment to abolitionism and voting rights for both African Americans and women, modern Americans may discover him to be a man before his time.

While residing in the wealthiest and most populous slaveholding state before the war, Underwood became one of the earliest leaders of the Republican Party, which was founded in opposition to the extension of slavery into the federal territories. A passionate foe of the "peculiar institution," Underwood's "pen and tongue were always busily employed in the advocacy of the right of the colored man to freedom," according to one of his closest colleagues. At the first Republican convention in Philadelphia in 1856, Underwood accused Virginia's statesmen of polluting "its fair land with the sweat and tears of unpaid labor." Later in his career, Judge Underwood recommended confiscating the land of leading rebels in order to provide the freedmen with a means to support themselves. Perhaps unsurprisingly, friends and family of Underwood feared for his life on numerous occasions. Virginians considered his opinions notorious in the 1850s and 1860s.

Underwood was born in Litchfield, New York, on March 14, 1809—just one month after Abraham Lincoln. His deeply religious parents raised him to loathe the injustices of slavery; abolitionism would be central to the young Underwood's development. After graduating from Hamilton College in 1832, he moved to Virginia where he worked as a teacher in the household of a powerful Virginia politician. Eventually, he'd marry one of his former pupils, a daughter of former Congressman Edward B. Jackson.

Throughout the 1850s, Underwood pursued various schemes in order to demonstrate the superiority of free labor. His fiery speech denouncing slavery in Virginia at the Republican convention of 1856 brought him considerable notoriety. Indeed, his neighbors in Clarke County, Virginia, recommended that he "leave the State as speedily as he can find it in his power to do so." Critics told him he had "broken the rules" of the Old Dominion. After initially supporting New York Senator William Seward for president in 1860, Underwood campaigned nationally on behalf of Abraham Lincoln of Illinois, who would win a historic victory that November. The new president rewarded Underwood's efforts with a position in the Treasury Department in 1861. Just two years later, Lincoln selected Underwood as a federal judge for eastern Virginia, a position he would hold until his death in 1873. For nine crucial years, a highly partisan, outspoken champion of the freedmen sat on the federal bench of the leading southern state—the birthplace of Washington, Jefferson, Marshall, *and* Robert E. Lee.

Lucius Chandler, a federal district attorney who worked closely with Underwood, noted there were extremely bitter feelings directed toward the judge during his time in Virginia. One observer referred to Underwood as the bête noir of Richmond, a man who was regarded with "horror and disgust." The Virginia press often referred to him as a Jacobin, and always reminded its audience that he originally came from up north. One rather childish editorial described him as an

Figure 3.1.   Judge John C. Underwood. *Source:* **Library of Congress.**

absurd, blasphemous, cowardly, devilish, empirical, fanatical, ghoulish, horrible, ignorant, jacobinal, knavish, lily-livered, maudlin, nondescript, odious, poisonous, querulous, rascally, sycophantic, traitorous, unrighteous, venal, witless, extravagant, yankeeish zero.[3]

Perhaps blinded by this type of hatred, some later writers have been sharply critical of Underwood. The renowned biographer of Salmon Chase, for example, described him as the "corrupt and vengeful district court judge, John Underwood."[4]

This view of Underwood is incorrect. Chandler understood that Underwood's "unpardonable sin was unsoundness, as it was called, on the slavery question." Bradley T. Johnson, a former Confederate general, who had been indicted for treason by a Maryland court, described him as "diligent, laborious, prompt, always ready and courteous to suitors & the bar."[5] After receiving a pardon, Johnson worked in the Virginia federal court system and emphasized that his opinion of Underwood was free of bias—he actually disagreed with the judge on every possible political issue imaginable. No doubt Underwood *was* a partisan on the major topics of the day, and he could be indelicate in his countless speeches and numerous letters to various publications. Yet, those who knew him best also describe him as hard-working and honest. Chandler declared that during their entire acquaintance, he had never seen him angry or "known him to speak with bitterness of any individual, or do an unkind or ungenerous act." John Curtis Underwood may have been a zealot, but he was an honorable zealot.

★   ★   ★

Just as Andrew Johnson began settling into his demanding new role, Underwood wrote him a letter on April 21 about prosecuting the rebel leadership during the next term of the US District Court in eastern Virginia.[6] Writing three days before their meeting at the Treasury Department, Underwood said he was ready for official action on his part and was interested in hearing both Johnson and Chief Justice Salmon Chase's views on whether to call a jury at this time and the number of persons to be prosecuted. He also noted that Lucius Chandler, district attorney for eastern Virginia, had "tasted the fruits of rebellion by a long confinement in the Libby prison for his loyalty," and would therefore "be certain to summon a jury that will properly and efficiently discharge their duties to the country." Underwood closed his letter by adding, "the returning rebels now swarming in our towns are so defiant in their conduct, that the condition of loyal men in this State will be not only uncomfortable but extremely unsafe unless the power of the Government to punish treason shall be fully demonstrated."

Attorney General James Speed, acting on Johnson's behalf, responded to Underwood three days later by agreeing that "the rebellious spirit now rampant must be subdued."[7] Speed also mentioned the new president's "earnest wish" that the Confederate leaders be brought to justice. Apparently, the failure to provide concrete plans by the administration's top lawyer was troubling to Underwood. He soon wrote to Chief Justice Chase complaining of the "gingerly and overcautious" letter of the attorney general.[8] Underwood argued that there mustn't be any delay in enforcing the laws punishing treason, believing that "a little vigor now would be worth much hereafter." Given everything he knew about Andrew Johnson, Underwood felt certain that Speed's letter did not reflect the president's views.

His instinct was correct. Former Senator Preston King, who was serving as Johnson's de facto chief of staff during the early days of his presidency, visited Underwood on April 28, 1865.[9] King asked that Underwood make a second trip to Johnson's rooms at the Treasury Department the following morning in order to discuss judicial proceedings against the rebel leadership. Both Johnson and King were eager to set the legal process in motion. Johnson had vowed on countless occasions to make treason odious, and he intended to fulfill that promise as soon as possible.

The meeting between Johnson, King, and Underwood occurred immediately after King's visit to the judge. Underwood told them that a court would convene in Norfolk, Virginia, during the May term, and that a grand jury would be ready at that time. Johnson and King then expressed their view that it was the duty of the court to present to the grand jury "the views of the Supreme Court of the United States as expressed by Mr. Justice Greer, that the late civil war was a rebellion, and that those who had been engaged in it were, not only enemies to the United States, but were also guilty of treason, and that the more prominent and guilty leaders ought to be indicted for their conduct."[10] They added that they both believed the conduct of the Confederate leadership ultimately resulted in the assassination of President Lincoln.

According to Bradley T. Johnson, the former Confederate general who wrote about this meeting many years later in the 1870s, Underwood needed to be convinced by Johnson and King that the war was a rebellion and not a larger conflict between two sovereign nations. Supposedly, Underwood had believed that "the great conflict had outgrown the character of a rebellion, and had assumed the dimensions of a civil war."[11] The distinction between a rebellion and a war between two sovereign powers was a considerable one. If the conflict was a rebellion, then the rebels could be justifiably charged with violating "Article III, Section 3" of the US Constitution, which reads:

> Treason against the United States, shall consist only in levying war against them, or in adhering to their enemies, giving them aid and comfort. No person shall be convicted of treason unless on the testimony of two witnesses to the same overt act, or on confession in open court.

> The Congress shall have power to declare the punishment of treason, but no attainder of treason shall work corruption of blood, or forfeiture except during the life of the person attainted.

If found guilty of treason, which is the only crime actually defined in the Constitution, the rebels would have faced capital punishment according to a congressional enactment of 1790, which declared that traitors "shall suffer death" for their crimes. Underwood apparently told Bradley Johnson years later that his "hostility to capital punishment" had made him hesitant to view the war as a rebellion.[12] In the end, he reluctantly agreed to advise the grand jury as Johnson and King recommended.

Bradley T. Johnson's account of the meeting between President Johnson, King, and Underwood raises some questions. As a former Confederate officer, Johnson had himself been indicted for treason by a Maryland court. After he was pardoned, he worked as an officer of the fourth circuit court under Chief Justice Salmon Chase. In 1872 and 1873, Johnson compiled a collection of cases involving Chase and it was as a result of those efforts that we learned the details of this meeting. Unfortunately, the notion that Underwood had to be talked into charging the leaders with treason seems unlikely.

In his letter to Chase, which was written before the meeting with King and Andrew Johnson, Underwood wrote, "our great need is a vigorous administration of the laws punishing treason." In his remarks during the meeting of the southern delegation with the president, Underwood clearly laid out the case for punishing traitors. Bradley Johnson may have misunderstood Underwood's account of that meeting from seven years earlier. Or perhaps Underwood's memory was flawed. One way or another, it seems much more likely that Underwood, King, and Andrew Johnson agreed completely on the need to charge the Confederate leaders with treason in the spring of 1865. At their meeting, they must have devoted considerable thought to determining who, precisely, would be charged.

★   ★   ★

America's constitutional law on treason went into effect in 1790. It borrowed heavily from England's Treason Act of 1351, a statute passed by Parliament during the reign of Edward III, which defined treason as

> [w]hen a Man doth compass or imagine the Death of our Lord the King, or our Lady his Queen or of their eldest Son and Heir; or if a Man do violate the

King's Companion or the King's eldest Daughter unmarried, or the Wife of the
King's eldest Son and Heir; or if a Man do levy War against our Lord the King
in his Realm, or be adherent to the King's Enemies in his Realm, giving to
them Aid and Comfort in the Realm or elsewhere.[13]

One can easily see the similarity in language between the American law and
the earlier English one. Both define treason in part as the act of "levying war"
or "giving aid and comfort" to enemies. In England, treason was considered
one of the worst possible crimes, and the prescribed punishment was truly
horrific.[14] First, the traitor was dragged across the ground by a horse. Then, he
would be hanged, disemboweled, beheaded, and cut into four sections. Female
traitors were burned.

The Jacobite Rising in 1745 provided Americans of the Civil War era
with a more recent example of how rebels were treated in Great Britain. In
the aftermath of the rebellion, officials of the Crown had many of the rebels
shot. Those who escaped had their homes plundered and burned. In addition,
numerous rebels were imprisoned, tried, and hanged. In the end, 3,471 men,
women, and children were imprisoned; of these, 120 men were executed.
Quite a few of the rebels were tried, found guilty, and then pardoned. As part
of their pardon agreement, they were sent off as indentured servants to the
New World. Interestingly, both commoners *and* aristocrats faced punishment
for their involvement with the Jacobite Rising. This contrasted with the Johnson administration approach, which would single out the Confederate leadership. To make the trials more manageable, the British government had the
ordinary soldiers draw lots "so that every twentieth prisoner would be tried
and punished."[15]

Despite the similarity of language, the development of American treason
law differed considerably from the English model.[16] During the early modern
period, English judges began to take a broader view of treason. Simply opposing the laws or speaking out against the monarch eventually became known as
"constructive treason." America's founding fathers were fearful of the arbitrary
nature of constructive treason, and were therefore careful to clearly define
treason in the Constitution. Recognizing the danger of "newfangled and arti-
ficial treasons" as James Madison described them, the convention took the
precaution of "inserting a constitutional definition of the crime." From the
1790s until the beginning of the Civil War, American courts took an increasingly narrow view of treason that required an actual levying of war against the
government for there to be evidence of the crime. As a result, treason cases

were extremely rare in the early Republic, with John Brown the only prominent figure to be convicted and hanged for the crime in the years prior to the Civil War.

The most famous and influential treason case in early American history was the United States versus Aaron Burr in 1807.[17] President Thomas Jefferson believed that Burr, who notoriously had killed Alexander Hamilton in a duel in 1804, had been plotting to separate the western territories from the United States as part of a larger scheme to make war on the Spanish empire in Mexico. After Burr's men resisted efforts to subdue them by a Virginia militia, Burr was arrested and charged with treason. Crucially, even though Burr was not present on the day his men opposed the militia, he was indicted for "levying war" against the US government, regardless of his actual whereabouts.

Chief Justice John Marshall, who presided over the Burr trial, underlined the importance of the case, "As there is no crime which can more excite and agitate the passions of men than treason, no charge demands more from the tribunal before which it is made a deliberate and temperate inquiry."[18] Marshall lived up to his word. Despite Burr's unpopularity at the time, Marshall challenged the government's position that Burr was "constructively present" during the standoff between his men and the militia. He argued, "there is no testimony whatever which tends to prove that the accused was actually or constructively present when that assemblage did take place."[19] According to Marshall, "To conspire to levy war, and actually to levy war, are distinct offenses."[20] Ultimately, Burr was acquitted. During the case, Marshall had determined that a treason charge required that "war must be levied in fact, that the object must be one which is to be effected by force," and "that the assemblage must be such as to prove that this is its object."[21] For the government to prove that Burr was involved in planning the treasonous act, it had to prove that "war had actually been levied." This the government could not do. Its failure resulted in a narrower interpretation of the American law of treason from 1807 to 1860. To be charged with treason under the US Constitution, the use of force would have to be present.

During the Civil War, another legal case would have a tremendous impact on the government's ability to prosecute rebels for treason. In the "Prize Cases" ruling in early 1863, the Supreme Court upheld by a 5–4 vote Lincoln's declaration of a blockade around the southern states.[22] Writing the majority opinion, Associate Justice Robert C. Grier supported Lincoln's view of the war as "domestic insurrection," which allowed him to establish a naval blockade. The court declared that the United States could treat the Confederacy as a belligerent power, which entitled both sides to the protection of the laws of war, *without* recognizing it as a sovereign power. President Johnson and Preston King cited this ruling when they advised Underwood on the need to charge the Confederate leaders with treason.

On the surface, the Prize Cases were simply about whether or not the United States could seize ships headed to Confederate ports prior to a formal declaration of war. More deeply, the case touched on a much larger, murkier dilemma of the war: should the rebels be treated as traitors or as enemies from a sovereign nation? The final ruling eventually gave the Lincoln and Johnson administrations extensive flexibility. According to Grier, the US government could treat the Confederacy as a belligerent during the war without giving up its sovereign rights over those states. He argued, "When the regular course of justice is interrupted by revolt, rebellion, or insurrection, so that the Courts of Justice cannot be kept open, civil war exists and hostilities may be prosecuted on the same footing as if those opposing the Government were foreign enemies invading the land." As a result of this ruling, the United States could treat the Confederacy like a sovereign nation during the war, while reserving the right to consider anyone who participated in the rebellion as traitors after the war. This provided a firm foundation for the treason charges in Judge Underwood's courtroom in May 1865.

★   ★   ★

Before the new president could prosecute Lee and his fellow officers who surrendered at Appomattox, he had to make sure that Lee's agreement with Grant didn't prohibit civil charges from being filed after the war was concluded. Soon after taking over as chief executive, Johnson, who viewed Lee as an "arch traitor," sought advice on this subject from General Benjamin Butler, a successful attorney from Massachusetts who had also played a prominent military role for much of the war. Butler had been relieved of his command of the Army of the James by Grant in January 1865, but was retained by the army as a source of legal expertise. On April 25, 1865, Butler wrote a lengthy memorandum to Johnson explaining why the parole Lee received from Grant did not protect him from being prosecuted for treason.[23]

After surveying the historical record, Butler argued that a parole was merely a military arrangement that allowed a prisoner "the privilege of partial liberty, instead of close confinement." It did not in any way lessen the possibility of being tried for crimes resulting from wartime activities. Having reviewed Lee's agreement with Grant, Butler asserted, "Their surrender was a purely military convention and referred to military terms only. It could not and did not alter in any way or in any degree the civil rights or criminal liabilities of the captives either in persons or property as a treaty of peace might have done." This point, Butler believed, would have clearly been obvious to Lee. With bemusement, he asked, "Is it to be supposed that Lee was at that moment negotiating for a pardon for crimes which up to that moment he had never acknowledged he had committed, with a General who he must have known could not pardon crimes?" Equally critical of Grant—who had been, it should be noted, responsible for taking Butler's command away—he declared, "Indeed the Lieutenant General [Grant] had not authority to grant amnesty or pardon even if he had undertaken so to do." Butler then concluded "that there is no objection arising out of their surrender as prisoners of war to the trial of Lee and his officers for any offenses against municipal laws." Attorney General James Speed and Francis Lieber—two additional legal authorities—agreed with Butler's conclusion.

By late May 1865, Andrew Johnson decided to begin prosecutions against the Confederate leaders. Jefferson Davis was an obvious first choice especially since the former Confederate president had never been a party to any military parole agreement. According to Attorney General Speed, "Immediately after the capture of Jefferson Davis, the President and the Cabinet, but the President more particularly, were anxious for a speedy and prompt trial of Jefferson Davis."[24] This too is unsurprising given the apparent hostility of Johnson toward Davis. When Johnson mentioned Davis's name in a speech at the Willard Hotel in Washington, DC, after the fall of Richmond to Union troops in April 1865, the crowd began yelling, "Hang him! Hang him!" to which Johnson replied, "Yes! I say hang him twenty times."[25]

Apart from any personal animosity, there were also very compelling reasons for quick trials of the rebel leadership. In a letter to Secretary of War Stanton, Virginia's Governor Francis Pierpont argued that Davis's conviction "will be easier now than at a future day" and "promptness is all important."[26] The governor believed the prosecution could win the case and added, "If the leading rebels are not promptly tried then the war is not ended, unless the North becomes humble flunkies to the pride of the South." The passage of time, many observers believed, would make treason trials less appealing to the public.

On May 26, 1865, a federal court in Washington, DC, indicted Jefferson Davis for treason.[27] In this case, the act of levying war was General Jubal Early's attack on Fort Stevens in Washington, DC, on July 12, 1864. Even though he directed the overall war effort from Richmond, Virginia, Davis was considered "constructively" present at the battle of Fort Stevens. In language derived from

English cases from the fourteenth century, the indictment declared that Davis, "with force and arms, unlawfully, falsely, maliciously and traitorously did compass, imagine and intend to raise, levy and carry on war, insurrection and rebellion against the said United States of America, for the subversion of the Government of the said United States of America." The words "compass" and "imagine" are curious ones that apparently meant "intend" during the reign of England's Edward III. By the mid-nineteenth century, however, these words had their current meanings for most Americans. In the clearest expression of the charges against Davis, the indictment concluded,

> Jefferson Davis, with the said insurgents so traitorously assembled, armed and arrayed as aforesaid, most wickedly, maliciously and traitorously did ordain, prepare, levy and carry on war against said United States of America, for the subversion of the Government of the said United States of America, contrary to the duty of his said allegiance and fidelity, against the Constitution, peace and Government of this United States of America, and against the form of the Statute of the said United States of America.

A second indictment for high treason was found at the same time against John C. Breckinridge, Confederate secretary of war and former US vice president under James Buchanan. Unlike Davis, Breckinridge was physically present during the battle of Fort Stevens. A bench warrant in the case of Breckinridge, who was attempting to avoid capture at the time, was asked for by District Attorney Edward Carrington, a judicial appointee of Lincoln's. Breckinridge eluded arrest by Union troops and made his way to Cuba less than a week after his indictment.

Soon after the proceedings against Davis and Breckinridge, the scene shifted to Judge Underwood's courtroom. On Wednesday, May 31, 1865, a federal grand jury gathered in Norfolk, Virginia, to begin deliberations on whether or not to indict prominent political and military leaders of the Confederate States of America for treason. Judge John C. Underwood, in his charge to the grand jurors, declared that the "eyes of the nation and all Christendom" were upon them, and that they'd be expected to "declare that treason, like all other crimes, shall be punished in this home of liberty and justice."[28] He reminded them, as Andrew Johnson had urged him to do in their earlier meeting, that the crime of treason was "clearly defined in our laws and constitution" even though it might seem "new and strange to our courts of justice."

Convening a grand jury was the first step in prosecuting a civil case against the former rebels.[29] The role of a grand jury was to accuse, while that of a petit jury was to ultimately convict or acquit. The grand jury system can be traced back to medieval England where juries of knights were brought together to use their local knowledge in identifying those guilty of committing crimes. The grand jury idea eventually was transported to America, where it became part of the Constitution just like American treason law. According to the Fifth Amendment, "No person shall be held to answer for a capital crime, unless on a presentment or indictment of a Grand Jury."

A mere month and a half after General Robert E. Lee's surrender at Appomattox Court House and President Abraham Lincoln's assassination, Judge Underwood passionately appealed for justice before his court. He defined treason as "wholesale murder" that "embraces in its sweep all the crimes of the Decalogue."[30] This horrific act, Underwood believed, had murdered tens of thousands of young Americans during the recent war, "by the slaughter on the battlefields, and by starvation in the most loathsome dungeons." He was outraged that the men most responsible for the rebellion— "with hands dripping with the blood of our slaughtered innocents and martyred President"—were yet still at large. Underwood felt the grand jurors must send a message to their countrymen that future rebellions would not be tolerated, declaring, "It is for you to teach them that those who sow the wind must reap the whirlwind; that clemency and mercy to them would be cruelty and murder to the innocent and unborn." He then concluded his instructions by advising that Robert E. Lee would not be protected from prosecution by his agreement with General Ulysses S. Grant at Appomattox on April 9, 1865.

Throughout his remarks, Underwood acknowledged that those rebels who were technically guilty of treason could be counted by hundreds of thousands and as a result, "a universal prosecution would be unreasonable and impossible." He further explained that the mass of southerners were not morally responsible for the rebellion since they have "been despotically controlled by their wicked leaders, and are, therefore, rather to be pitied than punished more severely than they have already." Keeping poor people in ignorance only made the Confederate leaders even guiltier in the eyes of Underwood. It would be up to the grand jury to determine how many of those leaders would have to "answer to the violated laws of the country."

After several days of deliberations, the Norfolk grand jury decided to indict thirty-seven leaders of the Confederacy for treason on June 7, 1865.[31] Robert E. Lee, the former general in chief of the Confederate armies, was the most prominent leader of the group. Among the others of stature were Lieu-tenant Generals James Longstreet and Jubal Early along with two of Lee's sons and his nephew Fitzhugh Lee.

One person on the list of those indicted raised a few eyebrows among Virginians. William N. McVeigh, who was indicted with Lee and the others, had been a citizen of Alexandria, Virginia, prior to the war. When McVeigh fled Alexandria after Union forces occupied the city, his home was confiscated by Judge Underwood's court. Shortly after, Underwood's wife Maria pur-chased McVeigh's former property for a considerable discount at an auction. Some Virginians saw the indictment charge against McVeigh as an attempt to ensure he wouldn't be able to regain the property. For his part, Underwood argued that he, personally, had "never purchased or leased out any confiscated property in this or any other city, county, or State." What his wealthy wife did with her own money was her business, he seemed to imply. He also noted that his own house and farm in rebel territory had been illegally seized and occu-pied for over three years.[32]

It should also be noted that one prominent Confederate leader was *not* on the list. Jefferson Davis, who had been charged in a federal court in Washing-ton, DC, in May 1865, was not indicted by the Norfolk court in June 1865. He would later be indicted by the same court in May 1866, which may help explain the subsequent confusion. Bradley Johnson, while compiling court records in 1872 for his book on Chief Justice Salmon Chase, was the first to mistakenly report that Jefferson Davis was indicted by Underwood's court in June 1865, writing, "the indictment against Mr. Davis and others for treason . . . has been lost from the records of the court during the summer of 1865."[33] Scholars continue to rely on Bradley Johnson's reporting, even though he's clearly mistaken on this particular detail.

Newspaper accounts at the time listed all those indicted by the Norfolk court in June 1865 and Jefferson Davis's name wasn't included on those lists. In testimony during the impeachment trial of Andrew Johnson, Underwood explained that Davis wasn't indicted at that time because several members of the grand jury believed that Davis "had been already indicted in the District of Columbia, and that it would be a work of supererogation to indict him over again."[34] When Attorney General Speed later made the decision that Davis must be tried in Virginia, Underwood's court indicted Davis at the next term in May 1866.

Lee's indictment was by far the most significant of the thirty-seven. Using the antiquated language of medieval England, Lee's entire indictment, which had been prepared by US District Attorney Lucius Chandler, reads as follows:

Records of the Norfolk Court
United States v. Robert E. Lee
Indictment for Treason
District of Virginia, to wit:
In the District Court of the United States of America, in and for the District
    of Virginia, at Norfolk.
MAY TERM, 1865.
The jurors of the United States of America, in and for the body of the District
of Virginia, upon their oath present, that **Robert E. Lee of the City of
Richmond, in the County of Henrico**, in the District aforesaid. **Yeoman**;
being an inhabitant of, and residing within the United States of America, and
owing allegiance and fidelity to the said United States of America, not having
the fear of God before his eyes, nor weighing the duty of his said allegiance,
but being moved and seduced by the instigation of the devil, wickedly devising
and intending the peace and tranquility of the said United States of America
to disturb, and the Government of the said United States of America to sub-
vert, and to stir, move and incite insurrection, rebellion and war against the
said United States of America, on the **first** day of **April** in the year of our Lord
one thousand eight hundred and sixty **five** in the County of **Dinwiddie**, in
the district of Virginia aforesaid, and within the jurisdiction of this Court and
of the Circuit Court of the United States for the Fourth Circuit in and for the
District of Virginia aforesaid, with force and arms, unlawfully, falsely, maliciously, and traitorously, did compass, imagine and intend to raise, levy, and
carry on war, insurrection and rebellion against the said United States of
America and in order to fulfill and bring to effect the said traitorous compass-
ings, imaginations, and intentions of him the said **Robert E. Lee**, he the said
Robert E. Lee afterwards, to wit, on the said **first** day of **April** in the year of
our Lord one thousand eight hundred and sixty **five** in the country of **Dinwiddie** aforesaid, in the District of Virginia aforesaid, and within the jurisdiction of this Court and the Circuit Court of the United States for the Fourth
Circuit in and for the District of Virginia aforesaid, with a great multitude of
persons, whose names to the jurors aforesaid are at present unknown, to the
number of five hundred persons and upwards, armed and arrayed in a warlike
manner, that is to say, with cannon, muskets, pistols, swords, dirks and other
warlike weapons as well offensive as defensive, being then and there unlawfully, maliciously and traitorously assembled and gathered together did falsely
and traitorously assemble and join themselves together against the said United
States of America, and there and then with force and arms did falsely and
traitorously and in a warlike and hostile manner, array and dispose themselves

against the said United States of America, and then and there, that is to say, on the day and year last aforesaid, in the County of **Dinwiddie** aforesaid, in the District of Virginia aforesaid, and within the jurisdiction of this Court, and of the Circuit Court of the United States for the Fourth Circuit in and for the said District of Virginia, in pursuance of such their traitorous intentions and purposes aforesaid, he the said **Robert E. Lee**, with the said persons so as aforesaid, traitorously assembled, and armed and arrayed in manner aforesaid, most wickedly, maliciously and traitorously did ordain, prepare, levy and carry on war against the said United States of America, contrary to the duty of the allegiance and fidelity of the said **Robert E. Lee to the said United States,** against the Constitution, Government, peace and dignity of the said United States of America, and against the form of the Statute of the United States of America in such case made and provided.

This indictment found on testimony of R.W.P. Garnett and C.C. Ballan sworn to in open Court and sent for by Grand Jury.

[Signed]

L.H. Chandler

United States Attorney for the District of Virginia.

Filed June 7, 1865[35]

The language of this indictment is almost identical to the one in the Jefferson Davis case in Washington, DC. Lee is accused of

> . . . not having the fear of God before his eyes, nor weighing the duty of his said allegiance, but being moved and seduced by the instigation of the devil, wickedly devising and intending the peace and tranquility of the said United States of America to disturb, and the Government of the said United States of America to subvert, and to stir, move and incite insurrection, rebellion and war against the said United States of America.

The indictment then concludes with the main charge:

> Robert E. Lee, with the said persons so as aforesaid, traitorously assembled, and armed and arrayed in manner aforesaid, most wickedly, maliciously and traitorously did ordain, prepare, levy and carry on war against the said United States of America, against the Constitution, Government, peace and dignity of the said United States of America, and against the Statute of the United States of America.

The key accusation here is that of levying war against the United States. And unlike Davis, Lee had actually waged war within the jurisdiction of the district court along with "five hundred persons and upwards." Finally, the indictment was founded on the testimony of two individuals, as required by the Constitution.

The news of the indictments was widely reported by the press, though several of the details were inaccurate.[36] Some accounts believed the proceedings took place in Richmond instead of Norfolk. And the *New York Times* reported there were fifty indictments, while the *New York Herald* said there were about forty. In general, reporters seemed to believe that the "abolitionist" Judge Underwood was acting independently of the Johnson administration, especially since they seemed convinced that the agreement with Grant protected Lee and his officers from prosecution by federal authorities.

Unsurprisingly, the southern press was outraged by the news that Lee had been indicted. In one scathing editorial titled "Judge Underwood and General Lee" in the *Petersburg News*, Underwood is portrayed as a carpet bagger whose "sentiments on the subject of slavery were obnoxious to the people" of Virginia. Somehow, this intruder had become "the highest judicial officer in the Eastern District of Virginia." Believing Underwood unworthy of even loosening Robert E. Lee's shoe laces, the editorial objected to the judge's charge to the jury—"which for violence, blasphemy, and unfounded aspersion of a brave and chivalrous people, beggars imagery, and defies comparison." Like many other accounts, this editorial erroneously believed that the Johnson administration was unwilling to raise a finger against Lee. Instead, "the foul deed was left for the congenial performance of an imported judge who, after maligning the State whose people gave him his bread in his poverty and consequence in his obscurity summons these people to aid him in hunting to his death their most eminent fellow citizen."[37]

On June 12, 1865, Underwood went to Washington, DC, to consult with Attorney General James Speed about how to proceed against the Confederate leaders now that they had been charged. For cases of such importance, it was assumed by legal experts that the attorney general would manage the prosecutions with Chief Justice Salmon Chase presiding as judge. Underwood brought with him all of the indictments that had only just been approved by the grand jury.

In just under two months, the Johnson administration had made considerable progress toward its goal of making treason odious. Davis and Breckinridge were now under indictment by a Washington, DC, court, while Robert E. Lee and thirty-six other leaders faced prosecution in a Virginia court. Meanwhile, the trial against the conspirators in the Lincoln assassination was nearing its conclusion in the nation's capital. So far, Andrew Johnson appeared to be a man of his word.

Table 3.1. Confederate Leaders Indicted at Norfolk, Virginia, June 1865.

Name	Rank/Position
Montgomery Dent Corse	Major
General Richard Snowden Andrews	Colonel and envoy to Germany
Henry B. Taylor	
Charles James Faulkner	Assistant Adjutant General; former Minister to France
William N. McVeigh	Civilian (Alexandria, VA)
William S. Winder	Captain
Robert Ould	Commissioner of Exchange of Prisoners
George Booker	Major
Cornelius Boyle	Major
W. H. Payne	Brigadier General
Thomas Turner	Commandant, Libby Prison
James A. Seddon	Secretary of War
William Burton Richards Jr.	Acting Quartermaster
Wade Hampton	Lieutenant General
Richard H. Dulany	Colonel
William H. Taylor	Adjutant to Robert E. Lee
John Debree	Paymaster (Navy)
James Longstreet	Lieutenant General
Robert E. Lee	General-in-Chief, C.S.A.
Oscar F. Baxter	Cavalryman
William Mahone	Major General
William Smith	Confederate Governor of Virginia
Eppa Hunton	Brigadier General
Roger Pryor	Brigadier General
David Bridgeford	Major
Charles K. Mallory	Colonel
George W. Custis Lee	Major General
Samuel Cooper	Adjutant General and Inspector General, C.S.A.

Table 3.1. (Continued)

Name	Rank/Position
William Henry Fitzhugh "Rooney" Lee	Major General
Henry A. Wise	Brigadier General and former Governor of Virginia
Benjamin Huger	Major General
George W. Alexander	Commandant of Castle Thunder, Richmond Prison
Richard Booker	Captain
Fitzhugh Lee	Major General
Thomas S. Bocock	Speaker of the Confederate States House of Representatives
Jubal Early	Lieutenant General
R. S. Ewell	Lieutenant General

Source: Compiled by author.

4

"WHEN CAN THESE MEN BE TRIED?"

While President Johnson and Judge Underwood prepared to prosecute Lee for treason, the former Confederate general was pondering his future. Where would he live now? How would he support his family? Would he pledge his loyalty to the US Constitution? Such questions preoccupied Lee's mind in the weeks after Appomattox.

During that time, Lee tried his best to recover from the traumatic and exhausting experience of combat over the previous four years. Though only fifty-eight years old, Lee looked like a much older man. The war had taken a heavy toll on his physical well-being. In the spring of 1863, right before the crucial battle of Gettysburg, he had experienced a heart attack and would continue to suffer from progressive atherosclerosis for the remainder of his life.[1] When he eventually accepted a position at Washington College in August 1865, he did so with the stipulation that he wouldn't be required to teach classes. He just didn't have the stamina for it. Lee had only enough energy to oversee administrative matters for the college.

Despite his desire for rest, Lee received numerous visitors at his rented house on East Franklin Street in Richmond during those initial days after the war. Among them was Union General George Meade who had been Lee's opposing commander at the Battle of Gettysburg. Calling on Lee in Richmond in early May, Meade tried to convince him of the "expediency and propriety of his taking the oath of allegiance, not only of his own account, but for the great influence his example would have over others." The oath Meade was referring to was part of the general requirements for pardons and amnesty that had been outlined by President Lincoln in December 1863.[2]

Lee told Meade that he didn't have any personal objections to taking the

71

oath and he fully intended to submit to the Constitution and the laws of the United States. Before taking any oath, however, he preferred to wait "until he could form some idea of what the policy of the Government was going to be towards the people of the South." No doubt Lee was aware of the hostility of many northerners toward the Confederate leadership. Perhaps he wanted to wait until those harsh opinions softened somewhat.

Meade argued with Lee over this point. He believed Lee should take the oath first. Once the government saw Confederate leaders were prepared to restore their allegiance, then it would be more likely to craft a conciliatory long-term policy toward the southern states. Lee seemed to cede some ground by admitting that "the Government of the United States was the only one having power and authority, and those who designed living under it, should evince their determination by going through this necessary form." Lee then spoke a "great deal about the status of the negro." Finally, after their long and stimulating talk, Meade reported feeling sad for the difficulties facing his former rival.

It's revealing that Lee spoke a great deal about the status of the freedmen with Meade. Around this time, Lee advised a cousin to "get rid of the negroes" on his plantation—there were approximately ninety or so women, children, and old men left on his cousin's estate after the war.[3] Lee believed the government would take care of them, adding, "I have always observed that wherever you find the negro, everything is going down around him, and wherever you find the white man, you see everything around him improving."[4] Lee had no desire to see the freedmen as part of Virginia's future. Not only would he deny them the vote, but he hoped to "get rid of them" altogether, as he would tell a congressional committee in early 1866.[5]

The endless stream of visitors in Richmond eventually proved to be too taxing on Lee and his family. He longed for a quiet little farm in the countryside where he could earn his daily bread, "the world forgetting, by the world forgot," quoting a favorite line from the poet Alexander Pope. In late May, he mounted his horse Traveller and set off by himself to inquire about possible properties in the nearby countryside. He began by visiting Colonel Thomas Carter, whose father was a first cousin of Lee's, at the "Pampatike Plantation," roughly twenty-five miles outside of Richmond.[6] While there, he played with the colonel's children, while also enjoying the company of close friends and relatives. According to one of Lee's sons, those days at Pampatike "were the happiest he had spent for many years."[7] The visit convinced Lee even more than before that he needed to purchase a country home.

During this pleasant bucolic interlude in late May and early June, Lee learned of momentous news from the nation's capital.[8] President Johnson had issued a "Proclamation Granting Amnesty to Participants in the Rebellion with Certain Exceptions" on May 29, 1865—the proclamation was announced about the same time the administration was bringing charges against the Confederate leadership. Lee was not yet aware of his impending indictment, however.

Upon hearing the news of Johnson's proclamation, Lee decided to return to Richmond to discover what would be required of him in order to comply with the amnesty provisions. His initial reaction, after learning more of the details, was one of hopefulness. He sincerely believed Johnson had provided a viable path forward for former Confederates to rejoin the Union—just the signal he had told General Meade he was looking for. The central questions dividing northerners and southerners had already been decided by the war, Lee believed, and he concluded "it to be the duty of every one to unite in the restoration of the country, and the reestablishment of peace and harmony."[9]

By applying for a pardon, Lee envisioned himself serving as a model for other southerners who may have been wavering on whether or not to return to the Union. On a personal level, a restoration of his civil rights might also allow Lee to regain his wife's property at Arlington.[10] During the war, Congress had passed legislation that allowed local authorities to collect real estate taxes in areas under rebellion. When neither Lee nor his wife were able to pay *in person* a tax of $92.07 on the Arlington property, the commissioners sold the estate to the federal government for $26,800, which was considerably less than the assessed value of $34,100. The government had received a pretty good bargain on the historic property that had once been the home of George Washington's adopted son, George Washington Parke Custis. The Lees, of course, received nothing for their family home.

Johnson's proclamation represented a highly detailed response to the ambiguous status of former rebels after the war.[11] Upon becoming president, Johnson asked Attorney General Speed if Lincoln's amnesty policy of 1863 was still sufficient in the new environment after Appomattox. Speed didn't believe it was and argued that a much more comprehensive proclamation was now needed. Lincoln's amnesty had been open to all Confederates and only excluded politicians and military leaders from its benefits. Johnson's plan, on the other hand, would "except" fourteen classes from the general amnesty and those excepted classes instead would be required to apply for a special pardon directly to the president of the United States. The word "pardon"—just to clarify—is an act of forgiveness given to an individual, while "amnesty" is the term for a general pardon covering a large number of persons.

Johnson's Amnesty Proclamation began with an explanation of why a new policy was deemed necessary. Many former rebels had so far "failed or neglected to take the benefits offered thereby," while others had been "justly deprived of all claim to amnesty and pardon thereunder by reason of their participation, directly or by implication" in the rebellion. Because there appeared to be much confusion and uncertainty as to who might be eligible for a pardon under Lincoln's policy, Johnson offered a clearer plan for those who desired "to apply for and obtain amnesty and pardon."[12]

The overwhelming majority of former Confederates received amnesty under this proclamation with "restoration of all property, except as to slaves." The only condition was that each person desiring the benefits of a pardon must take and keep the following oath:

> I, _____, do solemnly swear or affirm, in presence of Almighty God, that I will henceforth faithfully support, protect, and defend the Constitution of the United States and the Union of the States thereunder, and that I will in like manner abide by and faithfully support all laws and proclamations which have been made during the existing rebellion with reference to the emancipation of slaves. So help me God.

Such liberal terms for the vast majority of ex-rebels fit in with the overall policy of the Johnson administration. It would be impossible—and counter-productive—to bring treason charges against hundreds of thousands of south-erners for their role in the war. The policy that had evolved within the administration was that almost everyone would receive liberal terms *except* for the leaders of the rebellion.

Such thinking is reflected in the extensive list of excepted classes that didn't receive the benefits of this proclamation. Those individuals within these excepted classes would be expected to *apply* for a pardon in addition to taking an oath. Among the excepted classes were politicians, judges, military officers above the rank of colonel, and "all persons who have voluntarily participated in said rebellion and the estimated value of whose taxable property is over $20,000." Robert E. Lee, as a West Point educated officer with considerable assets, was excluded from the general amnesty by the third, fifth, eighth, and thirteenth exceptions. Excepted individuals like Lee had reason to be hopeful, however. They could make a "special application" for pardon to the president and clemency would be "liberally extended as may be consistent with the facts of the case and the peace and dignity of the United States."

On June 7, 1865, which was coincidentally the same date as the Norfolk indictments, Attorney General Speed announced additional rules for those excepted individuals wishing to apply for a pardon.[13] Before any application would be considered by the president, "it must be shown that they have respectively taken and subscribed the oath" as prescribed by the proclamation. And any pardon that might be issued would become invalid if the individual "shall hereafter at any time acquire any property whatever in slaves, or make use of slave labor."

Secretary of the Navy Welles reported in his diary that Speed and Stanton provided most of the content for Johnson's proclamation of May 29, 1865, though the rest of the cabinet vigorously debated all of the various components.[14] Not everyone agreed with the thirteenth exception, which denied the general amnesty to all those with assets of $20,000 or more. Grant, who often participated in cabinet discussions, had been opposed to that one, though he later conceded Johnson "was much nearer right on the twenty thousand dollar clause" than he had been.[15] The president, dedicated foe of wealthy planters and loyal supporter of white working men, wouldn't budge on the property exception. Judge Underwood was glad he remained resolute. Less than two weeks before the issuance of the proclamation, Underwood wrote Johnson advising him that those individuals who had made vast fortunes by supplying the rebel armies "should not be permitted to take the oath of amnesty."[16] Later that summer, Underwood wrote another note to Johnson thanking him for his firm stance against the "rich rebels of Richmond."[17]

★   ★   ★

It may not have been obvious to everyone at the time, but Johnson's Amnesty Proclamation was part of an overall strategic approach toward the defeated Confederates. The vast majority of them would be pardoned. A smaller but meaningful number of prominent rebels—judges, politicians, civil servants, and the like—would be expected to prove they would be loyal in the future, but then allowed to return to full citizenship. Finally, there were a relatively small number of Confederate leaders who would be prosecuted for their role in the rebellion and denied political rights in the future. Just three days before the announcement of the Amnesty Proclamation on May 29, Jefferson Davis and John C. Breckinridge had been indicted by a federal court in Washington, DC. A mere two days after the proclamation, Judge Underwood delivered his charge to the grand jury that would indict thirty-seven leading figures of the Confederacy. When Lee learned of Johnson's proclamation while at Pampatike, he was unaware of the impending charges about to be filed against him. Instead, he was encouraged by the Johnson administration's apparent magnanimity, and returned home hopeful about the future. He'd soon be disappointed.

Shortly after arriving in Richmond, Lee heard alarming news that he was about to be indicted for treason by a Norfolk grand jury. Seeking counsel, he immediately contacted his friend Reverdy Johnson, who offered Lee his legal services.[18] Johnson, a Democratic senator from Maryland, had remained loyal to the Union during the war. The senator's first move was to visit Colonel Adam Badeau, a military secretary to General Grant, on Lee's behalf. Johnson asked Badeau about Grant's thoughts on the indictment. Badeau told him that General Grant "was firm in his determination to stand by his own terms."[19] He added, however, that Grant believed Lee should still apply for a pardon "in order to indicate his complete submission."

Lee had mixed feelings after hearing Grant's response. He was entirely willing to apply for a pardon, but wanted some assurance in advance that Grant would support his application. Lee was almost always meticulous about the way events might *appear* and this case was no different. After learning of Lee's wishes, Badeau informed Reverdy Johnson of Grant's "readiness to endorse Lee's application favorably."[20]

After carefully securing Grant's support, Lee then forwarded him two documents on June 13, 1865.[21] One of them was an extremely brief application for pardon addressed to Andrew Johnson.

His Excellency Andrew Johnson
President of the United States
Sir: Being excluded from the provisions of the amnesty and pardon contained in the proclamation of the 29th ult., [May 29], I hereby apply for the benefits and full restoration of all rights and privileges extended to those included in its terms. I graduated at the Military Academy at West Point in June, 1829; resigned from the United States Army, April 1861; was a general in the Confederate Army, and included in the surrender of the Army of Northern Virginia, April 9, 1865. I have the honor to be, very respectfully,
Your obedient servant,
R. E. Lee

In less than a hundred words, Lee provided the bare minimum of information, unlike some petitioners whose applications consisted of thousands of words and numerous supporting documents. In Lee's case, it appeared he was grudgingly performing an unpleasant task and wasn't about to grovel before the tailor turned politician from Tennessee. Lee also failed to include an oath with his application, having been unaware at the time of the Attorney General's memorandum of June 7 requiring that each application for pardon include a certified oath. For many years, scholars assumed that Lee refused to take the oath. We now know, of course, that he did eventually take it and had it forwarded to the State Department in early October 1865.

The other letter Lee sent was addressed directly to General Grant. He wrote that he had "supposed that the officers and men of the army of N.Va., were by the terms of the surrender, protected by the U.S. Government from molestation so long as they conformed to its conditions."[22] While proudly, perhaps, noting that he "was ready to meet any charges" and "did not wish to avoid trial," he wondered if he was correct in believing that his parole protected him from prosecution. If that was indeed the case, Lee informed Grant he wished to comply with the provisions of the Amnesty Proclamation and asked that his enclosed application for pardon be considered.

Three days after receiving the documents from Lee, Grant forwarded them to Secretary of War Stanton with the following cover letter:

> In my opinion the officers and men paroled at Appomattox C.H. and since upon the same terms given to Lee, can not be tried for treason so long as they observe the terms of their parole. This is my understanding. Good faith as well as true policy dictates that we should observe the conditions of that convention. Bad faith on the part of the Governm't or a construction of that convention subjecting officers to trial for treason, would produce a feeling of insecurity in the minds of all paroled officers and men. If so disposed they might even regard such an infraction of terms, by the Government as an entire release from all obligation on their part.
>
> I will state further that the terms granted by me met with the hearty approval of the President at the time, and of the country generally. The action of Judge Underwood in Norfolk has already had an injurious effect, and I would ask that he be ordered to quash all indictments found against paroled prisoners of war, and to desist from further prosecution of them.[23]

Grant concluded the note by asking Stanton to present Lee's application to the president with his earnest recommendation that a pardon may be granted to the former general in chief. He also noted the oath wasn't included in the application because the order requiring it hadn't reached Richmond when Lee had forwarded his documents. After reading Grant's letter, Stanton noted on the docket, "Presented by Sec. of War & postponed for further consideration of Cabinet."[24]

Grant's communication to Stanton raises some questions about his understanding of the Johnson administration's legal strategy toward the Confederate leadership. First, it's clear that Grant believed the military paroles issued at Appomattox protected Lee's men from prosecution for their wartime actions even after the war was concluded. As we have seen, Johnson's legal advisors—Benjamin Butler, Francis Lieber, and Attorney General Speed—disputed this notion. Second, Grant implied that Judge Underwood had brought forward the charges independently of the administration and should be "ordered" to quash the indictments against the paroled prisoners. He also felt that Underwood should "desist from further prosecution of them," a belief showing a misunderstanding of a judge's role. Such actions in this case would, of course, rest with the Attorney General and the local District Attorney, Lucius Chandler. It appears that General Grant was more accustomed to the workings of military justice.

To be fair to Grant, it did sometimes seem like Underwood was collaborating a bit too closely with the Johnson administration. As we'll later see, Chief Justice Chase was far more careful than Underwood about the importance of appearing to be independent. Finally, Grant did make one very persuasive point that shouldn't be discounted. If the perception of bad faith led to renewed hostilities by the paroled Confederates, then the administration may have indeed erred by the indictments at Norfolk.

Lee and Grant didn't appear to be interested in political gamesmanship. They truly believed the paroles agreed to at Appomattox protected Lee's men from prosecution "so long as they observe their paroles and the laws in force where they may reside." Despite their sincerity, these beliefs about the paroles were almost certainly incorrect. As Butler convincingly pointed out, these were military arrangements over prisoners of war. Once the war ended, the paroles were no longer in effect. It's difficult to believe that an agreement hammered out between two generals on a battlefield could protect thousands of men from possible war crimes or other actions that might come to light after the war.

Surprisingly, both Lee and Grant knew all too well about the blurry line between military and civil matters. As we saw in chapter 1, Lee had written Grant, just one month before his surrender at Appomattox, suggesting a "military convention" of some kind where Lee and Grant might arrive at a "satisfactory adjustment of the present unhappy difficulties."[25] Grant forwarded Lee's idea to Stanton, who answered firmly, "you are not to decide, discuss, or confer upon any political question: such questions the President holds in his own hands; and will submit them to no military conferences or conventions."[26]

After receiving this note, Grant wrote Lee, "I have no authority to accede to your proposition for a conference on the subject proposed. Such authority is vested in the President of the United States alone."[27] This exchange shows that Lee and Grant were at least aware of the limits of military authority. Less than two weeks after Appomattox, Attorney General Speed underlined the administration's position by stating that Grant had only been acting in his capacity as a military officer, and "a prisoner exchange system became void once hostilities ceased."[28] Speed also challenged the extent to which a parole could indirectly serve as "protection" against future charges by writing that only a president could grant a pardon and his power "cannot be delegated; it is a personal trust, inseparably connected with the office of President."

The limitations on military authority had been illustrated once again when General Sherman attempted to make peace with General Joseph Johnston on April 18, 1865, just three days after Johnson became president. Sherman's agreement with Johnston had included a general amnesty and a restoration of property and voting rights for all southerners. The cabinet was unanimous in rejecting this agreement, and Grant was given the thankless task of telling Sherman that a new agreement would be necessary. On April 26, new terms were agreed to along the same lines as those accepted by Lee at Appomattox. Months later, the Judge Advocate in the trial of Captain Henry Wirz—the commandant at the notorious Andersonville Prison—would point to the rejection of Sherman's initial agreement as proof of the limits of military authority. As an example, the Judge Advocate raised the hypothetical possibility of a collaborator in the Lincoln assassination then joining Johnston's army in time to be included in the surrender terms. Would such a person be protected by his parole? The judge believed "the proposition was too monstrous for serious consideration"—only the president could pardon war crimes and treason.[29]

If Grant's "legal" case for his paroles was weak, his military argument was rather strong. He believed General Lee "would not have surrendered his army, and given up all their arms, if he had supposed that after the surrender he was going to be tried for treason and hanged."[30] It seemed like a good deal, according to Grant, to achieve peace by preserving "the lives of a few leaders." Indeed, he made this precise argument in a lengthy official report, begun on June 20, 1865, on Army operations during the last year of the war. He wrote, "Could he [Lee] have been persuaded that he was to be tried for treason, and pursued as a traitor, the surrender never would have taken place. Gen. Lee would this day be at large and a great part of the late rebel Armies would be scattered over the South, with Arms in their hands, causing infinite trouble."[31]

Grant eventually crossed out these lines and didn't include them in the final report.

There was another consideration for Grant as well. After having waged a brutal total war against the South, Grant wrote his wife in late April 1865 that he was "anxious to see peace restored, so that further devastation need not take place in the country."[32] He felt the suffering of the South in the future would "be beyond conception" and observed, "People who talk of further retaliation and punishment, except of the political leaders, either do not conceive of the suffering endured already or they are heartless and unfeeling and wish to stay at home out of danger while the punishment is being inflicted." In the official report mentioned earlier, Grant said, "Those who had to fight and risk their lives have learned moderation and forgiveness. Would it not be well for all to learn to yeald [sic] enough of their individual views to the will of the Majority to preserve a long and happy peace?"[33] He ended up striking out these lines as well. Perhaps he thought twice of angering those who vowed to punish traitors.

Johnson and Underwood actually would not have been too far apart from Grant's views. They too had no desire to further punish ordinary southerners. Instead, they aimed to hold accountable a relatively tiny number of Confederate leaders. Grant seemed to concede the need to punish the leadership, so perhaps the only real difference is that Grant wanted to protect the *military* leaders—particularly those who served with him at West Point—while Johnson and Underwood wanted to hold the military men accountable as well. The bonds forged at the military academy appeared to remain strong for Grant despite the stresses of a civil war. He certainly wasn't forgiving of the political leadership who he described as "guilty of the most heinous offenses known to our laws. Let them reap the fruit of their offenses."[34] Grant had even called for the execution of Jefferson Davis in 1861.[35] Was there really all that much difference between Lee's role in the rebellion and that of Davis's? Lee, of all people, didn't think so, a point he made on several occasions.

What happened next, during the several days after Grant forwarded Lee's documents to Stanton, remains somewhat of a mystery. Here is a basic outline. Between June 16 and June 20, 1865, Grant and Johnson met once or twice to discuss the indictment of Lee by the Norfolk grand jury. The two disagreed vehemently on how to handle Lee in the future. Johnson wanted to prosecute him, while Grant believed the paroles protected him from punishment for his wartime actions. Grant may have even threatened to resign his commission if Lee was arrested and prosecuted. Finally, on June 20, 1865, Attorney General Speed wrote Norfolk District Attorney Lucius Chandler, regarding the recently indicted Confederate leaders, "I am instructed by the President to direct you not to have warrants of arrest taken out against them or any of them til further orders."[36] Our knowledge of what may have transpired between Grant and Johnson comes from various—and often conflicting—accounts provided by Grant and his associates. Johnson never wrote about the discussions.

The most reliable account of Grant and Johnson's disagreement on Lee's indictment came from Grant himself, during his testimony before the House Judiciary Committee on July 18 and 20, 1867.[37] The committee was then considering bringing impeachment charges against President Johnson and it wished to question Grant about his commander in chief. Grant's responses to tough questions from the congressmen appear fair to the president, in hindsight. It should be remembered, however, that Grant would later support those who wanted to convict Johnson during his impeachment trial of 1868. He also had the opportunity to make corrections to his testimony.

Much of the questioning of Grant was devoted to the treatment of former rebels after the war. The policy toward Lee in particular was given the most attention by far. To an early question about the paroles of Lee and his men, Grant responded,

> I frequently had to intercede for General Lee and other paroled officers, on the ground that their parole, so long as they obeyed the laws of the United States, protected them from arrest and trial. The President at that time occupied exactly the reverse grounds, viz: that they should be tried and punished. He wanted to know when the time would come that they should be punished. I told him, not so long as they obeyed the laws and complied with the stipulation. That was the ground I took.

The congressmen challenged Grant's understanding of the meaning of a military parole and its relation to the civil courts. At one point, a clearly frustrated Grant replied testily, "I am not quite certain whether I am being tried, or who is being tried, by the questions asked."

On the central question of whether Johnson insisted General Lee be tried for treason, Grant answered, "He contended for it." He added that they didn't really argue about it. Rather, Johnson asserted that Lee should be tried. When asked if he remembered when these discussions occurred with Johnson, Grant said,

> The conversations were frequent upon the inauguration of Mr. Johnson. I cannot give the time. He seemed to be anxious to get at the leaders to punish them. He would say that the leaders of the rebellion must be punished, and that treason

must be made odious. He cared nothing for the men in the ranks—the common men. He would let them go, for they were led into it by the leaders.

Grant concluded his testimony about Lee by saying he hadn't spoken with Johnson about the case since 1865.

Decades later, the stories about those conversations between Johnson and Grant about Lee became more dramatic. One such story, a seemingly accurate account, was provided by Adam Badeau, Grant's military secretary, in the 1880s.[38] According to this account, Grant went in person to talk with Johnson about the documents Lee had sent on June 13, 1865. Apparently, Johnson was unimpressed by the documents—he wanted "to make treason odious" and asked, "When can these men be tried?" Grant responded, "Never, unless they violate their paroles." The president then had his attorney general write an official letter opposing Grant's view, according to Badeau. In response, Grant threatened to resign his commission in the Army, telling Badeau at the time, "And I will keep my word. I will not stay in the army if they break the pledges that I made." Badeau concluded his account by stating that the president "gave way, for he found a will more stubborn, or at least more potent with the people, than his own, and orders were issued to discontinue the proceedings against Lee." The so-called orders Badeau referred to resulted in the already mentioned letter to District Attorney Lucius Chandler where Speed directs him to not arrest Lee and his men "til further orders." The entire letter is quoted here:

Washington, June 20, 1865

Lucius H. Chandler, Esq.
U.S. District Attorney
Norfolk, Va.
Sir: I learn that many of the rebel officers and soldiers that were paroled by capitulation have been indicted. I am instructed by the President to direct you not to have warrants of arrest taken out against them or any of them til further orders.
I am, sir, very respectfully, your obedient servant,
James Speed
Attorney General[39]

Many historians, perhaps relying too heavily on Badeau who didn't quote the letter, have often believed that this communication "quashed"—to use Grant's term—any future prosecution of Lee. We will later see in correspondence between Johnson and Chase, for example, that this view is mistaken. Johnson may have been convinced by Grant, however, that Lee's parole was still valid as long as the war hadn't been *officially* declared over. This interpretation is supported by a letter from Speed's assistant attorney general to a sheriff in New Orleans on June 13:

> The Attorney General has heretofore expressed the opinion that officers who are at large under the capitulations of Generals Lee and Johnson [*sic*] ought not to be tried or arrested by the Courts of the United States for treason until the President has officially proclaimed the suppression of the rebellion and announced that the war is at an end. When such proclamation is issued the present inclination of the mind of the Attorney General is, that the said capitulations do not in law further protect such officers from prosecutions by the Government of the United States. That point, however, has not yet been officially determined.[40]

This letter makes it clear that both Johnson and Speed believed they could still prosecute Lee once the end of the war was declared. Of course, Johnson may have also prudently felt not quite ready to thwart the will of the immensely popular General Grant. Regardless, the phrase "til further orders" meant Johnson was keeping his options open.

Outside of Grant himself, Badeau was likely the most believable reporter of those conversations, though we must remember he had a personal interest in protecting the image of Grant as the magnanimous victor of Appomattox. Surprisingly, Badeau offered one of most negative views of Lee at that time, describing him as

> [e]laborate, specious, elusive, not free from the besetting sin of the South—a tendency to duplicity—but the stubborn, valiant, and arrogant, Lee was on the whole a fitting representative of a cause which, originating in treason, based on the enslavement of a race, and deriving its only chance of success from men who had been false to their military oaths, was, in reality, a rebellion against the rights of man, and a defiance of the instinct and judgment of the civilized world. He fought with the splendid energy of that arch rebel who was expelled from heaven, and his downfall was as absolute.[41]

Most historians report Badeau's view of the conversation between Johnson and Grant—and except for a few details, his version was compatible with Grant's testimony before the Judiciary Committee.

The writer Hamlin Garland's widely read biography of Grant, published in 1898, appeared to borrow Badeau's account with some dramatic rhetorical flourishes thrown in. Of Grant's intervention on behalf of Lee, Garland declared, "nothing could be franker, manlier, or more generous than this."[42] When Grant told Johnson that Lee could never be tried, Garland wrote, "Johnson persisted in the contention. 'I would like to know,' he said *sneeringly*, 'by what right a military commander interferes to protect an arch-traitor from the laws' " (italics added). Garland then described Grant as firm in his stance on the matter: "Upon this rock of his inflexible resolution, the rage of the President broke without effect." Finally, Garland concluded that the indictments were dropped right then and there and never heard of again.

An even more dramatic account, with several wildly different details, was provided by the railroad executive, John W. Garrett, in an interview published in 1885. Garrett, who was president of the Baltimore and Ohio Railroad Company, was a close friend of both Lee and Grant. In the interview, he told a reporter, "I don't think that it was ever known how near Lee came to being arrested as one of the conspirators in the plot to assassinate President Lincoln and his Cabinet."[43] Garrett then shared a shocking, somewhat unbelievable, detail:

> I know that Andy Johnson in some unaccountable way got the idea in his head that Lee was in that conspiracy. Somebody had told Johnson something. I have some reasons for believing that led him to think so. Johnson wanted Lee arrested at once and I know that he proposed if Lee was found guilty to have him beheaded. Johnson told me that Lee couldn't be hanged, shouldn't be shot, and he would order him beheaded.

Obviously, the notion that Johnson wanted Lee beheaded seems implausible to say the least. Garrett, as the CEO of a major American railroad, *should* be a reasonably reliable source, however.

Garrett goes even further with his story. Upon hearing of Johnson's intentions after the Lincoln assassination, he met Grant to tell him the news. He remembered, "I have seen men black with anger, but I never saw such anger as Grant then showed." Grant then responded, "This is infamous—infamous! I will throw up my commission if there is the slightest attempt to do it." Garrett recalled advising Grant to share his views with the cabinet, which Grant soon did. Garrett said Grant was very stern with Johnson, saying, "Lee has given me his parole, sir. You can trust every West Point officer who gives his parole." These remarks, if true, wouldn't have impressed Johnson, who had been a fierce critic of West Point during his days in Congress. Finally,

Garrett told his interviewer that Johnson was moved "and a little frightened, too," by Grant's threat to resign his commission. If not for Grant's intervention, Garrett believed, "Lee might have been at serious peril."

One final account comes from Richard Wise, son of Henry Wise, a former governor of Virginia and Confederate general who was indicted by the Norfolk grand jury.[44] Wise remembered an anecdote from a conversation with Grant on a train ride, two decades after the event. In this account, it was Secretary of War Edwin Stanton, and not Johnson, who was insistent on prosecuting Lee. According to Wise, Stanton said, "This is the civil part of the matter; I will attend to that." When Stanton persisted, Grant threatened to resign unless the prosecutions were dropped. Stanton then withdrew his support, Wise remembered, and the indictments fell through.

Just to make everything even murkier, Joseph Fowler, a senator from Tennessee and friend of Andrew Johnson, felt this story in all its numerous variations was mostly boasting by Grant.[45] Fowler believed Johnson was pursuing a clear policy that was supported by most Americans, and that he was a more faithful friend to the South than Grant. Fowler was even skeptical of Grant's testimony before the House Judiciary Committee.

So, where does the truth lie? Grant's testimony before the Judiciary Committee, despite Fowler's view, is probably the most accurate account, especially since President Johnson was still alive at that time and could have easily disputed his narrative if it was untrue. Over the years, one suspects, Grant's friends found it all too tempting to embellish the basic story with details that enhanced Grant's reputation as the forgiving warrior from West Point. This tale of Grant's magnanimity is what many people remember today. Perhaps that's how Americans prefer to recall that difficult summer after the war.

Grant may or may not have threatened to resign, but his political power in June 1865 was real. Andrew Johnson could be stubborn, but he knew how to play the political game. Grant's opposition led him to put the prosecution of Lee and the others aside "til further notice." Johnson wasn't done with them yet, however.

5

"THE WORLD FORGETTING, BY THE WORLD FORGOT."

Lee learned Grant had endorsed his application for pardon in a letter from the Union General written on June 20. While he appreciated Grant's efforts, Lee didn't know what to expect from President Johnson. In correspondence with one of his former assistants, he said, "I have no wish to avoid any trial the Government may order, and cannot flee."[1] Writing to his middle son Fitzhugh a month later, Lee remained unsure of his status, though he hinted he believed time was on his side:

> As to the indictments, I hope you, at least, may not be prosecuted. I see no other reason for it than for prosecuting all who ever engaged in the war. I think, however, we may expect procrastination in measures of relief, denunciatory threats, etc. We must be patient, and let them take their course. As soon as I can ascertain their intention toward me, if not prevented, I shall endeavor to procure some humble, but quiet, abode for your mother and sisters, where I hope they can be happy.[2]

Lee would continue to wonder about his status throughout the summer of 1865. Unfortunately for him, very few details were forthcoming. He had to put his dream of purchasing a home in the countryside on hold until his status was finally decided. As he wrote his youngest son, Robert E. Lee Jr., in late June, "I can do nothing until I learn what decision in my case is made in Washington."[3]

Luckily, a close family friend recognized Lee's plight and offered him a small cottage on her estate in the country outside Richmond. Lee welcomed the opportunity to escape the bustle of the city and made the move out there with his family in late June 1865. During the remainder of the summer, he "spent several months of quiet and rest, only interrupted by the calls of those who came in all honesty and sincerity to pay their respects to him."[4] The countryside allowed him to ride Traveller daily and attend local church services regularly.

During this time, Lee corresponded with many former Confederate colleagues about the best way to proceed in the aftermath of the war. He consistently expressed his belief that southerners should resist the temptation of exile. Instead, they should remain home so they could help rebuild their broken and beloved South. In a letter to Colonel Richard Maury, who was considering emigrating to Mexico, he wrote, "Although prospects may not now be cheering, I have entertained the opinion that, unless prevented by circumstances or necessity, it would be better for them and the country to remain at their homes and share the fate of their respective States."[5]

Lee also frequently encouraged his fellow southerners to take the oath as prescribed by Johnson's Amnesty Proclamation, and if a particular individual was a member of one of the excepted classes, Lee advised applying for a pardon directly to the president as required by the new guidelines. When Captain Joseph Tatnall wrote him in August 1865 expressing concerns about taking the oath, Lee provided a clear expression of his views at that time:

> I have, since the cessation of hostilities, advised all with whom I have conversed on the subject, who come within the terms of the President's proclamations, to take the oath of allegiance, and accept in good faith the amnesty offered. But I have gone further, and have recommended to those who were excluded from their benefits, to make application under the proviso of the proclamation of the 29th of May, to be embraced in its provisions.[6]

Lee would even tell former soldiers that he himself had applied for a pardon on June 13, 1865. Unfortunately, he had to add, "I have not received an answer, and cannot inform you what has been the decision of the President." Lee enclosed a copy of his own letter to Johnson as an example for Tatnall, and expressed confidence that the captain would eventually discover the "proper course to be pursued."

Members of the excepted classes were slow at first to submit pardon applications to President Johnson. Eventually, more and more of them sought pardons in late summer and early fall. All in all, roughly 15,000 individuals from the excepted groups applied for a pardon, of which 13,500 were successful.

Another two hundred thousand oaths from individuals not in the excepted classes were received by the State Department. Southerners gradually realized that complying with Johnson's proclamation would be necessary if they were to have their civil rights and property restored.[7]

By July 1865, more and more southerners were heading to Washington, DC, to obtain pardons. Hotels filled up and the president's "ante-room was crowded with Senators and Representatives of the late rebel Congress, seeking interviews with the President and beseeching that their pardons might be hurried up."[8] The legal scholar Francis Lieber, who had been meeting individually with cabinet members during this time, was shocked to see all of the pardon seekers in Johnson's office when he came to call on the president. Lieber urged Johnson to spend less time on this demeaning activity. "The nation does not set up the presidency for this abominable thing."[9]

Johnson could be defensive about such criticism. In early August during a discussion of the pardon question, he said, "few had been granted, notwithstanding the clamor that was raised."[10] According to Gideon Welles, everyone at the meeting that day understood "neither Davis, Stephens, nor any member of the Rebel Cabinet should be paroled." Despite Johnson's protests in late summer, the volume of applications soon picked up considerably. The scale of the pardoning project was much larger than anticipated and it proved to be tiring, time-consuming work.

As the president's reconstruction plan began to be implemented in the former Confederate states, many of the excepted classes wanted to ensure that they could once again participate in the political process. To deal with increasing numbers of applications, M. F. Pleasants, a former Confederate Colonel, was appointed pardon clerk.[11] Seated in the attorney general's office, his job entailed reviewing the incoming petitions and preparing them for the president's consideration. According to General L. C. Baker, chief of the National Detective Police, the appointment of Pleasants resulted in applications coming "forward in great numbers." Once former Confederates learned that a fellow southerner would be receiving the applications, they apparently became more willing to send them in.

Despite Johnson's leniency to the vast majority of pardon seekers, he remained determined to punish the conspirators in the Lincoln assassination along with the leading rebels. In early July, the military commission in the assassination trial reached its verdict. Among the papers the commission sent to Johnson for his signature was a recommendation of mercy for Mrs. Surratt, who had been found guilty and sentenced to hang. Johnson rejected the plea for mercy and she was hanged along with the others shortly after 1:00 p.m. on July 7, 1865.[12]

Many observers had assumed the president would eventually commute Mrs. Surratt's sentence to imprisonment for life. Much of the evidence against her was circumstantial and the public was ambivalent about capital punishment for women. According to the *New York Times*, however, "no one who knew the President and his unmovable nature supposed for an instant that the sentence would be changed in jot or tittle."[13] Judge Advocate General Holt, immediately after discussing the subject of mercy with Johnson, reported the president saying,

> She must be punished with the rest . . . women and men should learn that if women committed crimes they would be punished; that if they entered into conspiracies to assassinate, they must suffer the penalty; that were this not so, hereafter conspirators and assassins would use women as their instruments; it would be mercy to womankind to let Mrs. Surratt suffer the penalty of her crime.[14]

The president's firm stance in this instance was intended to send a clear message to the nation. Assassins and the worst traitors should not expect forgiveness from the Johnson administration.

Johnson's alleged rejection of the military commission's recommendation of mercy for Mrs. Surratt would ultimately create a scandal. According to Judge Holt, he showed the recommendation to Johnson on July 5 and Johnson declined the request. Years later, Johnson disputed Holt's account and said he never saw the military commission's recommendation. One of Johnson's biographers notes he had been severely ill at the time and may have not even realized he saw it when he was reviewing documents related to the case.[15] Regardless, it's hard to believe Johnson would have commuted her sentence even if he had seen the recommendation. The decision to hang Mrs. Surratt especially angered Robert E. Lee. A family friend remembered that it was one of the few times Lee got upset that summer about a public event.[16]

Johnson demonstrated his firmness another time when General James Longstreet, one of Lee's most trusted lieutenants, applied for a pardon. Longstreet, who had been indicted by the Norfolk court along with Lee, was also a close personal friend of General Grant. Indeed, Longstreet actually served as a groomsman at Grant's wedding. In his memoir, Longstreet tells the intriguing story of his pardon application.[17]

While in Washington, DC, in November 1865, Longstreet paid a visit to

General Grant, who soon asked him if he'd like a pardon. Longstreet said he was "not guilty of an offense that required pardon." But then he added, he "intended to live in the country, and would prefer to have the privileges of citizenship." Grant told his friend that he'd talk with Stanton and Johnson about the matter.

The next day Grant told Longstreet he had spoken to both Stanton and Johnson in addition to writing a letter to Johnson on his behalf. In the letter, Grant wrote, "I have no hesitation in recommending General Longstreet to your Excellency for pardon. I will further state that my opinion of him is such that I shall feel it as a personal favor to myself if this pardon is granted."[18] Both men were reasonably hopeful that this intercession would do the trick.

Johnson and Longstreet had a lengthy conversation about the matter on the following day. The president wasn't quite ready to make a decision and asked Longstreet to visit him again the next day at noontime. Then, they had another long discussion until Johnson finally said, "There are three persons from the South who can never receive amnesty: Mr. Davis, General Lee, and yourself. You have given the Union too much trouble."[19] Longstreet replied, "You know, Mr. President, that those who are forgiven most love the most." "Yes," Johnson said, "you have very high authority for that, but you can't have amnesty." So despite Grant's request of a favor in this matter, Johnson remained resolute.

★   ★   ★

Lee had no idea about Johnson's attitude on his pardon application throughout the summer of 1865, however. From his refuge at "Derwent"—as his country house was called—he became more hopeful and soon decided it was time to return to work. He needed the money and figured he'd be a positive model for his fellow southerners. During this time, he also decided to work on a narrative of the war, though he refused to make it a commercial enterprise.

Fortuitously, one day in August a gentlemen knocked on Lee's door—out of the blue—with a job opportunity. Judge John W. Brokenbrough arrived at Lee's temporary home with a letter from the Board of Trustees of Washington College notifying Lee of his election to the presidency of that institution in Lexington, Virginia.[20] The salary would be $1,500 per year—a significant amount in those lean times—plus a house and garden. The president also received one-fifth of the tuition of the students, who paid $75 each per year.

The college had begun as an academy in 1749. George Washington gave it an endowment, which resulted in the institution changing its name from "Liberty Hall Academy" to "Washington Academy," later "Washington College." After a difficult four years during the war, the college had only four professors and forty students. Lee gave serious consideration to this attractive opportunity before responding to the trustees on August 24. Lee first mentioned that he could only undertake general administration and supervision of the institution, and then shared his concerns:

> Being excluded from the terms of amnesty in the proclamation of the President of the U.S. of the 29th May last, and an object of censure to a portion of the country; I have thought it probable that my occupation of the position of President might draw upon the College a feeling of hostility, and I should therefore cause injury to an institution which it would be my highest desire to advance.[21]

He also added that it was "particularly incumbent on those charged with the instruction of the young to set them an example of submission to authority, and I could not consent to be the cause of animadversion [criticism] upon the college."

In particularly artful phrasing, Lee then provided his answer: "Should you, however, take a different view, and think that my services in the position tendered to me by the board will be advantageous to the college and the country, I will yield to your judgment and accept it; otherwise, I must most respectfully decline the office."[22] It's safe to say Lee knew the board would enthusiastically desire his services, but he somehow felt the need to make a show of declining the offer. As expected, the board of trustees responded quickly to Lee's letter, urging "him to enter upon his duties as president at his earliest convenience." In late September, Lee summoned Traveller and headed to Lexington.

Not everyone thought Lee should be allowed to accept the position after the news was made public on September 1. Theodore Tilton, editor of the *Independent*, wrote,

> As president, he must look after the morals of his young men. If he desires to impress upon them the obligations of truthfulness, he can remind them of the oath he took to support and defend the Government of the United States, and how he has kept that oath the last four years . . . the bloodiest and guiltiest traitor in all the South, that man we make president of a college.[23]

The highly respected British M. P. John Bright, in a letter to Senator Charles Sumner, lamented, "Now, nobody is punished. Lee is allowed to become Principal of a College to teach loyalty to your young men, and I suppose bye and bye Davis will be free."[24] An angry citizen wrote Andrew Johnson, "Aren't you ashamed to give Lee the privilege of being a President of a college? Satan wouldn't have him open the door for fresh arrivals."[25]

On October 2, Lee took his oath of office in the company of professors and students, as required by the rules of the college. In front of everyone, he said, "I do swear that I will, to the best of my skill and judgment, faithfully and truly discharge the duties required of me by an act entitled, 'An act for incorporating the rector and trustees of Liberty Hall Academy,' without favor, affection or partiality."[26]

Lee had taken another oath earlier that day. In his acceptance letter to the trustees in August, he had said it was important for those charged with teaching young people to "set them an example of submission to authority."[27] So on the morning prior to his inauguration as president of the college, Lee finally took the amnesty oath as required by Johnson's proclamation of May 29. He appeared before a young attorney and notary public in Lexington named Charles Davidson, and signed his name to the following oath:

> I, Robert E. Lee of Lexington, Virginia do solemnly swear, in the presence of Almighty God, that I will henceforth faithfully support, protect, and defend the Constitution of the United States, and the Union of the States thereunder, and that I will, in like manner, abide by and faithfully support all laws and proclamations which have been made during the existing rebellion with reference to the emancipation of slaves, so help me God.[28]

A week later, on October 9, Davidson sent Lee's oath along with twelve others to Secretary of State Seward with the following note: "I have the honor to report that the following named gentlemen have taken before me the Oath of Amnesty prescribed by the Proclamation of President Johnson." The news of Lee taking the oath was reported in the *New York Times* on October 16, 1865; a transcription of the oath would later be published in various newspapers across America.

The oath was filed at the State Department where it remained until it was moved to the National Archives in the twentieth century. Over the years, scholars and public officials began to assume Lee never took the oath. For some historians, the missing oath provided the only plausible explanation as to why Johnson chose not to pardon Lee. Somehow, the real history of this period had been forgotten. President Johnson, as we have seen, had no intention of pardoning Lee in 1865, oath or no oath. Regardless, Lee felt he had done his duty in the hours before assuming the presidency of the college—a role he'd perform until his death five years later.

Robert E. Lee's decision to apply for a pardon and later take the oath was a difficult one. He professed to friends and colleagues that he had done nothing wrong, yet he made the application anyway. Attorney General James Speed had determined that "the acceptance of a pardon is a confession of guilt, or of the existence of a state of facts from which a judgment of guilt would soon follow."[29] Lee may not have agreed with Speed, but he surely knew many Americans would view his application as an admission of guilt. He went forward with it, regardless, because he believed his example would serve as encouragement for his fellow southerners, who needed to move past the war and rebuild their lives. Amidst all of the glory he earned on various Civil War battlefields, it's easy to overlook a seminal fact about his life: the day Lee took the amnesty oath was one of his finest hours.

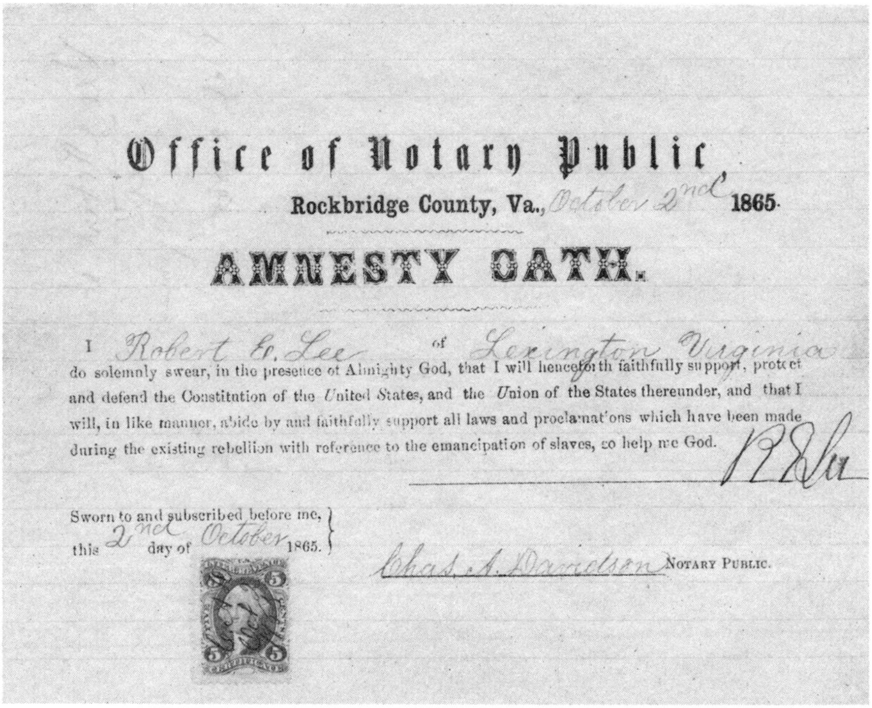

Figure 5.1.   Lee's Amnesty Oath. *Source:* **National Archives.**

Just one day after taking on his new role, Lee revealed his state of mind in a letter to General P. G. T. Beauregard. After first expressing regret that Beauregard's war-related papers had been lost, Lee then told the general that he had applied for a pardon, though he hadn't heard if his application was successful. Lee then provided an elaborate defense of his actions during the war:

> I need not tell you that true patriotism sometimes requires of men to act exactly contrary, at one period, to that which it does at another, and the motive which impels them—the desire to do right—is precisely the same. The circumstances which govern their actions change; and their conduct must conform to the new order of things. History is full of demonstrations of this. Washington himself is an example. At one time he fought against the French at Yorktown, under orders of the Continental Congress of America, against him. He has not been branded by the world with reproach for this; but his course has been applauded.[30]

Here, Lee explains how he had come full circle—the hero of the Mexican War who later became the general in chief of the Confederacy was now once again a loyal American. He had been the same person all along, of course; only the circumstances had changed. One senses Lee was trying extremely hard to convince himself of this fact. It's also apparent that he doesn't enjoy being viewed as a traitor by many of his countrymen. In October 1865, there were still many good reasons for Lee to feel sensitive about his reputation, as we'll soon see. Despite his desire to retreat to the countryside—"the world forgetting, by the world forgot"—we see a man at this time who wished to defend his actions.[31]

As Lee took his amnesty oath on October 2, he must have wondered about Andrew Johnson's attitude toward his application for pardon. He would have been unhappy to learn the answer. In a surprising coincidence, Johnson wrote a letter to Chief Justice Chase on October 2 inquiring about when the indicted Confederates—Lee and the thirty-six others—could be prosecuted:

Dear Sir,

It may become necessary that the Government prosecute some high crimes and misdemeanors, committed against the United States within the District of Virginia.

Permit me to enquire whether the Circuit Court of the United States for that District is so far reorganized and in condition to exercise its functions that yourself, or either of the Associate Justices of the Supreme Court will hold a term of the Circuit Court there during the autumn or early winter for the trial of causes.[32]

It should be remembered here that Lee had already been indicted in Virginia; Jefferson Davis had not. Johnson hoped to move forward with the treason cases, regardless of Grant's intervention on behalf of General Lee.

6

". . . RATHER AS A DEMON THAN A MAN."

On the morning of November 10, 1865, the prisoner was escorted out of his tiny room at the Old Capitol Prison. A sign on the door read: "No. 9—Wirz, H., Captain, C.S.A." He was led down the stairs and then out to the prison yard where a scaffold had been hastily erected. Troops lined the perimeter of the yard, while additional soldiers waited on rooftops and trees in order to witness the ghastly proceedings to come. There had been one thousand applications for the two hundred tickets that had been issued for the event. Spectators arrived several hours early with hopes of getting a good vantage point.[1]

Captain Henry Wirz, the notorious commandant of Andersonville Prison, climbed the stairs to the scaffold and took a seat on a small stool. For eighteen minutes, he was forced to listen to a reading of the highly detailed findings of the military court. During those anxious moments, soldiers in the treetops began yelling, "Hang the scoundrel" and "Remember Andersonville." Finally, Wirz was asked if he had anything to say. He said nothing.

Soldiers pinioned the prisoner's hands and legs with straps and adjusted the noose. At precisely thirty-two minutes past ten, a military detective pressed the fatal spring that resulted in Wirz dangling in the air. It was over quickly and soldiers started cheering when it became clear Wirz was dead. Within minutes, relic hunters began cutting splinters from the scaffold and clipping off pieces of the rope. Wirz's body was taken down and would eventually be buried next to Lincoln conspirator George Atzerodt in the Old Arsenal Penitentiary. All that was left in his room after the execution was some clothing,

Figure 6.1.   The execution of Captain Henry Wirz, 1865. *Source:* **Library of Congress.**

tobacco, whiskey, a Bible, and a cat, which had been his companion during his trial.

★   ★   ★

Andrew Johnson had remained inflexible in the face of demands for clemency for Wirz. A week before the execution, Johnson approved the findings and sentence handed down by the military court. And in the waning moments before the hanging, Johnson rejected a last-second appeal by Wirz's attorney. The suffering of the Union soldiers at Andersonville Prison had been too great for mercy to be shown to Wirz. *Someone* had to be punished for the outrageous violations against the laws of war that had been committed at the prison. This was the view of an overwhelming majority of northerners at the time.

Andersonville Prison, located in southwest Georgia, was built in early 1864.[2] With all fighting focused around Richmond, Virginia, at that time, the

Davis administration believed Georgia offered a more secure location for housing prisoners. Throughout the fourteen months of its existence, roughly thirteen thousand Union soldiers died there due to insufficient food and atrocious living conditions. During the trial of Wirz, almost 150 witnesses testified that Wirz had "violated the laws of war by not only withholding available food and supplies, but also by issuing orders that directly resulted in the death of prisoners of war."[3] Judge Advocate Holt and Secretary of War Stanton blamed the senior Confederate leadership for the conditions at the camp, but ultimately decided to prosecute the camp commandant first.

Despite the desire to focus solely on Wirz for the time being, the original indictment—prepared by a Stanton appointee—included Robert E. Lee and others as co-conspirators who allegedly attempted to kill Union prisoners. The first charge, announced on the opening day of the trial in late August, accused Wirz of

[m]aliciously, willfully and traitorously, and in aid of the then, existing armed rebellion against the United States of America, on or before the 1st day of March, A.D. 1864, and on divers other days between that day and the 10th day of April 1865, combining, confederating and conspiring together with Robert E. Lee, James A. Seddon, John H. Winder, Lucius D. Northrup, Richard B. Winder, Joseph White, W. S. Winder, B. B. Stevenson, _____ Moore, and others, unknown, to injure the health and destroy the lives of soldiers in the military service of the United States, and in the military prisons thereof, to the end that the armies of the United States might be weakened and impaired, in violation of the laws and customs of war.[4]

Generally, there were two overarching charges against Wirz. The first was that he entered into a conspiracy with the top Confederate leadership to harm prisoners in violation of the laws of war. The second was that he committed murder on multiple occasions both personally and by giving orders to his subordinates.

Stanton was livid when he learned of the initial charges that were read out in court.[5] He was still collecting evidence against Jefferson Davis and the other leading rebels and wasn't quite ready to prosecute them for possible war crimes. He insisted that the indictment be changed and three days later, a new one was submitted that didn't include the Confederate leaders in the charges. This would eventually cause problems for the prosecution, however. Why was only Wirz on trial if he was part of a greater conspiracy hatched in Richmond by senior politicians and military leaders?

★   ★   ★

The trial of Captain Henry Wirz, a Swiss émigré, began on August 21, 1865, and ended on October 24, lasting sixty-three days. According to newspaper accounts, the prisoner was in his early forties and was stoop shouldered with a sallow face, pinched nose, and dark blue intelligent eyes. He wore "old, shabby-genteel clothes," and his face was described as "denoting much intelligence, but impressing you with the idea that its owner was a man of iron will, determined in purpose, and heartless in the execution of it." The comprehensive testimony of almost 150 witnesses was ultimately published in a volume of 850 single-spaced pages.[6] Supporters of the Union, already outraged by the treatment of its prisoners, would be further horrified by what they learned.

Throughout the trial, which took place in the rooms of the Court of Claims in the basement of the Capitol building, there were numerous accounts of Wirz personally shooting prisoners. There were also reports of Wirz bragging of killing more damned Yankees than Lee was killing at Richmond.[7] Surprisingly, the raw numbers actually supported that obscene boast—more Union soldiers died at Andersonville than were killed at Gettysburg, Antietam, Second Bull Run, Chancellorsville, and the Wilderness *combined*. The descriptions of starving, suffering prisoners would have been particularly upsetting to those who followed the trial. One anecdote about General Howell Cobb, a Confederate leader with close ties to Jefferson Davis, was shocking in its ghoulishness. He allegedly told his soldiers in front of fifteen thousand Union prisoners that "I would treat the prisoners well, I would feed them well, I would care for them"—but then he pointed to a nearby graveyard, which seemed to indicate the true meaning of his words.[8]

In a letter to President Johnson presenting the findings and sentence of the military commission, Judge Holt was scathing in his remarks on the case. He wrote of ferocious dogs tearing Union prisoners to shreds and unarmed captives being gunned down by their captors. As a result of Wirz's crimes, over thirteen thousand prisoners lay "dead, buried, naked, maimed, and putrid, in one vast sepulcher."[9] It was made all the more horrible, according to Holt, by the fact that "this work of death" seemed to "have been a saturnalia of enjoyment for the prisoner, who amid these savage orgies evidenced such exultation and mingled with them such nameless blasphemy and ribald jests, as at times to exhibit him rather as a demon than a man."

Of course, Holt strongly believed that Wirz was working in tandem with the rebel leadership in Richmond. Only by looking at Confederate prisons like Andersonville, he told Johnson, can we "best understand the inner and real life of the rebellion, and the hellish criminality and brutality of the traitors who maintained it."[10]

Holt's view was a common one in the North in 1865, even if the truth was somewhat more nuanced than that. Critics of the Wirz trial—both at the time and subsequently—have pointed out that there were irregularities in the way the military commission prosecuted the case.[11] Some witnesses for the defense were blocked from testifying and much of the evidence was imprecise and even contradictory at times. Perhaps most importantly, historians have noted the insurmountable challenges involved with caring for tens of thousands of prisoners while the southern economy was breaking down in 1864 and 1865. By 1865, the Davis administration could barely feed its own soldiers let alone provide for all of its prisoners of war. Regardless of the academic debate, northerners in 1865 were united in believing war crimes had been committed at southern prison camps. The Wirz trial only reinforced that belief.

The trial also did not appear to change anyone's mind as to the culpability of the Confederate leadership for the horrors of Andersonville. Two months before the trial, Congressman George Boutwell had declared that Jefferson Davis and Robert E. Lee were "responsible to the country for the slow murder of our soldiers in prison."[12] Six months after the execution of Wirz, Congressman George Washington Julian stated on the floor of the House of Representatives that Robert E. Lee was "guiltier by far than the Christless wretch who obeyed his orders in starving our soldiers at Andersonville."[13] Many years later, in another speech in the House, Congressman James Blaine would say, "Wirz deserved no mercy, but at the same time as I have often said, it seemed like skipping over the president, superintendent, and board of directors in a great railroad accident and hanging the brakeman on the rear car."[14]

The findings of the military commission in the trial of Wirz supported the belief that the Richmond leaders were involved. As mentioned earlier, the leadership was struck from the first indictment of Wirz after Stanton had complained he was still gathering evidence against them. In the final charges, however, Jefferson Davis, Secretary of War James Seddon, and Howell Cobb had been included as co-conspirators once again by Judge Advocate Norton Parker Chipman, the prosecutor in the case. Robert E. Lee, however, was not added to the final charges, after his removal from the original indictment.[15]

Stanton, Holt, and Chipman believed they had clear evidence connecting Jefferson Davis to the abuses at Andersonville. By not including Lee as a co-conspirator in the final charges, we can possibly surmise they couldn't make a similarly convincing case against him. Chipman still treated Lee as a co-conspirator, however, and refused to admit his testimony into the trial. Presumably, Chipman didn't wish to introduce Lee's denials into the court record without having the chance to cross-examine him.

One widely shared anecdote appeared to suggest the government was desperate to charge Davis for his actions in relation to Andersonville. According to a fellow prisoner at the Old Capitol Prison, Wirz had been approached by a government official with a deal on the evening before his execution. The official, who was never named, allegedly offered Wirz his freedom if he would "testify against Mr. Davis, and criminate him with the charges against Andersonville Prison."[16] According to the story, Wirz refused the deal and bravely accepted his fate rather than commit "treason" against the South.

Decades later, Judge Advocate Chipman ridiculed Davis for repeating the tale, saying that "history is not made of such unsubstantiated figments of the imagination."[17] In his book *The Tragedy of Andersonville*, published in 1911, Chipman argued that the government had plenty of evidence against Davis and didn't need the support of such a witness as Wirz. Regardless, Chipman pointed out that Wirz himself had claimed during the trial that "he was obeying the orders of his superiors, and that the Richmond authorities were responsible and not he." The Judge Advocate found it impossible to believe that such a "dastardly" story could gain credence given the true facts of the case. Like the effective prosecutor he was, Chipman added that the government had intended, in any event, to try Davis for high treason and not war crimes, even though he was guilty of those, too.

The trial and execution of Captain Wirz had been extremely troubling to Robert E. Lee on multiple levels. In November 1865, the English author Herbert Saunders wrote, after a long visit with Lee in Lexington, "On only one subject would he talk at any length about his own conduct, and that was with reference to the treatment of Federal prisoners who had fallen into his hands."[18] Lee was hurt, according to Saunders, by the "backhanded stigma cast upon him by having been included by name in the first indictment framed against Wirz, though he was afterward omitted from the new charges." From Saunders's account, which was not made public during Lee's lifetime, the general was insistent that he had acted honorably in regard to Union prisoners.

After big battles like the Second Bull Run, Fredericksburg, and Chancellorsville, for example, Lee said he had taken care to send wounded Union soldiers over to the enemy. Lee also argued that the Confederates had always been proponents of doing away with the necessity of retaining prisoners by emphasizing the benefits of the exchange system that had been in place. When the Union representatives ended the exchange in 1863, the South "found themselves with 30,000 prisoners for whom they were quite unable to do as much as they wished in the way of food." Finally, Lee told Saunders that he had nothing to do with the management of prisons and didn't even know Wirz was in charge of Andersonville until after the war was over.

Not wanting to stir up trouble, Lee insisted that Saunders keep his comments from the interview private. Later, in public testimony before Congress in early 1866, Lee reiterated many of the same points he had made to Saunders. When Senator Jacob Howard, a Radical Republican from Michigan, asked Lee about his knowledge of the suffering of prisoners, Lee replied, "I never had any control over prisoners, except those that were captured on the field of battle."[19] Those prisoners he would send to the proper officer, he added. After he dispatched the prisoners, he had no more control, telling Howard, "It was entirely in the hands of the War Department."

Lee also testified that he knew nothing about Andersonville except for what he read in the newspapers. When asked if he had heard anything about the scenes of cruelty in places like Andersonville, he replied,

Nothing in the world. As I said before, I suppose they suffered from the want of ability on the part of the Confederate States to supply their wants. At the very beginning of the war I knew that there were sufferings of prisoners on both sides, but, as far as I could, I did everything in my power to relieve them, and urged the establishment of the cartel which was established.[20]

From his interview with Saunders and his appearance before Congress, we see Lee absolving himself from any responsibility for the suffering of Union prisoners. He believed he had done all in his power to alleviate the strains on Confederate prisons by promoting the prisoner exchange cartel, which eventually broke down in the summer of 1863. Not everyone agreed, however, that Lee was blameless, especially since he upheld a policy that directly led to the breakdown of the exchange system.

★   ★   ★

Early in the war, northerners supported the exchange of prisoners from both sides as opposed to letting captured soldiers languish in poorly constructed prison camps. Giving in to public pressure, the Lincoln administration agreed to the Dix–Hill Cartel in 1862 that allowed for prisoners to be exchanged man for man and officer for officer. If there was surplus on one side that couldn't be exchanged, those prisoners would be paroled, which allowed them to return to their side as long as they didn't take up arms again. They would remain paroled prisoners until properly exchanged. The cartel worked reasonably well in late 1862 and early 1863. Prisons in both North and South began to empty.

The cartel eventually broke down, however, as a result of Confederate treatment of black prisoners. In July 1862, the US Congress gave permission to the president to recruit African American soldiers. The administration began deploying them after the Emancipation Proclamation, which went into effect on January 1, 1863.

Shortly after the proclamation, Jefferson Davis characterized the measure as one "by which several millions of human beings of an inferior race, peaceful and contented laborers in their field, are doomed to extermination."[21] He advised the Confederate Congress that black soldiers and their white officers would be "dealt with in accordance with the laws of those States providing for the punishment of criminals engaged in exciting servile insurrection." Several months later, on May 1, 1863, the Confederate Congress, in an attempt to codify Davis's remarks, passed draconian legislation in relation to black prisoners and their officers. Section 4 of the joint resolution read as follows:

> That every white person, being a commissioned officer, or acting as such, who, during the present war, shall command negroes or mulattoes in arms against the Confederate States, or shall arm, train, organize, or prepare negroes or mulattoes for military service against the Confederate States, or who shall voluntarily aid negroes or mulattoes in any military enterprise, attack, or conflict in such service, shall be deemed as inciting servile insurrection, and shall, if captured, be put to death, or be otherwise punished at the discretion of the court.[22]

Additionally, section 7 held that "all negroes and mulattoes" who were engaged in war and were captured would be delivered to the states where they were captured to be "dealt with according to the present or future laws of such State or States." The legislation did not make any distinction between recently freed slaves and freedmen, even though roughly one-third of the 180,000 black soldiers who eventually served in the Union army during the war had been free prior to 1861. All *black* soldiers along with their white officers, it was determined, would be punished severely. Soon after the passage of the resolution, in July 1863, the Confederates made it operational, refusing to exchange several prisoners who had been part of a battle involving black troops.

President Lincoln responded swiftly to the new provocation. On July 30, 1863, he announced General Order No. 252, which stated, "The law of nations, and the usages and customs of war, as carried on by civilized powers, permit no distinction as to color in the treatment of prisoners of war as public enemies."[23] The order also stipulated that the United States would not tolerate the enslavement of captured black soldiers. Such an offense would "be punished by retaliation upon the enemy's prisoners in our possession." For every Union soldier killed in violation of the law, a Confederate soldier would be killed. And for every Union soldier enslaved, a rebel prisoner would be required to perform hard labor at public works. General Order No. 252 was never quite fully put into practice, but it did put an end to the cartel agreement until the rebels would agree to treat black prisoners with traditional rights under the laws of war. The Confederate government refused to change its policies at the time, and the prison populations, on both sides, rose dramatically throughout 1864.

Despite the joint resolution passed by the Confederate Congress, the actual treatment of captured black soldiers varied considerably during the remainder of the war. Some black soldiers were given "no quarter" and were massacred upon being captured. Others were enslaved or put to hard labor. Toward the end of the war, some free black prisoners were even provided the same treatment as their white comrades, though they weren't officially recognized as prisoners of war.

One of the most notorious instances of killing black soldiers, who were attempting to surrender, occurred at Fort Pillow in western Tennessee in April 1864. General Nathan Bedford Forrest led roughly three thousand Confederates in an attack on the fort. One Confederate soldier described what happened when Union troops tried to surrender:

> The slaughter was awful. Words cannot describe the scene. The poor deluded negroes would run up to our men fall upon their knees and with uplifted hands scream for mercy but they were ordered to their feet and then shot down. The whitte [sic] men fared but little better. Their fort turned out to be a great slaughter pen.[24]

After it was all over, almost three hundred Union soldiers had been killed. A Congressional committee ultimately determined that "the atrocities committed at Fort Pillow were not the result of passions excited by the heat of conflict, but were the result of a policy deliberately decided upon, and unhesitatingly announced."[25] The committee also declared that "the testimony herewith submitted must convince even the most skeptical that it is the intention of the rebel authorities not to recognize the officers and men of our colored regiments as entitled to the treatment accorded by all civilized nations to prisoners of war."

Fort Pillow, alas, was not an isolated event. At the battle of Olustee in Florida in February 1864, rebel soldiers shot and clubbed to death roughly fifty wounded African American soldiers. One Georgian remembered that African American soldiers "would beg and pray, but it did them no good."[26] At the battle of the Crater on July 30, 1864, 436 black soldiers died—many of them after having tried to surrender. A Confederate general recalled, "Some of the Negro prisoners who were originally allowed to surrender . . . were afterward shot by others and there was, without doubt, a great deal of unnecessary killing of them."[27]

The inconsistent and muddled Confederate policy toward black prisoners of war can be illustrated by the shifting outlook of James Seddon, who served as secretary of war of the Confederate States from 1862 until January 1865. Seddon, who had been a staunch advocate of secession before the war, laid out his thinking on African American soldiers in a letter to General Beauregard just ten days after becoming secretary of war in November 1862:

> The question as to the slaves taken in Federal uniform and with arms in their hands . . . has been considered in conference with the President. Slaves in flagrant rebellion are subject to death by the laws of every slave-holding State, and did circumstances admit without too great delays and military inconvenience might be handed over to the civil tribunals for condemnation. They cannot be recognized in any way as soldiers subject to the rules of war and to trial by military courts; yet for example and to repress any spirit of insubordination it is deemed essential that slaves in armed insurrection should meet condign punishment. Summary execution must therefore be inflicted on those taken, as with the slaves referred to by General Mercer, under circumstances indicative beyond doubt of actual rebellion.[28]

By August 1863, Seddon had changed his opinion ever so slightly. In another letter to Beauregard, he stated that "free negroes should be either promptly executed or the determination arrived at and announced not to execute them during the war."[29] In other words, Seddon was now searching for a policy that could be followed *consistently* throughout the South. While he still didn't think black soldiers should be treated a prisoners of war, he now believed the best approach might be to hold "them to hard labor during the war." By late 1864, Seddon was even beginning to worry about the effect on international opinion of a rigid enforcement of the joint resolution of the Confederate Congress. He also feared northern retaliation for the mistreatment of free black soldiers.

After the war, Seddon was indicted for treason, though not for violations of the laws of war, along with Lee by the Norfolk grand jury in June 1865. Unlike Lee, Seddon was held in a military prison before being released in November 1865. In a letter to President Johnson asking for his release, a friend of Seddon wrote,

> During my visit to Mr. Seddon in his prison he disclaimed, in the most solemn manner, every feeling of unkindness, much less of cruelty, towards prisoners who fell into their hands; and, from what I know of his character from an acquaintance of 33 years, I am satisfied he is incapable of any deliberate or willful act of inhumanity.[30]

It's hard to fathom how someone who called for the "summary execution" of black soldiers could be viewed by a colleague as "incapable of any deliberate or willful act of inhumanity." Perhaps only within a culture that did not consider African Americans to be fully human could such remarks make any sense at all.

★　★　★

Approximately one hundred black prisoners ended up at Andersonville. There, they were treated even worse than the white prisoners. At certain times, "prison commander Henry Wirz allowed local planters to go inside the pen and inspect black prisoners, claiming any they thought to be theirs."[31] Some of the seriously wounded black prisoners received no medicine or medical treatment. One white prisoner reported that the guards "seemed to have a particular spite toward the colored soldiers, and they had to go without rations several days at a time on account of not daring to go forward and get them."[32]

Robert E. Lee may not have been aware of the day-to-day operations of Andersonville, but he certainly upheld, as the South's leading general, Confederate policies toward African American prisoners. Correspondence between Lee and General Grant in October 1864, just five months after the Fort Pillow massacre, revealed a great deal about Lee's thinking. After some fighting southeast of Richmond in late September, Lee proposed a prisoner exchange to Grant who was open to the idea. Grant did enquire, however, about the status of black troops, saying, "Before further negotiations are had upon the subject I would ask if you propose delivering these men the same as white soliders?"[33] On October 3, 1864, Lee responded as follows:

In my proposition of the first Inst: to exchange the prisoners of War belonging to the armies operating in Viga [*sic*] I intended to include all captured soldiers of the U.S. of whatever nation Colour under my Control—Deserters from our Service, & negroes belonging to our Citizens are not Considered Subjects of exchange & were not included in my proposition. If there are any Such among those stated by you to have been Captured around Richmond & they can not be returned.[34]

Clearly, Lee stood by the official position that former slaves were not entitled to prisoner of war status. By this time, however, the Confederates had modified their official policy in practice and were willing to exchange those black prisoners who had been free prior to 1861. Grant declined the proposed exchange, saying, "the Government is bound to secure to all persons received into her Armies the rights due to soldiers."[35] After the war, Lee would feign ignorance of Grant's position on the matter, telling the congressional inquiry, "I did not know why it [the cartel] was suspended."[36] That was an extremely misleading point, of course. General Lee could often be cagey when defending himself.

Lee and Grant corresponded again later in the month. Grant complained to Lee that black prisoners had been deployed to work on fortifications that were exposed to Union fire. In a long response to Grant, Lee noted that placing the men there had been an error, but then went on to explain Confederate policies on black prisoners.[37]

Lee began by reiterating a recent change in policy that would treat free blacks as prisoners of war who would be "proper subjects of exchange." Fearing retaliation from the North, Secretary of War Seddon had decided to ignore the part of the Joint Resolution of May 1, 1863, threatening to enslave or kill free blacks. Former slaves, however, would still be subject to the harsh measures laid out by the Confederate Congress. Lee added, "all such slave property identified as belonging to citizens of any of the Confederate States, or to persons enjoying the protection of their laws, will be restored like other captured private property to those entitled to them." In response, Grant said it was his duty "to protect all persons received into the army of the United States, regardless of color or nationality." For his part, General Lee left little doubt that he was protecting the Confederate social system, regardless of his personal opinion on slavery.

Remarkably, supporters of the Confederacy actually blamed General Grant for the problems in southern prisons. They pointed to evidence that Grant disliked the cartel system, believing it allowed the South to replenish its ranks with returning soldiers whether by exchange or parole. Because of Grant's opposition to exchanges, the critics argued that the end of the exchange system created overcrowding at southern prison camps and eventually led to diseases and illnesses resulting from a lack of food, fresh water, and medical care. Confederate apologists made much of a letter from Grant to General Benjamin Butler on August 18, 1864, which stated,

> It is hard on our men held in Southern prisons not to exchange them, but it is humanity to those left in the ranks to fight our battles. Every man we hold, when released on parole or otherwise, becomes an active soldier against us at once either directly or indirectly. If we commence a system of exchange which liberates all prisoners taken, we will have to fight on until the whole South is exterminated. If we hold those caught they amount to no more than dead men. At this particular time to release all rebel prisoners North would insure Sherman's defeat and would compromise our safety here.[38]

This quote was considered so telling (and damning) that an excerpt of it was subsequently engraved on a monument to Captain Wirz that was dedicated by the United Daughters of the Confederacy in the town of Andersonville, Georgia, in 1909.

The complete documentary evidence, however, does not support the view that Grant was responsible for the breakdown of the prisoner exchange system. We have already seen that it collapsed in July 1863 over Confederate treatment of captured African American soldiers. Grant did not even take overall command of Union forces until the spring of 1864. And by the time of Grant's letter to Butler, there were already thirty thousand Union soldiers at Andersonville.

The Confederate leadership was never willing to offer *all* black troops as part of any exchanges. As Colonel Robert Ould, Confederate Commissioner for the Exchange of Prisoners of War, once remarked, "We will die in the last ditch before giving up the right to send slaves back to slavery."[39] Such an attitude was unacceptable to the Lincoln administration. The Union army's exchange agent, General Butler, eloquently expressed the administration's position when he said, "The wrongs, indignities, and privations suffered by our soldiers would move me to consent to anything to procure their exchange, except to barter away the honor and the faith of the Government of the United States, which has been so solemnly pledged to the colored soldiers in its ranks."[40]

★ ★ ★

The topic of Civil War prisoners is a contentious one. In the immediate aftermath of the war, dozens of memoirs were written about experiences in southern prisons. One former prisoner wrote in 1865, "I send out this book trusting that whatever influence it may exercise will aid in bringing the guilty leaders of Treason to just punishment for their enormous crimes against humanity."[41] The author forgave ordinary southerners, but blamed "Jeff Davis, Robert E. Lee and other rebels high in authority and the monsters whom they placed in command of the prisons."[42] The leaders, he argued, deserved a "just and condign punishment." The numerous memoirs were quite similar in portraying horrific treatment by sadistic guards and describing monstrous commandants like Captain Wirz. At the pinnacle of this "diabolic plot" were Jefferson Davis, his cabinet, and Robert E. Lee.

The treatment of African American prisoners may not have received as much attention right after the war, but it too raises moral questions about the Confederate States of America.[43] The Confederate Congress' decision not to treat black soldiers wearing the Union blue as prisoners of war ultimately culminated in the breakdown of the cartel, which in turn led to overcrowding at southern prisons like Andersonville. While Robert E. Lee may not have been operationally involved with Andersonville Prison, he *was* responsible for overseeing the war effort on behalf of a regime determined to preserve a "social organization" based on slavery. Resolutions like the one on black prisoners of war issued by the Confederate Congress on May 1, 1863, were representative of the values of the Confederate States of America.

To the modern observer, the abuses inflicted on black prisoners during the Civil War appear to be war crimes.[44] Federal prosecutors in 1865 wouldn't have used that precise term, but they too recognized the laws of war had been violated by the rebel leadership. In Francis Lieber's "General Order No. 100" that had been distributed to all Union officers in the field in 1863, Article 57 stated, "No belligerent has a right to declare that enemies of a certain class, color, or condition, when properly organized as soldiers, will not be treated by him as public enemies." Article 58 added, "The law of nations knows no distinction of color, and if an enemy of the United States should enslave and sell any captured persons of their army, it would be a case for the severest retaliation, if not redressed upon complaint."[45] General Benjamin Butler argued similarly in 1864 that "upon no ground of national law . . . can it be claimed for a moment that to any slave from any State, when found within our lines, any right of property can attach in behalf of his former master."[46]

Alas, in the immediate aftermath of the war, there was very little appetite for prosecuting Confederate leaders who may have been involved in re-enslaving African American prisoners, thereby violating the laws of war. This story seems to have been lost to Americans over the past century and a half. Yet, it has always been the "missing" context when considering Lee's plea of "innocence" in relation to the mistreatment of Union prisoners of war.

7

"THERE IS GENERAL LEE, AS HUNGRY FOR THE GALLOWS AS DAVIS."

On November 17, 1865, exactly one week after the hanging of Captain Wirz, George Washington Julian delivered a fiery address before the Indiana legislature in Indianapolis. Congressman Julian, a Radical Republican who served Indiana's fifth congressional district, had been asked to answer the question, "do you agree or disagree with the policy of President Johnson?"[1] Local supporters of Johnson were apprehensive about the abolitionist's possible answer, and they tried, unsuccessfully, to stop the speech. They had good reason to be worried.

Puckishly, Julian began his remarks by addressing head on the question of whether or not he agreed with Johnson: "If the House had told me what, in their opinion, the policy of President Johnson is, I could then have told you precisely whether I agree or disagree with him."[2] Clearly, he was jesting. In fact, Julian had been extremely critical of Johnson, believing the president was far too lenient in his handling of former rebels. On this point, he agreed with many of his fellow Radical Republicans at the time. If treason was a crime, Julian argued, then "at the end of the war you ought to make a fit example of these traitors, and thus render a repetition of their crime difficult in the future."[3] President Johnson had said something similar on numerous occasions in the days after the assassination of Lincoln. Somehow, it seemed, Johnson had reversed course. He now appeared to be letting the Confederates off easy. Was the president reneging on his vow to make treason odious?

Julian rehearsed a familiar argument to his audience. With murderers and

Figure 7.1.   Columbia: Shall I Trust These Men, And Not This Man? Pardon. Franchise Columbia, 1865. *Source:* Ben and Beatrice Goldstein Foundation, Thomas Nast collection. Library of Congress.

pirates, you indict them and then punish them. Traitors like Davis and Lee, who killed hundreds of thousands of men, were far worse, however. "Each one of these leaders was a national assassin, with his dagger in his hand, aiming it at the nation's vitals," according to Julian. Jefferson Davis, for example, should receive a fair and decent trial, and then, Julian added, "I would convict him and then build a gallows and hang him, in the name of God." The abolitionist had no desire to dispense mercy at the expense of justice.[4]

Warming to his topic, Julian told his audience he wouldn't stop with Davis:

Why should I? There is General Lee, as hungry for the gallows as Davis. He is running at large up and down the hills and valleys of Old Virginia, as if nothing at all had happened; and lately I have heard that he has been offered the presidency of a college: going to turn missionary and schoolmaster, I suppose to "teach the young idea how to shoot!" At the same time, as we are informed, he is to write a history of the rebellion. Gentlemen, I would not have him write that history. I would have it written by a loyal man, and I would have him put in a chapter giving an account of the hanging of Lee as a traitor.[5]

Outraged that Lee was still free, Julian felt the Confederate general in chief should be "in the ninth or lowest hell, where Dante says all traitors are found." He continued by making a timely reference to recent events in the nation's capital. Noting that Wirz had asked for a copy of Baxter's *Call to the Unconverted* right before he was hanged, Julian said he'd provide Lee with a copy of the same book but would also "let the gallows have him, and leave God to determine what should be done with his soul." Then, in words that would anger southerners for many years to come, Julian promised, "Nor would I stop with Lee. I would hang liberally, while I had my hand in. I would make the gallows respectable in these latter days, by dedicating it to Christian men."[6]

Talking for two hours, Julian also considered the need to seize the estates of southern aristocrats and dole out their land to loyal soldiers, poor white southerners, and freedmen. He also methodically laid out the case for black suffrage, and concluded his pugnacious address by stating, "The glorious fruits of our victory are within our grasp. We have only to reach forth our hands to possess them."[7] With the 39th Congress finally about to meet in early December, it was time for northerners to stand firm and dictate the peace. The president's soft approach to reconstruction had appeared ineffective so far. The Radical Republicans had a harsher plan in store for the secessionists.

Julian's talk received an enthusiastic response both inside and outside the hall. The speech first appeared in print in the *Cincinnati Gazette* and later was published as a pamphlet. Critics of the congressman, perhaps unsurprisingly in light of some of the rhetoric, were enraged and exasperated. Editors at the conservative *Indianapolis Journal* were particularly incensed by the speech, describing Julian as having "the temper of a hedgehog, the adhesiveness of a barnacle, the vanity of a peacock, the vindictiveness of a Corsican, the hypocrisy of Aminadab Sleek and the duplicity of the devil."[8]

Not all of the responses, alas, were as harmless as the childish editorial from the local newspaper. Several days after the talk, an angry rival viciously assaulted Julian, while he waited for a train in Richmond, Indiana.[9] The congressman intended to travel from Richmond to Washington, DC, for the opening of Congress. He was confronted on the platform by Solomon Meredith, a political opponent and former general in the Union army during the war. After exchanging words, the six-foot, seven-inch Meredith struck Julian on the head with a piece of iron and then hit him a dozen more times while he lay defenseless on the ground. Finally, the general whipped the congressman unconscious with a piece of cowhide. All the while, Meredith's gang of ruffians yelled, "Flog the damned abolitionist." "Give him what he deserves."

One local paper speculated that Julian's political enemies were angry about the positive reception to his speech in Indianapolis: "Determined to silence him at all events, and every other resource having been exhausted, they have resorted to a cowardly attempt on his life."[10] The brutal assault reminded many observers of the beating of Senator Charles Sumner on the Senate floor by Congressman Preston Brooks in 1856. Both before and after the war, it was extremely dangerous being an abolitionist in America.

★ ★ ★

George Washington Julian was one of the more extreme members of the Radical Republicans, a group that included Charles Sumner, Thaddeus Stevens, and Benjamin Butler among many others. This faction of the Republican Party had led the fight to emancipate the slaves and was now united by a desire to secure suffrage for the freedmen. In April 1865, the Radicals had been hopeful they had an ally in the new president. Over the course of the summer of 1865, however, they gradually became disillusioned with Andrew Johnson.

Shortly after the assassination of Lincoln, Johnson had vowed countless times, as we have seen, to "make treason odious." Yet, by late summer and early fall, he was pardoning former rebels freely and liberally. Over a span of nine months, more than fourteen thousand pardons would be granted. The Radical Republicans couldn't bear the idea that many of these pardoned rebels, who had only recently been trying to destroy the Union, might soon be in the halls of Congress obstructing any attempts at reconstruction. Many observers at the time wondered why Johnson had apparently changed course so abruptly. Why had he become so lenient toward the rebels? And why was he so keen on having traitors back causing mischief again at the US Capitol?

Johnson rejected the belief that he had somehow changed course. All along, he'd argue, he wanted to prosecute and severely punish roughly forty or fifty of the leaders, while pardoning all the rest. He was also committed to returning the southern states to the Union as quickly as possible, believing somewhat dogmatically that the southern states had never actually left *in theory*.[11] In the months before Congress was to convene in December 1865, Johnson began implementing a plan, which would allow for the rapid restoration of the Union. Former rebel politicians and soldiers would be elected to the upcoming Congress under this approach. Johnson also made it clear he wouldn't support black suffrage. In some respects, apart from his commitment to prosecuting the Confederate leadership, his plan was the polar opposite of what the Radicals were hoping for.

The Radicals believed Johnson's strategy—his "experiment" as it was known—made a bad situation much worse. Whitelaw Reid, an editor of the *New York Tribune*, argued that, in May and June, the Johnson administration "could at that time have prescribed no conditions for the return of the Rebel states which they would not have promptly accepted. They expected nothing; were prepared for the worst; would have been thankful for anything."[12]

Instead, Johnson offered overly generous terms to the Confederate States. Reid wrote, "The President had lustily proclaimed treason a crime, but the Southern people took his actions in preference to his words, and were confirmed in their own view that it was but a difference of opinion on a constitutional point, in which, under the circumstances, they were ready to yield."[13] Throughout the South that summer and fall, Robert E. Lee was highly praised and commonly referred to as "that great and good man."[14] Some Virginians even talked about him as a possible governor of the "Old Dominion."

The Radical Republicans were incredulous. They felt Johnson's leniency had emboldened former secessionists who eventually became far less willing to submit to policies that might, for example, improve the dire condition of the freedmen. John Minor Botts, a Virginia Unionist who testified before the Joint Committee on Reconstruction in February 1866, stated that Johnson's "indiscriminate system of pardoning" resulted in the former rebels becoming "bold, insolent, and defiant."[15] Of the forty-four individuals who were asked about this topic before the committee, forty-two agreed with Botts's assessment.[16] One Congressman tried to explain Johnson's apparent reversal by saying the president enjoyed pardoning his former social superiors. By being lenient, Johnson would somehow "attain the goal of his highest ambition; he would conquer the haughty enemy who during all these years of his public career had been able to fix upon him the badge of social inferiority."[17]

The Radical Republicans spoke frequently of the need to punish the Confederate leaders and offered a far more comprehensive approach than either Johnson or Lincoln, while he was still alive. Senator Charles Sumner, speaking in the Senate in 1862, advised Lincoln to "strike down the leaders of the rebellion and lift up the slaves."[18] The gentlemanly senator, who was the moral leader of the Radicals, thought "the tallest poppies must drop" and their land seized.[19] In May 1865, Sumner favored driving roughly five hundred or so former rebels out of the country where they would learn "how to appreciate the crime they have committed."[20] Jefferson Davis and a few others deserved harsher treatment, however. Indeed, Sumner told Chief Justice Chase, "I never cease to regret that Jeff. Davis was not shot at the time of his capture."[21] By October 1865, Sumner was seriously concerned about so many "late Rebels coming into power."[22] On December 2, 1865, just two days before Congress met, Sumner and Andrew Johnson had a heated discussion about reconstruction matters. Johnson got so agitated during the two-and-half-hour meeting that he used Sumner's silk hat as a spittoon.[23]

Like Sumner, General Benjamin Butler also spoke of punishing the leaders, while at the same time "lifting up" the freedmen.[24] At a speech in June 1865 at Lowell, Massachusetts, Butler—who Andrew Johnson believed was "the most daring and unscrupulous demagogue" he had ever seen—urged the idea of confiscating the land of the leading rebels and giving it directly to African American veterans.[25] Thaddeus Stevens, perhaps *the* most talented politician of the time, developed this controversial idea even further in a speech in early September 1865.

An enfeebled seventy-four-year-old, Stevens wore a brown wig, deliberately tilted cockeyed atop his head. Born in Vermont, he had moved to Pennsylvania where he eventually was elected to the House of Representatives. During the 1860s, he dominated the House with his wicked wit and uncompromising stance on abolition. Throughout his life, he was a dedicated foe of slavery and was an early voice in Congress for universal, uncompensated emancipation. Stevens had always been wary of Andrew Johnson. When Lincoln told Stevens he intended to select Johnson as his vice president in 1864, Stevens told him, "Mr. President, Andrew Johnson is a rank demagogue, and I suspect at heart a damned scoundrel."[26] Described as a "Pennsylvania Caliban," Stevens made countless enemies. One leading historian of the period has described him as "a hater of the South."[27]

At a speech in his hometown of Lancaster, Pennsylvania, that the *New York Times* labeled "The Great Topic of the Hour," Stevens discussed the interrelationship between Reconstruction and the punishment of the secessionists. Up until this point, President Johnson and his cabinet had been making all decisions regarding the former Confederate states. Stevens, who believed Johnson had been far too eager to make amends with traitors, asked his audience, "Is then all lost? Is this great conquest to be in vain?"[28] To those questions, Stevens replied that all will depend on "the virtue and intelligence of the next Congress." That body would ultimately determine Reconstruction—it alone should be responsible for "giving law to the vanquished."

Stevens agreed with Butler that the property of wealthy rebels should be confiscated and given to the freedmen. Indeed, the "Old Commoner" offered a surprisingly detailed proposal. By seizing the estates of the leading secession-ists, he calculated the government would obtain 394 million acres. This would be sufficient to provide every male freedman with farms of forty acres. After disbursing all that land, there would still be roughly 350 million acres left over. This land could then be sold with the proceeds used for paying down the national debt and funding pensions for veterans. According to Stevens's logic, it was "far easier and more beneficial to exile 70,000 proud, bloated and defiant rebels, than to expatriate four millions of laborers, native to the soil and loyal to the government."

In retrospect, it shouldn't be surprising that the former lawyer also offered some insightful commentary on the legal issues involved with punishing rebels and confiscating their land. Stevens pointed out there would be too many obstacles for justice to be served if the former Confederate states were treated as if they had never left the Union. For example, according to the Constitu-tion, Jefferson Davis would have to be tried in Virginia by an impartial jury. Of course, no southern jury would ever dream of convicting him unless it was "packed." A packed jury, however, would be "judicial murder" according to Stevens.[29]

The solution to the problem, Stevens believed, was to treat the southern states as "conquered enemies." Then, the rebel leadership could be tried and punished by a "courts-martial"—precisely how the government was proceed-ing against Captain Wirz in September 1865. Stevens believed the nature of the Civil War allowed the victor "to execute, to imprison, to confiscate." To support the idea of confiscation, he quoted the Swiss legal expert Emer de Vattel,

> A conqueror, who has taken up arms not only against the sovereign but against the nation herself, and whose intention it was to subdue a fierce and savage people, and once for all to reduce an obstinate enemy, such a conqueror may, with justice, lay burdens on the conquered nation, both as a compensation for the expenses of the war, and as a punishment.

A large number of wealthy rebels would have their land seized under Stevens's plan, while a relative handful would also face capital punishment. Stevens con-fessed, "I am not fond of sanguinary punishments, but surely some victims must propitiate the manes of our starved, murdered, slaughtered martyrs."

One the eve of the 39th Congress, the challenge of how best to punish the rebels was at the top of the Radical Republican agenda. How many former rebels should be punished? Should fifty, five hundred, or ten thousand of the senior leaders of the rebellion be brought to justice? Should they be tried and hanged for treason? Sent into exile? Or should they merely lose political rights like voting and holding office? If the land of the leading rebels was to be seized, should it be allotted to the freedmen? These were just some of the questions that would be debated as the people's representatives gathered in Washington for a highly anticipated opening of Congress.

★   ★   ★

The day everyone had been waiting for came at last. The chamber of the House of Representatives teemed with activity on the morning of the opening of Congress on Monday, December 4, 1865. Within the main hall, "members, pages, office-holders, office seekers, and a miscellaneous crowd, swarmed over the new carpet and among the desks."[30] In less than an hour after the call to order, Thaddeus Stevens, the driving force in the House of Representatives, issued a clear challenge to the Johnson administration.

First, it was determined, contrary to the wishes of the president, that the representatives from the former Confederate states would not be seated in Congress. Next, it was announced that a congressional caucus, having met the previous night, had agreed to the creation of a joint committee of fifteen members, "who shall inquire into the conditions of the States which formed the so-called Confederate States of America, and report whether any of them are entitled to be represented in either House of Congress."[31]

The committee of fifteen, which eventually became known as the Joint Committee on Reconstruction, consisted of six senators and nine members of the House of Representatives. Among the senators on the committee were Jacob Howard (Republican, MI) and Reverdy Johnson (Democrat, MD)—Reverdy was Lee's friend who had previously offered to provide him with legal assistance. Among the members from the House were Thaddeus Stevens (Republican, PA), Roscoe Conkling (Republican, NY), and Henry Blow (Republican, MO). To get a better sense of the condition of the South, the Joint Committee embarked on an extensive effort to gather testimony from former secessionists, southern Unionists, freedmen, and northerners, who were temporarily residing in the South. Overall, 137 individuals would be interviewed between January and May 1866. Robert E. Lee, who was examined by Howard, Blow, and Conkling, appeared before one of its subcommittees on February 17, 1866. Other luminaries appearing before subcommittees included the former Confederate Vice President Alexander Stephens, Judge John C. Underwood, and Clara Barton. Testimony from all of the interviews would be published in an 814-page report consisting of "pages of type too fine for an old man to read."[32] The final report would also contain 260 pages of documentary evidence.

On the day after the opening of Congress, President Johnson submitted his first annual message. This surprisingly conciliatory address, from the usually combative Johnson, was mostly well received by both the Senate and House. The judicious document had been prepared by George Bancroft, a famous historian and former cabinet member from the Polk administration.[33]

The message began by noting the death of Lincoln "by an act of parricidal treason." It then devoted extensive detail on Johnson's highly nuanced thoughts on the relationship between the states and the Constitution.[34] As expected, there was also much discussion of taxes, foreign relations, and various issues relating to the recently freed slaves.

Midway through the address, Johnson explained his policy on punishing the leading rebels. He believed,

> It is manifest that treason, most flagrant in character, has been committed. Persons who are charged with its commission should have fair and impartial trials in the highest civil tribunals of the country, in order that the Constitution and the laws may be fully vindicated, the truth clearly established and affirmed that treason is a crime, that traitors should be punished and the offense made infamous, and, at the same time, that the question may be judicially settled, finally and forever, that no State of its own will has the right to renounce its place in the Union.

Johnson was telling both Congress and the nation that those rebels charged with treason—Davis, Lee, and the others indicted by Underwood's grand jury—would receive a fair trial in a civil court, as opposed to a military tribunal like the one that tried Wirz. Johnson also advised Congress that the circuit courts in the former Confederate States would not be held until Congress had "an opportunity to consider and act on the whole subject."

On this last point, Johnson was quoting directly from a letter he had received from Chief Justice Chase. In early October, as we have already seen, Johnson had told Chase that he wanted him to preside over the prosecution of "some high crimes and misdemeanors committed against the United States within the District of Virginia." Here, Johnson is referring specifically to Lee and the thirty-six other indicted leaders. Davis, at that time, had only been indicted in the District of Columbia. Chase replied by saying, first, his schedule wouldn't allow for him to oversee a circuit court trial in November 1865. Second, and more importantly, he didn't wish to appear in a circuit court in a state like Virginia, which was still subject to martial law. At that time, Supreme Court justices also had circuit court responsibilities—Chase served in the fourth circuit comprising Virginia, North Carolina, and Maryland. Until it was clear that the war was officially over, Chase wouldn't appear in his circuit. Also, Chase believed Congress should "consider and act" on this subject. In his annual message, Johnson revealed that it was Chase that was holding up the prosecution and punishment of the leading rebels. The president was ready and willing to go forward with trials as soon as possible.

The Radical Republicans could be blinded by their own rhetoric on occasion. In the roughly eight months or so between the death of Lincoln and the opening of Congress, the Johnson administration had actually constructed, in fits and starts, a fairly clear policy on punishing the leading rebels. Attorney General James Speed summarized the administration's approach in a letter to Johnson on January 6, 1866, that was intended to be shared with the Senate. All along, Johnson and Speed had sought the advice of leading legal thinkers like Butler and Lieber, who were allied with the Radicals.

Speed believed it would be "a direful calamity if many whom the sword has spared the law should spare also."[35] After consulting with Francis Lieber, Speed had contended within the cabinet that civil courts, rather than military courts, must be used for treason trials. Civil courts would provide far greater legitimacy for an eventual verdict. Johnson's cabinet members eventually agreed on this particular point after considerable debate. They also concurred that future trials, according to the Constitution, must be held in the state and district "wherein the crime shall have been committed." Speed argued against the notion that a rebel leader could somehow be "constructively present" while directing armies in faraway locations.

It was in this letter that Speed publicly clarified the cabinet's view of the paroles that had been granted to Lee and his men. The administration believed the paroles only provided protection as long as the war had not been legally ended. Once peace was formalized, however, the paroles would no longer be valid and Lee's men could be prosecuted. The chief justice had also made it quite clear that he refused to preside in a circuit court until the war was formally over. Speed was particularly adamant that any treason trial must be conducted before the chief justice.

From a purely legal perspective, Judge Underwood *could* have presided over a treason trial without the chief justice present. Speed rejected that idea, however, declaring, "I never would have consented to try such a case before Judge Underwood in that district."[36] Obviously, there was historical precedent involved here—Chief Justice Marshall, for example, had presided over the treason trial of Aaron Burr. There was also evidence to suggest that Speed believed Underwood was too partisan and perhaps not trustworthy. We saw earlier that Underwood had been accused of improperly confiscating a property that was later purchased by his wife. In a letter to District Attorney Chandler, Speed mentioned reports of overly aggressive confiscations in Underwood's district. He added, "The charge is plainly made that the seizures are initiated not with the purpose of promoting justice, and reestablishing the authority of the law, but for private ends and private gain."[37] Speed clearly had suspicions about Underwood. Any future treason trials would require the presence of Chief Justice Salmon Chase, who would sit in the circuit court alongside Judge Underwood.

★ ★ ★

As part of the Joint Committee on Reconstruction's investigation of conditions in the South, a subcommittee was formed, led by Jacob Howard, Roscoe Conkling, and Henry Blow, to examine Virginia, North Carolina, and South Carolina. The subcommittee would eventually question forty-nine residents of Virginia. Surprisingly, thirty-eight of those residents were Republicans and nine or so were conservatives. Obviously, this was extremely unrepresentative of Virginia, which was overwhelmingly made up of former rebels and rebel sympathizers.

Judge John C. Underwood became one of the first individuals to testify, appearing before the subcommittee on January 31, 1866.[38] Subsequent witnesses would offer similar testimony to that provided by the Judge. He noted there was increasing bitterness between those who had been loyal to the Union and those who had supported the Confederacy. He also testified that, "Sooner than see the colored people raised to a legal and political equality, the southern people would prefer their total annihilation." Underwood also believed Andrew Johnson's policy on pardons and amnesties had made the rebels more "malignant" toward Union men in Virginia.

After some preliminary questions, Underwood was asked about the likelihood of winning a treason trial against former rebels in Virginia. This was a particularly intriguing line of questioning, in light of the fact that Underwood, along with Chief Justice Chase, would likely preside over such a trial in the 4th Circuit Court. That extremely relevant detail wasn't disclosed during the hearing, however. Asked if he could call a jury in Virginia that would convict a man of treason, Underwood replied,

It would be perfectly idle to think of such a thing. They boast of their treason, and ten or eleven out of the twelve on any jury, I think, would say that Lee was almost equal to Washington, and was the noblest man in the State, and they regard every man who has committed treason with more favor than any man in the State who has remained loyal to the government.

Later, Underwood explained that the only way that Davis or Lee could be convicted of treason would be with a "packed jury." When questioned about whether he could pack a jury to convict Davis, Underwood answered, "I think it would be very difficult, but it could be done; I could pack a jury to convict him; I know very earnest, ardent Union men in Virginia."

The idea of "packing" a jury in order to win a conviction in a treason case sounds sinister to the modern ear. Indeed, it had extremely negative connotations back then, too. Thaddeus Stevens, we have seen, believed that packing a jury was the equivalent of "judicial murder."

In fairness to Underwood, he seemed to be using the term "packing" in a specifically local context. On one occasion he wrote to a colleague that in many counties in Virginia, juries were selected by sheriffs and marshals, "or in professional language, have packed juries instead of drawing them from a box of names selected by other officers, as is done in most States." As a former New Yorker, Underwood admitted he had been skeptical initially of this local practice, but then conceded that it seemed to work just fine. Regardless of the ethics relating to jury packing, trying a treason case before a Virginia jury promised to be an exceedingly difficult task. One can imagine most prosecutors would have been hesitant to pursue such a case.

The subcommittee scheduled a hearing for Robert E. Lee for February 17, 1866.[39] Lee hadn't been to Washington, DC, since meeting with his mentor, General Winfield Scott, right before resigning his commission from the US Army in April 1861. He reluctantly agreed to appear before the subcommittee, checking in to the Metropolitan Hotel in Washington on the day before his hearing. He later remarked that he could see his former home in Arlington on the other side of the Potomac River; it was a "house that any one might see with half an eye."[40] Numerous old acquaintances called on him at his hotel and he received numerous cards and notes from well-wishers.

On the morning of his hearing, he walked to the Capitol, with a large crowd following in his wake. Dressed in one of his gray Confederate uniforms, Lee entered the high-ceilinged room at 11:30 a.m. With his hand on a Bible, he swore to tell the truth. He was not given immunity while testifying—anything he said would be fair game in a future treason trial. In his poem "Lee in the Capitol," Herman Melville described Lee's entrance into the committee room,[41]

The meeting follows. In his mien
The victor and the vanquished both are seen—
All that he is, and what he late had been.
Awhile, with curious eyes they scan
The Chief who led invasion's van—

After having been sworn in, Lee sat in a chair facing Senator Jacob Howard, who started the questioning. Like Thaddeus Stevens, Howard had been born in Vermont. Later, he moved to Detroit, Michigan, to practice law, and eventually entered the Senate in 1862. Known as "Honest Jake" back home, he was described as "an excellent debater and a bitter partisan."[42] Howard was also recognized as one of the leading constitutional lawyers in the Senate.

Unsurprisingly, Lee was guarded and not especially forthcoming in many of his answers. Unlike most of the previous witnesses, he believed Virginians were supportive of Johnson's "policy in regard to the restoration of the whole country." Lee always used the word "restoration" instead of "reconstruction." He hoped that Virginia's relations to the Union could be similar to those that existed before the war.

The exchanges between Howard and Lee on the question of treason would have been especially helpful for those lawyers who might be involved in a future prosecution of Lee. Composed and careful in his language, the former Confederate general in chief would have been a formidable opponent in a courtroom. He also reiterated the view that a Virginia jury would be unlikely to return a guilty verdict in a treason case. The following is a fascinating back and forth between Howard and Lee on this subject:

Question: You understand my question: Suppose a jury was impanelled in your own neighborhood, taken up by lot; would it be practicable to convict, for instance, Jefferson Davis for having levied war upon the United States, and thus having committed the crime of treason?

Answer: I think it is very probable that they would not consider he had committed treason.

Question: Suppose the jury should be clearly and plainly instructed by the court that such an act of war upon the United States, on the part of Mr. Davis, or any other leading man, constituted in itself the crime of treason under the Constitution of the United States; would the jury be likely to heed that instruction, and if the facts were plainly in proof before them, convict the offender?

Answer: I do not know, sir, what they would do on that question.

Question: They do not generally suppose that it was treason against the United States, do they?

Answer: I do not think that they so consider it.

Question: In what light would they view it? What would be their excuse or justification? How would they escape in their own mind? I refer to the past.

Answer: I am referring to the past and as to the feelings they would have. So far as I know, they look upon the action of the State, in withdrawing itself from the government of the United States, as carrying the individuals of the State along with it; that the State was responsible for the act, not the individual.

Concluding this line of questioning, Howard asked Lee how he personally saw the question of treason:

Question: State, if you please, (and if you are disinclined to answer the question you need not, do so) what your own personal views on the question were?

Answer: That was my view; that the act of Virginia, in withdrawing herself from the United States, carried me along as a citizen of Virginia, and that her laws and her acts were binding on me.

Question: And that you felt to be your justification in taking the course that you did?

Answer: Yes, sir.

Here, Lee was making a point he had made in the past. The Confederate leadership didn't commit treason, he believed. Instead, they felt their primary loyalty lay with their respective states. The notion that the war was about "states' rights" had first been put forward by Lee in his interview with the *New York Herald* shortly after the war. That view would eventually become a core belief of the "Lost Cause" tradition. Would the government be willing to risk losing a treason trial against Davis or Lee?

Of course, Lee's understanding of the Constitution may not have been relevant in a future case. Howard makes this clear when he asks how a jury would respond if they were instructed by the court on the meaning of treason under the Constitution. Lee seemed quite honest when he replied, "I do not know, sir, what they would do on that question." That answer may have been worrying for anyone hoping to bring a civil case against Davis, Lee, or some of the other leaders of the Confederate States of America. We have seen that Attorney General James Speed had already committed the administration to trying treason cases in civil courts, as opposed to military tribunals. After hearing the testimony from Underwood, Lee, and many of the others before the subcommittee, the odds of success in a civil trial seemed long.

Lee's testimony relating to freedmen might shock modern Americans. When asked by Congressman Charles Blow about black suffrage, Lee replied, "My own opinion is, that, at this time, they cannot vote intelligently, and that giving them the right of suffrage would open the door to a great deal of demagogism, and lead to embarrassments in various ways." Later, Blow asked about the future of freedmen in Virginia,

Question: What is your opinion about its being an advantage to Virginia to keep them there at all? Do you not think that Virginia would be better off if the colored population were to go to Alabama, Louisiana, and the other southern States?

Answer: I think it would be better for Virginia if she could get rid of them. That is no new opinion with me. I have always thought so, and have always been in favor of emancipation—gradual emancipation.

Lee revealed himself to be a traditional southern conservative of that time, who preferred a Virginia without African Americans. As the most revered man in the South—then and for many years to come—his attitudes carried great weight, however. In postwar Virginia, there were five hundred thousand freedmen whose status remained uncertain. Nearly three-quarters of them were now homeless. On the pressing topic of how to best integrate these freedmen into a new society, the South's leading voice wished Virginia "could get rid of them." Sadly, this view had actually been the law of the land in Virginia prior to the war. According to the Virginia Code of 1849, all freedmen had been required to leave the state within one year of emancipation.

Seven freedmen would eventually appear before the committee—all on the same day. The duration of their testimony combined possibly took less time than that of Lee's. The committee did learn from one freedman that "the spirit of the whites against the blacks is much worse than it was before the war." Another African American added, "The only hope the colored people have is in Uncle Sam's bayonets."[43] The historian Richard Lowe believes that as a result of the committee overlooking the experience of African Americans in postwar Virginia, "The opportunity to develop a unique, firsthand perspective on Reconstruction through the testimony of Virginians of African descent was lost."[44]

After two and half hours, the questioning of Lee ended at around 2:00 p.m. Melville described the conclusion dramatically,

> He ceased. His earnestness unforeseen.
> Moved, but not swayed their former mien;
> And they dismissed him. Forth he went
> Through vaulted walks in lengthened line
> Like porches erst upon the Palatine:
> Historic reveries their lesson lent,
> The Past her shadow through the Future sent.

Lee walked back to his hotel, once again with a crowd following him the entire way. He returned to Lexington shortly after. The day after the meeting his wife, Mary, wrote a friend, "You will probably see by the [news]papers ere this reaches you that the Genl has been summoned to Washington to appear before the Reconstruction Committee. They should more properly be called the Destruction."[45]

The many hagiographers of Lee have seen his performance before the subcommittee as a shining, if somewhat unpleasant, moment for their hero. Douglas Southall Freeman, for example, emphasized Lee's calm and thoughtful responses to aggressive questioning, and concluded that the "committee failed to accomplish its purpose."[46] Freeman can barely hide his disdain for Howard and Blow.

Weeks after the hearing, a writer from the *Chicago Tribune*, which had been quite critical of Lee, was struck by all the things that General Lee did not know and had never heard of. The reporter sarcastically surmised that Lee didn't know anything about anything.

The truth probably lies somewhere between these two extreme assessments. Lee, who wasn't given immunity, needed to be careful in his testimony, and he was. For their part, Howard and Blow saw the hearing as a great opportunity to examine one of the leaders who was "at the head of the rebellion." On the topic of treason—which was the most important question relating to Lee—it's very unlikely that anyone's mind was changed one way or another by the general's testimony.

Lee's comments relating to the freedmen sound particularly harsh from a modern perspective. "Getting rid" of the freedmen would have been unfathomably cruel and disruptive so soon after emancipation, even if it was possible, which it was not. This cold side of Lee has been hidden to subsequent genera-tions, perhaps because it reflects so poorly on his reputation as a Christian gentleman.

Several weeks after his visit to Washington, he wrote a highly revealing letter to his cousin Markie Williams:

> In my late visit to Washington, knowing how our God mixes in the cup he gives us to drink in this World, the sweet with the bitter, I had hoped I might have found you there. But you were far beyond my reach. The changed times and circumstances did recall sad thoughts, but I rejoiced to think, that those who were so prominent in my thoughts, at former periods when returning from long and distant excursions, and whose welcome was so grateful, were now above all human influences and enjoying eternal peace and rest. I saw however other friends, whose kind reception gave me much pleasure, yet I am now considered such a monster, that I hesitate to darken with my shadow, the doors of those I love best lest I should bring upon them misfortune.[47]

Almost a year after the war, Lee believed he was considered "a monster" by many northerners and avoided calling upon old friends. He may have even wondered if all those questions about treason trials by his Radical Republican interrogators indicated a greater likelihood of prosecution in the future.

He had good reason to be concerned. The Johnson administration still wished to try him for treason and many northerners believed, more than ever before, that he had been complicit in the mistreatment of prisoners of war. Lee also told Markie that he "did not approach Arlington nearer than the railway. I know very well how things are there." His family estate, which had been founded by George Washington's adopted son, was now a federal cemetery. Melville wrote,

> Reasons of state, 'tis claimed, require the man.
> Demurring not, promptly he comes
> By ways which show the blackened homes,
> And—last—the seat no more his own,
> But Honor's; patriot grave-yards fill
> The forfeit slopes of that patrician hill,
> And fling a shroud on Arlington.

The price of joining the Confederacy had been very costly indeed for the former colonel in the US Army.

8

"GEN. LEE A WOMAN WHIPPER."

"Why, Tom, you couldn't possibly have earned, by your work, such
clothes and such living as I have given you."

"Knows all that, Mas'r St. Clare; Mas'r's been too good; but, Mas'r, I'd
rather have poor clothes, poor house, poor everything, and have 'em
mine, than have the best, and have 'em any man's else,—I had so,
Mas'r; I think it's natur, Mas'r."

—Harriet Beecher Stowe, *Uncle Tom's Cabin*, 1852

Upon returning to Lexington after testifying before the Joint Committee
on Reconstruction, Lee wrote a letter to Amanda Parks, a former slave
from his Arlington estate who had tried to visit him while he had been in
Washington, DC,

Amanda: I have received your letter of the 27th ult., and regret very much that
I did not see you when I was in Washington. I heard on returning to my room,
Sunday night, that you had been to see me; and I was sorry to have missed you,
for I wished to learn how you were, and how all the people from Arlington
were getting on in the world. My interest in them is as great now as it ever was,
and I sincerely wish for their happiness and prosperity. At the period specified
in Mr. Custis's will—five years from the time of this death—I caused the liberation of all the people at Arlington, as well as those at the White House and
Romancoke, to be recorded in the Hustings Court at Richmond; and letters of
manumission to be given to those with whom I could communicate who
desired them. In consequence of the war which then existed, I could do nothing

131

more for them. I do not know why you should ask if I'm angry with you. I am not aware of your having done anything to give me offense, and I hope you would not say or do what was wrong. While you lived at Arlington you behaved very well, and were attentive and faithful to your duties. I hope you will always conduct yourself in the same manner. Wishing you health, happiness, and success in life, I am truly, R.E. Lee[1]

This friendly note revealed a warm and paternal Lee who seemed genuinely interested in the well-being of all the slaves that had been part of the estate of his father-in-law, George Washington Parke Custis. Admiring biographers of Lee have been right to showcase the letter as evidence of his solicitude toward his slaves.

It's possible there might be more to it than just that, however. The letter indirectly raises several questions worth considering in greater detail. Why does it appear that Amanda Parks was unaware of the details relating to the manumission of Custis's slaves? It had been over three years since she and the others had been legally freed by Lee. Also, why did Parks think Lee might be angry with her? Was it because Lee chose not to visit Arlington during his trip to Washington or was it for some other reason? Finally, when Lee said, "I hope you would not say or do what was wrong," did he have any particular reason for concern about Amanda or was that merely well-meaning advice from a kindly elder? A subsequent development just over two weeks after this letter was sent would make these questions especially relevant.

★　★　★

On March 26, 1866, the *New York Daily Tribune*—a widely read anti-slavery newspaper founded by Horace Greeley—published a shocking account of Lee's actions in 1859 by a former Arlington slave named Wesley Norris.[2] Here is the testimony in its entirety:

> My name is Wesley Norris; I was born a slave on the plantation of George Parke Custis; after the death of Mr. Custis, Gen. Lee, who had been made executor of the estate, assumed control of the slaves, in number about seventy; it was the general impression among the slaves of Mr. Custis that on his death they should be forever free; in fact this statement had been made to them by Mr. C. years before; at his death we were informed by Gen. Lee that by the conditions of the will we must remain slaves for five years; I remained with Gen. Lee for about seventeen months, when my sister Mary, a cousin of ours, and I determined to run away, which we did in the year 1859; we had already reached

Westminster, in Maryland, on our way to the North, when we were apprehended and thrown into prison, and Gen. Lee notified of our arrest; we
remained in prison fifteen days, when we were sent back to Arlington; we were
immediately taken before Gen. Lee, who demanded the reason why we ran
away; we frankly told him that we considered ourselves free; he then told us he
would teach us a lesson we never would forget; he then ordered us to the barn,
where, in his presence, we were tied firmly to posts by a Mr. Gwin, our overseer, who was ordered by Gen. Lee to strip us to the waist and give us fifty
lashes each, excepting my sister, who received but twenty; we were accordingly
stripped to the skin by the overseer, who, however, had sufficient humanity to
decline whipping us; accordingly Dick Williams, a county constable, was called
in, who gave us the number of lashes ordered; Gen. Lee, in the meantime,
stood by, and frequently enjoined Williams to "lay it on well," an injunction
which he did not fail to heed; not satisfied with simply lacerating our naked
flesh, Gen. Lee then ordered the overseer to thoroughly wash our backs with
brine, which was done. After this my cousin and myself were sent to Hanover
Court-House jail, my sister being sent to Richmond to an agent to be hired;
we remained in jail about a week, when we were sent to Nelson county, where
we were hired out by Gen. Lee's agent to work on the Orange and Alexander
railroad; we remained thus employed for about seven months, and were then
sent to Alabama, and put to work on what is known as the Northeastern railroad; in January, 1863, we were sent to Richmond, from which place I finally
made my escape through the rebel lines to freedom; I have nothing further to
say; what I have stated is true in every particular, and I can at any time bring at
least a dozen witnesses, both white and black, to substantiate my statements: I
am at present employed by the Government; and am at work in the National
Cemetary [*sic*] on Arlington Heights, where I can be found by those who desire
further particulars; my sister referred to is at present employed by the French
Minister at Washington, and will confirm my statement.

Before analyzing these charges in detail, it's worthwhile to summarize the key
elements of Norris's statement. Sometime in late May 1859, Wesley Norris,
his sister Mary, and their cousin George Parks attempted to run away from the
Arlington estate due to their belief they had already been freed by Custis.
Wesley Norris was twenty-nine years old at the time; his sister Mary was just
sixteen. George Parks, it should also be noted, was the brother of Amanda
Parks.

    The three runaways were eventually caught near the Pennsylvania border
and returned to Robert E. Lee. On leave from the army at the time, Colonel
Lee was managing, on behalf of the Custis estate, the 63 slaves at Arlington in
addition to another 136 slaves at two other properties. Norris alleged that Lee

had the three slaves brutally whipped, urging the constable to "lay it on well." Cruelly, Lee had their backs washed with brine afterward, according to Norris. Eventually, all three of them were hired out to other slave owners far away from Arlington. Finally, Norris noted that he had subsequently returned to Arlington, working at the new National Cemetery.

Wesley Norris's statement in 1866 wasn't the first time these charges had been leveled at Lee. The *Tribune* had initially published, in June 1859 shortly after the events in question, two anonymous letters alleging brutality by Lee toward Wesley Norris, Mary Norris, and George Parks. Varying accounts of the episode would appear in numerous publications between 1859 and 1866, but the testimony provided by Wesley Norris in March 1866 purported to be the first time one of the victims had given *their* version of events.[3] Norris's declaration that "what I have stated is true in every particular, and I can at any time bring at least a dozen witnesses" gave his story the appearance of being a damning indictment of Lee's behavior as a slave master. Perhaps Lee, viewed by many in the South as a true Christian soldier, was no different than any other prewar slave driver who had been corrupted by the peculiar institution.

Obviously, the *New York Daily Tribune*, a dedicated champion of the freedmen, had a vested interest in questioning Lee's credibility soon after he had testified before the Joint Committee on Reconstruction in Washington, DC. As historian Elizabeth Varon wisely points out, the publication of Norris's statement occurred "at the very moment when the fate of the Civil Rights bill hung in the balance."[4] The bill would eventually pass on April 9, 1866, over President Johnson's veto. Shortly after Norris's testimony appeared in the *Tribune*, another antislavery periodical, the *Independent*, published an excerpt for "the admirers of General Robert E. Lee" under the headline, "Gen. Lee a Woman Whipper."[5] That particular piece concluded with the line, "A woman whipper a Christian gentleman!" Exposing Lee as a hypocrite appeared to be a preferred line of attack for the Radical press.

We don't know if Norris approached Greeley's paper or if it was the other way around. One possibility might be that an editor from the influential newspaper heard Norris had returned to Arlington and then contacted him to take down his testimony on this long-standing allegation. Was Amanda Parks, who was also living at Arlington at the time, aware of the decision to publish her cousin's testimony in the *Tribune*? Is it possible she attempted to warn Lee about this matter during his stay in the nation's capital? Finally, we don't know if Norris was "coached" into saying certain things or if his account was heavily edited in order to have a more powerful impact on public opinion. Perhaps he wrote it all himself.

Regardless, Lee was extremely unhappy with the publication of Norris's account, perceiving it as an unprovoked attack by the northern press. Shortly after the story appeared, Lee told his friend George Fox that "the same statement had been published at the North for several years."[6] He added,

> The statement is not true; but I have not thought proper to publish a contradiction, being unwilling to be drawn into a newspaper discussion, believing that those who know me would not credit it and those who do not would care nothing about it. I cannot now depart from the rule that I have followed. It is so easy to make accusations against the people of the South upon similar testimony, that those so disposed, should one be refuted, will immediately create another; and thus you would be led into endless controversy.

Lee concluded by asking Fox to treat his letter as private. Not only was Lee unwilling to publicly defend his treatment of his father-in-law's slaves, but he also didn't want others to mount a defense on his behalf. Lee hoped national reconciliation would ultimately result in a correction of the record sometime in the future.

Lee's postwar correspondence makes it clear he believed northern advocates of the freedmen were unfair in their criticism of white southerners who had supported the Confederacy. When he stated to Fox that it is "so easy to make accusations against the people of the South upon similar testimony," one senses Lee's frustration in early 1866. He may have had good reason to feel that way. The attacks on his behavior as a slave owner were intended to call into question Lee's character and integrity. It had to sting him considerably when an editorial writer wondered how a Christian gentleman could be a woman whipper. Less than a year earlier, Lee had been indicted for treason before an abolitionist judge in a federal courtroom. Now, he faced a *moral* indictment by an abolitionist newspaper for his treatment of his former slaves. For a man who cared a great deal about his personal honor, this must have been an extremely difficult burden. He also intuitively knew that defending himself in the pages of northern newspapers was an unwise strategy. Lee chose to wait for the personal attacks to eventually abate.

Like almost all southerners, Lee always had an intense dislike of abolitionists. Prior to the war, he viewed them as meddlesome and responsible for provoking the national crisis over slavery. He and his wife, Mary, also blamed abolitionists for encouraging many of their slaves—including Wesley, Mary, and George—to run away shortly after the death of George Washington Parke Custis. Mary Lee wrote, "Scarcely had my father been laid in his tomb when two men were constantly lurking about here tampering with the servants & telling them they had a right to their freedom *immediately.*"[7] Several years before the war, in a letter to his wife, Lee chastised abolitionists for their arrogance and hypocrisy. Lee conceded that slavery would be abolished someday but then declared,

> We must leave the progress as well as the result in His hands who sees the end and who chooses to work by slow things and with whom a thousand years are but as a single day; although the abolitionist must know this, and must see that he has neither the right nor the power of operating except by moral means and suasion; and if he means well to the slave, he must not create angry feelings in the master. That although he may not approve the mode by which it pleases Providence to accomplish its purposes, the result will nevethelessr be the same. . . . Is it not strange that the descendants of those Pilgrim Fathers who crossed the Atlantic to preserve the freedom of their opinion have always proved themselves intolerant of the spiritual liberty of others?[8]

Lee's belief that God "chooses to work by slow things and with whom a thousand years are but as a single day" provides context for his statement before the Joint Committee that he had "always been in favor of emancipation— gradual emancipation."[9] As we'll see, the notion of "gradual emancipation" didn't appear to involve any meaningful concessions on the part of slave owners during the 1850s. In the years before the war, Lee wanted abolitionists to leave southerners alone. Reforming the institution of slavery would someday, it was believed, come from southerners themselves over a long time. Perhaps because he was a soldier and not a politician, Lee never specified precisely how that might work.

There's little doubt that some northern newspapers delighted in exposing Lee as a hypocrite for his treatment of the Arlington slaves. The story of the brutal whipping of three runaways seemed like it came directly from the pages of *Uncle Tom's Cabin.* No one was accusing Lee of acting illegally, of course. According to Virginia law, it was entirely legal to whip runaways—the state's legal code prescribed that the punishment shouldn't exceed "thirty-nine stripes" for each offender. No, the real charge against him was that of *cruelty.*

Is there evidence to suggest Lee was a heartless slave master? Lee's leading biographer, Douglas Southall Freeman, pronounced, "There is no evidence, direct or indirect, that Lee ever had them or any other Negroes flogged. The usage at Arlington and elsewhere in Virginia among people of Lee's station forbade such a thing."[10] Freeman, who described the "libel" as an example of the "extravagance of antislavery agitators," presumably didn't believe Norris's statement counted as evidence. A more recent biographer of Lee, Elizabeth Brown Pryor, thought Wesley Norris's account "rings true."[11] After a thorough examination of all of the evidence, she determined that "every detail of it can be verified."

We may never know exactly what happened to Wesley, Mary, and George that day in the barn at Arlington, but a closer examination of the facts of the case tells us a great deal about slavery on the eve of the Civil War. It also provides us with a better understanding of Lee's relationship to the social system he fought so tenaciously to uphold.

★　★　★

The *Carol County Democrat* first reported the news of the runaway slaves on June 2, 1859. A brief article announced that four slaves, owned by Colonel Robert E. Lee, had been apprehended in Westminster, Maryland, just shy of the Pennsylvania border. We now know, of course, that only three slaves, not four, had escaped Arlington. Perhaps an additional runaway from another estate had joined Lee's slaves during the escape. Mostly likely, they had departed sometime in late May.[12]

Three weeks after the report in the *Carol County Democrat*, two letters to the editor were published in the *New York Daily Tribune* that provided troubling details about what happened to the slaves after they returned to Arlington. Both letters were scathing in their criticism of "Col. Lee." Lee's first name was never mentioned in either letter and it's uncertain how many readers would have known who he was, even though he had been a hero in the Mexican War over a decade previously. Unlike Wesley Norris's account in 1866, the two letters were probably not published solely to attack Lee. Instead, their purpose may have been to highlight the abuses of slavery in general on an estate that had once belonged to George Washington's adopted son.

The first letter, written on June 21, 1859, made numerous allegations against Lee. First, the writer claimed Lee—the new proprietor of Arlington—had ignored the wishes of Custis who allegedly had freed all of his slaves on his deathbed. Then a litany of additional charges were made—slaves were now worked harder than ever before; three older women were denied their customary tea and coffee breaks; and one eighty-year-old slave had been returned to the fields after having been "retired" while Custis had been alive. The most shocking allegations, of course, related to Lee's treatment of the three slaves when they were brought back to Arlington. First, it was alleged they had been taken to a barn, where the two male slaves were given thirty-nine lashes each—the prescribed limit for their offense under Virginia law. When the slave whipper refused to whip the "girl," Lee himself supposedly "administered the thirty and nine lashes to her." The letter concluded by asking, "Shall 'Washington's body guard' be thus tampered with and never a voice raised for such utter helplessness?"

The second letter, written on June 19, made similar accusations and was signed, "A. Citizen." This letter writer also claimed that the slaves "were set free at the death of Custis, but are now held in bondage by Lee." In this particular telling of the whipping of Mary Norris, "Col. Lee stripped her and whipped her himself." The author said that he or she learned these facts from near relatives of the men who were whipped. One additional detail is added in this particular letter: "Custis had fifteen children by his slave women. I see his grandchildren every day; they are of a dark yellow." The mention of Custis's apparent sexual relations with his slaves and Lee stripping Mary Norris would have outraged many northerners who already believed that the typical plantation was a site of immorality and sexual exploitation. *The Liberator*, an influential abolitionist newspaper founded by William Lloyd Garrison, concisely summarized northern attitudes when it declared, "The sixteen slave states constitute one vast brothel."[13]

A third letter to the editor defending "Col. Lee" was published a few days later. Going by the name of "Justice," the writer declared "the whole story a malicious fabrication by some personal enemy of Col. Lee."[14] The author, however, only challenged the notion that Custis had set his slaves free upon his death, and never mentioned the brutal treatment of Wesley, Mary, and George. Like Lee and his wife, the letter writer believed that abolitionists were behind all this mischief.

A master who personally stripped and whipped a slave woman would have seemed especially cruel even in 1859. Unsurprisingly, almost all subsequent historians have refused to believe Lee was capable of such brutality. The fact that Wesley Norris reported that the constable, not Lee, administered the whippings—fifty lashes for the men and twenty-five lashes for Mary, according to his account—seemed to be sufficient evidence for scholars to absolve Lee from the charge of flogging Mary himself.

Scholarly opinion is most likely correct on this point. Yet, the story of Lee personally whipping Mary Norris remained persistent both during and after the war. Apparently, abolitionist editors and writers during that time were not quite as inclined as more recent scholars to give Lee the benefit of the doubt on these charges. One particularly damning account appeared in the press in the spring of 1863—at the height of Lee's military success during the war. A Union soldier named Samuel P. Putnam had visited Arlington and had spoken with Leonard Norris, the father of Wesley and Mary Norris.[15] Putnam detailed the conversation in private letter to his father. His letter was then published in various newspapers across the country in May 1863.

According to Putnam, Leonard Norris said, "Gen. Lee was more dreaded by his slaves than were any of his overseers" and reported that Lee personally whipped Mary Norris, snatching the whip from the overseer in order to do the bloody work himself. Leonard's telling of the incident differs considerably on important details from some of the other accounts. According to him, four boys and one girl were flogged. They were allegedly punished for having gone out without permission to find something to eat. Leonard also spoke of his children having been "sold" by General Lee, but he most likely meant that they had been "hired out."

Shortly after the publication of Putnam's letter, yet another soldier had a summary of one of his conversations with an Arlington slave published in a Massachusetts newspaper:

> At the cook house for the overseer's family I noticed an octoroon, nearly white, with fine features. She told me that her mother, long since dead was a quadroon and Gen. Lee's housekeeper at Arlington, and to the question, "Was your father a colored man?" she answered without hesitation "No—master's my father." And this father and master now leads an army, the sole purpose of which is to establish a government founded on an institution which enslaves his own children, making his own flesh and blood saleable property[16]

According to the historian John Neff, it's more likely that the response "master's my father," was referring to George Washington Parke Custis.[17] No doubt Lee would have been embarrassed and outraged if he heard of the insinuation by the soldier.

In August 1865, Emily Howland, an abolitionist who had taught slaves and freedmen at Arlington during the war, wrote about the Norris incident after having had numerous conversations with "Aunt Sally." Aunt Sally's full name was Sally Norris. She was Leonard's wife and the mother of Wesley and Mary Norris. Howland described Aunt Sally as one who could "tell how Lee defrauded her children, with all the rest of the bondmen of Custis, of the freedom which he gave them at his death."[18] Howland also reported that Sally showed her the barn where Lee took Mary Norris and, "finding the official whom he had summoned, unwilling to whip the woman, that flower of chivalry lashed her back himself; when sufficiently lacerated to suit him, it was salted, and she sent to Richmond to serve five years." Two things are worth noting about this particular account. One is that Aunt Sally, as the mother of two of the victims, should have been extremely familiar with the events in question. Second, Emily Howland, as an educator who worked on the premises during the war, *should* be a reasonably reliable source.

Lee offered a few details of his own immediately after the events under consideration. Writing to his oldest son on July 2, 1859, he said, "I do not know that you have been told that George Wesly and Mary Norris, [*sic*] absconded some months ago, were captured in Maryland, making their way to Pennsylvania, brought back, and are now hired out in lower Virginia."[19] Lee's irregular punctuation is confusing, but he almost certainly meant to say, "George Parks, Wesley Norris, and Mary Norris." He stated they had run away and that he hired them out in lower Virginia after they returned—these are facts everyone can agree on at the very least. Lee also told his son that the "*N.Y. Tribune* has attacked me for my treatment of your grandfather's slaves, but I shall not reply. He has left me an unpleasant legacy." Lee didn't categorically deny, at this time, all of the allegations that appeared in the *Tribune*, though he did remark on the difficulties he faced in managing Custis's slaves.

A somewhat less believable version of the story appeared in the *British Quarterly Review* over six years later in October 1865.[20] In this account, written by the English minister Robert Vaughan, Lee ordered Mary Norris to strip herself. Lee then looked on while she was tied to a post and given nearly two hundred lashes—roughly five times the legally prescribed amount! Vaughan apparently learned these details from a "Mrs. Grey"—likely Selina Grey who was a trusted servant of Mary Lee and sister of Mary Norris. Vaughan presumed that "General Lee may be a chivalrous and estimable man, but so much the worse for the slave system if this be true of him and I have no doubt of its truth." When a correspondent called Lee's attention to Vaughan's account in January 1866, he adamantly denied it, saying, "there is not a word of truth in it, or any ground for its origins."[21] Lee then added, "No servant, soldier, or citizen that was ever employed by me can in truth charge me with bad treatment."

Three years after the war, the *Independent* published additional testimony from one of Lee's former slaves that challenged Lee's profession of innocence. When asked by a reporter if Lee had been a good master, a female slave responded, "He was the worst man I ever see. He used to have po' souls cut most to pieces by de constable out here, and afterwards he made his oversee' wash dere backs wi' brine."[22] She later added of Lee and his wife, "Dey sold all my children off Souf, and dey keep five years of my time and my old man's." Finally, the *Independent*'s reporter said that all of the slaves at Arlington remembered "Gen. Lee as a cold-blooded, exacting military master."

The belief that "dey keep five years of my time" was a source of considerable confusion shortly after the death of George Washington Parke Custis. His slaves—and any outsiders who may have spoken with them—seemed to think Custis had promised them their freedom upon his death. Lee disputed this idea and could easily defend his position by pointing to Custis's actual will, which had been submitted to the Alexandria Court for probate on December 7, 1857.[23] According to the legal document, the slaves were not immediately freed and could possibly be held for up to five years. For whatever reason, the slaves didn't quite understand Custis's legal provisions for them. According to a later petition to the circuit court regarding questions surrounding the will, Lee believed that "evil-disposed persons . . . for unlawful and mischievous purposes, and imposing on the ignorance and credulity of said slaves have infused into their minds the idea that they are entitled to immediate freedom, under the terms of the Estate's will."[24] Lee was evidently upset by the inclination on the part of many of the slaves to prematurely end their obligations toward his family. He found it difficult to imagine they may have had a natural desire for liberty.

The controversy surrounding Custis's intentions was exacerbated by an attack against his heirs in a piece published by the *Boston Traveler* in December 1857. The paper described the final moments of George Washington's adopted son. Some of the slaves "were called into the room, and stood by the deathbed of their master, and that after having taken leave of them personally, he told them that he had left them, and all his servants, their freedom."[25] The writer also claimed that it was well known around town that Custis intended to free his slaves at his death, and then added, *"no white man was in the room, and the testimony of negroes will not be taken in Court"* (italics in original). Finally, the author hinted that the will had been deliberately hidden and the slaves were to be sold further south.

Despite his personal vow not to engage with press attacks, Lee did respond on this particular occasion. In a letter to the editor, he attempted to set the record straight. First, Lee stated that Custis had left his property to his daughter and her children. Then, he noted that the will was available for all to see at the Alexandria courthouse. Finally, he concluded his concise, straightforward letter by saying, "There is no desire on the part of the heirs to prevent the execution of its provisions in reference to the slaves, nor is there any truth or the least foundation for the assertion that they are being sold South."[26] Lee's letter is remarkable for its brevity—more than half of it is devoted to summarizing the charges with the remainder being a simple refutation of them in several sentences.

According to the will, Custis gave the Arlington estate to his only child, Mary Anna Randolph Lee, for use during her natural life.[27] Upon her death, the property would pass to his eldest grandson, George Washington Custis Lee—Mary and Robert E. Lee's oldest son. To Lee's four daughters—Mary, Ann, Agnes, and Mildred—Custis left $10,000 each. To his grandson William Henry Fitzhugh Lee (Rooney), Custis left his estate called "White House"; to his grandson Robert E. Lee Jr., he left his estate known as "Romancock"—Lee Sr. would later change the name to "Romancoke." Additional lands were marked out to be sold in order to fund the granddaughters' legacies. Surpluses at the estates of Romancoke and the White House were to be also allocated toward funding the legacies.

At the end of the document, Custis provided instructions relating to his slaves:

> And upon the legacies to my four granddaughters being paid, and my estates that are required to pay the said legacies being clear of debt, then I give freedom to my slaves, the said slaves to be emancipated most expedient and proper, the said emancipation to be accomplished in not exceeding five years from the time of my decease.

One reading of this highly complex sentence was that Lee, who eventually became the sole executor of the estate, had up to five years to deploy the slaves in paying down Custis's debt and funding his daughters' legacies. Lee, however, felt it was possible to read that sentence in such a way that he'd be able to utilize the slaves until all of the debts and legacies were paid off in their entirety, even if that took longer than five years. Indeed, his wife Mary believed it would take ten years to meet the obligations laid out by the will. Regardless of which interpretation was true under the law, Lee's job was made even harder by the fact that Custis's slaves thought—for some reason—they had been freed upon his death. We don't have conclusive proof that Custis ever made such a promise and it wouldn't have been legally binding, in any event. In this particular case, it appears the law was in conflict with the understandable yearning of the slaves to be free right away.

Lee took his responsibilities as executor quite seriously. He received a temporary leave from the army, so he could devote himself completely to improving the various estates bequeathed to his wife and children. His task had been made more difficult by the fact that his father-in-law had left behind roughly $11,000 to $12,000 in debt.[28] In addition, any excess capital required for investing in the properties would have to come out of the salary of an army colonel. After visiting the White House property in February 1858, Lee jotted down in his notebook, "buildings, dilapidated, no funds, no corn." He then went on to Romancoke and "found things there were more dilapidated than at White House—nothing looking well."[29]

Lee would also learn that the physical and emotional well-being of the roughly two hundred slaves across three properties represented another serious problem. During the year of his death, Custis had been "greatly pained, disappointed and mortified to hear" about the deprivations of his slaves, and remarked, "it ought not to be so, my negroes have been heavier worked than any slaves in Virginia, so much so, that neighbors of my Estates, have addressed to me anonymous letters, complaining of the subject."[30] Historians like Douglas Southall Freeman mistakenly believed that life was easy for the slaves under Custis's stewardship, but his own assessment indicated otherwise. Several months after Custis's death, his daughter would surprisingly describe these same slaves as "a host of idle & thankless dependents."[31] Perhaps they had been pushed to their limit. Soon after Lee took charge, some of the slaves became unruly and tried to run away. From a purely operational perspective, Lee had a difficult task ahead of him.

Upon assuming the day-to-day management of Custis's properties, Lee sought "proper guidance and direction" from the circuit court for Virginia on several matters relating to the will.[32] In a petition to the court, Lee admitted he "had experienced great difficulty in the control and management of the slaves at Arlington," and had been "embarrassed in the discharge of his duties as Executor in regard to said slaves, and other matters connected with said estate."

One of the most important questions asked by Lee in this document was "When will the slaves belonging to said testator's [Custis] estate be entitled to their freedom, and in what manner are they to be manumitted by your orator [Lee]?"[33] He also asked what would happen if he was unable to fund the legacies within five years. The circuit court responded on May 25, 1859, by declaring that "the slaves are entitled to their freedom at the expiration of five years from the death of the testator, or sooner if the legacies are paid off."[34] According to the decision, the slaves must be freed regardless of whether or not the legacies had been adequately funded.

Lee's personal lawyer, Francis L. Smith, sought additional clarification on this point from the Supreme Court of Appeals of Virginia in October 1859.[35] After summarizing the will, Smith noted that the estate had debts between

$11,000 and $12,000, of which $6,000 had already been paid by Lee. Among several points raised, Smith asked, "Are the slaves then to be free absolutely at the expiration of five years, or are their services to be contributed to aid in raising these legacies?" Smith wondered if Custis would have wanted such obligations funded "without the benefit of the labor of slaves, so essential in their cultivation." Arguing on behalf of Lee, Smith declared, "I submit that the emancipation of the slaves should be postponed till the said legacies are raised, and the debts of the estate are paid off." Here, Lee is clearly asking the court to place the economic interests of his wife and children above the liberty of almost two hundred slaves. He believed Custis would have wanted it that way.

In November 1861, almost six months after the beginning of the Civil War, the Virginia Court of Appeals finally ruled that the "slaves if not necessary for the payment of debts are entitled to their freedom at the expiration of five years."[36] Lee wondered if the legacies might actually be considered debts of the estate, but Smith advised him that the intention of the court was "to liberate the people at the end of five years."[37] Lee accepted the decision and began taking steps in early 1862 to emancipate all of Custis's slaves that hadn't yet escaped or been freed. By December 1862—right after the battle of Fredericksburg, one of his greatest military triumphs—Lee expressed his desire to liberate "the people" before the end of the year.[38] Fortunately for the Lee family, the legacies had been funded and the debt had been paid after all, despite their fears. He now wished to "close the whole affair."

On December 29, 1862, Lee filed a deed of manumission before a justice of the peace.[39] The document began, "Know all men by these presents, that I, Robert E. Lee, executor of the last will and testament of George W. P. Custis deceased, acting by and under the authority and direction of the provisions of said will, do hereby manumit, emancipate and forever set free from slavery the following named slaves." Then, 197 slaves were listed from Arlington, the White House, and Romancoke. It's a testament to Lee's extraordinary fastidiousness that he fulfilled all of the requirements of the will, while also commanding the Army of Northern Virginia. Alas, the freed slaves would have theoretically been required to leave Virginia within twelve months under the existing laws of the state.

Coincidentally, Abraham Lincoln's Emancipation Proclamation was signed a mere three days later on January 1, 1863. It declared all slaves within those Confederate states still in rebellion against the United States "shall be then, thenceforward, and forever free." Lincoln's Proclamation also announced the acceptance of African Americans into the military. Despite having just freed Custis's slaves, Lee was horrified by Lincoln's executive order. Fulfilling the demands of a will under existing law was one thing. Freeing all of the slaves across the rebel states by military fiat was quite another thing altogether. For Lee, slaves were assets that were legally at the disposal of their rightful owners. Writing to Secretary of War James Seddon in January 1863, Lee said,

> In view of the vast increase of the forces of the enemy, of the savage and brutal policy he has proclaimed, which leaves us no alternative but success or degradation worse than death, if we would save the honor of our families from pollution, our social system from destruction, let every effort be made, every means be employed, to fill and maintain the ranks of our armies, until God, in His mercy, shall bless us with the establishment of our independence.[40]

Worries about "degradation" and "pollution" were common among many Virginians who feared the consequences of former slaves possibly having sexual intercourse with whites, after being released from their masters. Lee therefore urged a renewed effort to "save the honor of our families from pollution, our social system from destruction." Here, the general is revealed as a conservative Virginian who was intent on defending a "social system" based on slavery. Lee would rather die than witness the success of Lincoln's policy for Virginia and the other slaveholding states.

★   ★   ★

How should we assess Lee's tenure as a slave owner and manager? Was he as cruel as the abolitionists would have us believe? Or was he a reluctant master who actually disliked being actively involved with the institution? Sympathetic historians have tended to downplay his connection to slavery, but the record shows he had been involved with the "peculiar institution," one way or another, for most of his adult life.

Lee became a slave owner in 1829 after his mother died, leaving her thirty slaves to her three sons.[41] Young Lee most likely sold some of them and "hired out" the rest. Renting out slaves was far more common than selling at the time. Hired slaves performed all kinds of jobs, often on one-year contracts. Such an arrangement suited a professional soldier like Lee. He would receive a steady income, while outsourcing the day-to-day management of the slaves to the hirer.

By 1847, tax records revealed that Lee owned just four slaves, who were over the age of twelve.[42] Lee quite possibly had invested the money he had received by the sale and hiring out of his slaves. According to his last will and testament drawn up in 1846, Lee had accumulated a portfolio of $38,750, consisting mostly of securities like bank stocks and railway bonds.

When Lee took over the responsibility of managing approximately two hundred slaves after his father-in-law died, he began hiring out slaves as a means to raise funds for the legacies and get rid of the most recalcitrant servants.[43] This apparently had not been a common practice under George Washington Parke Custis's stewardship. Of the thirty-five slaves over twelve years old at Arlington in 1858, Lee hired out eleven of them that year. Over time, he would hire out even larger numbers, sending them to Richmond and other locations in lower Virginia. In his appeal to the Virginia Supreme Court in 1859, Lee asked if he could hire out his slaves even further south outside the boundaries of Virginia. He argued that some of the slaves had become insubordinate and that hiring them out down south would make it more difficult for them to run away. The court declined his request. According to Wesley Norris's statement, he eventually was hired out in Alabama, which would have been contrary to the guidance of the court.

Hiring out slaves may have made financial sense from a purely entrepreneurial perspective, but it was perceived as a harsh practice by the slaves. A letter Lee wrote to one of his agents, William Overton Winston, illustrated the cold nature of the hiring out system:

> I Send down three Negro men belonging to the Estate of G.W.P. Custis, viz: Reuben, Parks & Edward, whom I wish you to hire in Virginia, to good and responsible men, for the year or a term of years, not exceeding 31 Decr 1862, or Such terms as may be in your judgement most advantageous., I do not wish these men returned here during the usual holy days, but to be retained until Called for.[44]

Being sent away for an indeterminate period, without the opportunity to return home during the Christmas holidays, was undeniably unsettling and disruptive for the vast majority of slaves. Frederick Douglass described slaves being overcome with "deep consternation" as they anticipated being sent away to work for new masters who may or may not treat them well. Many slaves suffered greatly by being separated from friends and family members. At Arlington, almost every slave family had been broken up as a result of this practice on the eve of the Civil War.[45]

Lee could be extraordinarily unsentimental when it came to deploying his slaves most profitably and often seemed unfeeling when talking about his slaves. In one letter to Mary about their servants, he wrote, "But do not trouble yourself about them as they are not worth it."[46] He described Reuben—mentioned above in the letter to Winston—as "a great rogue & rascal whom I must get rid of some way." In a letter to his son in 1861 urging him to hire out as many of the servants as possible, he said, "I should think that Harry, Amanda & Sarah, might at all events be put to service, to their benefit & mine, & much to your Mothers [sic] relief."[47] Amanda, it should be remembered, was the former slave who attempted to visit Lee, while he was in Washington, DC.

We will never really know for certain if Lee had Wesley Norris, Mary Norris, and George Parks whipped and then had their backs washed in brine. The evidence isn't strong enough to allow us to pass judgment, one way or another. Could Wesley Norris have made it all up? We have no idea. Without more direct testimony from the victims, it's pointless to speculate about what might have happened.

We do have plenty of evidence, however, that Lee optimized the value from his slaves by sending them away from their homes and families to work for hirers in lower Virginia. Just because it was a traditional practice in the South at the time doesn't make it any less harsh, from the perspective of the slaves. Even if Wesley, Mary, and George were never whipped, we do know they ran away in order to be free only to be captured, jailed, and sent away from their community. The bare facts of their story alone are heartbreaking enough.

Historians have traditionally focused on Lee's role as a dutiful and conscientious executor of his father-in-law's will. And there really is much to admire in the way he stoically went about making the best of "unpleasant legacy." This is only part of the story, however. It must not be forgotten that Lee was also a *beneficiary* of Custis's substantial estate. As the husband of Mary Anna Randolph Lee, he too received the "use and benefit" of Arlington during the course of her natural life. Improvements in that property would only make it even more valuable to his family and the eventual heir, his son George Washington Custis Lee. Anyone who has ever visited the grounds of Arlington today will appreciate the magnificence of the property. In many respects, it was and remains a priceless piece of land. At one point Lee urged his son to save money so he might "have the means to build up old Arlington & make it all we would wish."[48]

Utilizing the value of slave labor at Arlington and the other Custis properties for as long as legally possible—either directly or indirectly by hiring them
out further south—made perfect sense from a purely business outlook. It does
Lee no discredit, however, to note that there was a serious conflict of interest
here. Making sure his daughters received their legacies and his sons received
their estates in fine condition also provided intangible benefits for Lee as a
father. Who knows, he may have been especially driven by the fact that his
own father, "Light Horse Harry" Lee, had left only debts behind after his
inglorious death.

So yes, Lee was a dutiful executor. But here his sense of duty was in
complete alignment with his own financial self-interest. Soon after Custis died,
Lee told Colonel Albert Sydney Johnston that he'd prefer to stay in the army
rather than manage the estate, but he felt "a man's family has its claims, too."[49]
Unsurprisingly, his family's economic well-being came *before* the best interests
of the 197 slaves on the Custis properties. That fact was axiomatic in a social
system where slaves were treated primarily as an economic asset. Regardless of
what Lee said or did not say about slavery, he and his family clearly benefited
tremendously from the institution. Ironically, several months before his death,
Custis told one of his agents that improving the conditions of his slaves was an
extremely urgent priority.[50] That wouldn't be the case once his son-in-law
took over.

★   ★   ★

An understanding of Lee's personal experience with slavery—he owned
or managed slaves for over thirty years—helps us to better evaluate his postwar
comments on the institution. As we saw earlier in chapter 1, Lee had declared,
just days after the war, that "the best men of the South have long been anxious
to do away with the institution, and were quite willing to-day to see it abolished." Lee added that the South had only supported slavery because there
hadn't been a plan to "dispose" of the "negroes." Eight months later, in his
testimony before the Joint Committee on Reconstruction, Lee stated that he
wished Virginia could get rid of its "negroes" and that he had "always been in
favor of emancipation—gradual emancipation." Like many Americans after
the war, Lee preferred to move forward as if he had been opposed to slavery
all along.

Before and during the war, there does seem to be evidence that Lee
disliked slavery in *theory*. He also believed, however, it was necessary for the

improvement of African Americans and any attempt to end it would be contrary to God's wishes. The most famous of Lee's prewar pronouncements on slavery appeared in a letter to Mary in December 1856, shortly after the election of President James Buchanan. It's here that Lee said, "In this enlightened age there are few, I believe, but will acknowledge that slavery as an institution is a moral and political evil in any country."[51] Admirers of Lee often point to this line as evidence that he had been opposed to slavery before the war. It's important, however, to place that quote within the context of the entire letter.

Lee continued his remarks to Mary by saying that "the blacks are immeasurably better off here than in Africa, morally, socially, and physically." He then added, "The painful discipline they are undergoing is necessary for their instruction as a race, and I hope, will prepare and lead them to better things." For Lee, only God knew how long "their subjection may be necessary" and the abolitionists' attempts at reform were against God's wishes.

This idea that slavery was merely part of God's overall design was echoed in a letter from January 1865, during the closing months of the war. Lee was writing about the possibility of providing freedom to those slaves who might be willing to serve in the Confederate armies:

> Considering the relation of master and slave, controlled by humane laws and influenced by Christianity and an enlightened public sentiment, as the best that can exist between the white and black races while intermingled as at present in this country, I would deprecate any sudden disturbances of that relation unless it be necessary to avert a greater calamity to both.[52]

This statement is actually consistent with his postwar comments. Lee believed the institution of slavery was a necessary evil, ordained by God, as long as there wasn't a plan in place to resettle African Americans elsewhere after they obtained their freedom. One consistent theme for Lee was that white southerners and freedmen would never be able to live together harmoniously. Slavery at the very least provided order and stability. Who knew what emancipation would bring?

A year before his death, Lee apparently offered additional thoughts on slavery to the Reverend John Leyburn. Sixteen years later, in May 1885, Leyburn published the interview in *The Century*, a popular monthly magazine in the nineteenth century. According to Leyburn, Lee was hurt by northerners who "insisted that the object of the war had been to secure the perpetuation of slavery."[53] Lee told the reverend that this wasn't true, and that he had never been an advocate of slavery. Indeed, he was happy that slavery was abolished, and would "cheerfully have lost all I have lost by the war, and have suffered all I have suffered, to have this object attained." Lee concluded the interview by asking that journalists use their pens to "see that justice is done us."

The views put forward in the interview with Leyburn, alas, are not consistent with Lee's actions and statements during his adult life. Most likely, Reverend Leyburn embellished Lee's remarks somewhat, fifteen years after his meeting with the Confederate hero. Or perhaps Lee didn't want his memory tarnished by a former connection with increasingly reviled institution. Inexplicably, by 1885, despite overwhelming and conclusive evidence to the contrary, Lee had become a quasi-abolitionist in the minds of many of his admirers. Even today, this is the Lee that many Americans still honor and remember.

9

"IT USED TO BE FASHIONABLE
TO TRY A MAN BEFORE
THEY HANGED HIM."

I feel uneasy about President Davis for fear that he will be tried, sentenced and the sentence shall be executed.

—Jubal Early to Robert E. Lee, May 1866

In the spring of 1866, Robert E. Lee was still under federal indictment for treason and the Johnson administration remained committed to prosecuting the case. Until this point, Lee's parole at Appomattox had protected him from prosecution as long as the war hadn't been officially declared over. Lee's status changed, however, when President Johnson proclaimed on April 2, 1866, the "insurrection in certain southern states" was henceforth concluded. War was now legally at an end in all southern states, except for Texas.[1] As a result, the government could now try the indicted military leaders who had been paroled by Grant in April 1865, almost a year earlier. In a letter to Jubal Early around this time, Lee sensed trouble ahead, telling his former lieutenant that all controversy "will only serve to prolong angry and bitter feeling and postpone the period when reason and charity may resume their sway."[2] He seemed to have adopted a wait-and-see attitude on whether he'd actually stand trial for treason. For his part, Early took no chances and chose to live in Canada after the war.

The Johnson administration eventually decided that the first treason case it would prosecute would be against Jefferson Davis. It made sense to begin treason trials with the former Confederate president, who was often referred

Figure 9.1.   Petit Jury Pool for the May 1867 session of the US Circuit Court, District of Virginia, 1867. *Source:* **Cook Photograph Collection, The Valentine, Richmond, Virginia.**

to as an "arch traitor" by the northern press. Davis was currently being held at Fortress Monroe in Virginia and was believed by many Americans to have been connected to the conspirators in the Lincoln assassination. If the government couldn't win a case against Davis, then future treason trials against the rest of the Confederate leadership would be untenable, to say the least.[3]

Lee suspected Davis would be the first to be tried. In a letter to Davis's wife, Varina, Lee stated that Davis's trial might now be near and believed "the exhibition of the whole truth in his case will prove his defense and justification."[4] Lee also expressed sadness for the misfortune of Davis, telling Varina, "I have felt most keenly the sufferings and imprisonment of your husband, and have earnestly consulted with friends as to any possible mode of affording him relief and consolation." Additionally, Lee defended himself against charges of mistreating prisoners in response to a comment by Mrs. Davis about recent remarks on the subject by the Speaker of the House of Representatives.

The plight of Jefferson Davis, during the spring of 1866, appeared very grim indeed. Still incarcerated at an impregnable fortress at Hampton, Virginia, he had little hope of being freed in the near future. At first, Davis had actually been held in irons, before being detained in a casemate overlooking the fort's moat. Eventually, he had been moved to more comfortable quarters. His health had suffered considerably, however, while imprisoned. Apparently, he also had been extremely troubled by the execution of the Lincoln conspirators, remarking that President Johnson was "quick on the trigger." The one bright spot in this desperate situation was that he had a strong legal team representing him, led by Charles O'Conor, one of the most celebrated lawyers in the country. A firm believer in states' rights, O'Conor, who lived in New York City, sympathized with the southern states during the Civil War.[5]

As we have already learned, the Johnson administration, by early 1866, had decided treason trials must be held before a civil court rather than a military tribunal. Attorney General James Speed had also persuaded the cabinet that any trial must occur where the crime was actually committed, thereby rejecting the notion of "constructive presence." According to Article III of the Constitution, all trials, except in cases of impeachment, were to be by jury and "shall be held in the State where the said Crimes shall have been committed." In the cases of Davis and Lee, of course, the appropriate venue would be in the state of Virginia. With peace finally at hand, all those persons under indictment could now be "tried for such high crimes and misdemeanors as may be alleged against them," according to Speed.[6] The cabinet was in complete agreement that Chief Justice Salmon Chase must preside over treason trials, along with Judge John C. Underwood, in the circuit court serving Virginia in Richmond.[7] Everyone believed the chief justice would provide legitimacy to any guilty verdicts that might be found. Plus, Judge Underwood was viewed as too polarizing, by most members of the cabinet, to handle the cases on his own.

The government chose to try Davis on treason charges, though it had been also considering prosecuting him for complicity in the assassination of President Lincoln. Johnson, Stanton, and Holt suspected Davis was somehow involved in that infamous crime, but the evidence linking Davis to the conspiracy wasn't especially persuasive or reliable.[8] Francis Lieber, who was painstakingly examining stacks of Confederate documents, had yet to find any smoking guns, though he had noticed some items that raised eyebrows. Conspiracy charges in the assassination would have to be put aside.

To informed observers in 1866, there appeared to be a real possibility Jefferson Davis could be found guilty of treason by a jury in the Circuit Court of Virginia. Judge Underwood—one of the judges who would preside over the trial—felt strongly treason had indeed been committed by Davis, Lee, and the other Confederate leaders. He was also confident, as he declared before the Joint Committee on Reconstruction, he could pack a jury that would convict them all.[9] Chief Justice Chase—the other judge who would be hearing the cases—agreed treason had been committed. In a letter to Horace Greeley, Chase told the editor it was clear the leading rebels were guilty of treason, arguing, "There is the Constitution, and it is so plain that it can't be made plainer."[10] Chase differed from Johnson and Underwood in that he didn't seem to mind if the traitors were forgiven in the end. He was opposed, however, to ignoring the true meaning of the law.

★   ★   ★

Prior to the war, Chase had been one of the leading antislavery voices in the nation. Early in his law career in Ohio, he had been known as the "attorney-general for runaway negroes."[11] After becoming governor of Ohio in 1855, Chase hoped to run for president. After failing to generate support in the election of 1860, he agreed to serve as Secretary of the Treasury in Lincoln's administration. He later became chief justice of the Supreme Court after Roger Taney died. Upon joining the Supreme Court, it was expected Chase would be one of the strongest voices on behalf of the freed slaves.

Andrew Johnson was perhaps the most eager person of all for a speedy trial of Jefferson Davis. The president had vowed to punish traitors and he especially disliked Davis after their time together in Congress. Johnson's attorney general, James Speed, also believed it would be "a direful calamity if many whom the sword had spared the law should spare also."[12] Unlike other members of the administration, however, Speed was somewhat skeptical that an "impartial" Richmond jury would convict the rebel leaders. The district attorney for Virginia, Lucius Chandler, was more confident of success on this point than the attorney general, however.

The administration put together an exceptionally talented team to prosecute the Davis case. Speed would lead the effort in tandem with special counsel William Evarts, former Governor John Clifford of Massachusetts, and Lovell Rousseau of Kentucky. Evarts, in particular, was a gifted and respected lawyer who had recently won several high-profile cases. Chandler would also provide the team with invaluable local assistance from his base in Virginia.

Some Radicals sensed danger, however. After sifting through piles of Confederate correspondence, Francis Lieber remarked, "The trial of Jefferson Davis will be a terrible thing—volumes, a library of the most infernal treason will be belched forth—Davis will not be found guilty and we shall stand there as completely beaten. The time was lost and can never be recovered."[13] Senator Jacob Howard, who had questioned Lee before the Joint Committee for Reconstruction, expressed similar concerns in a speech before Congress. Howard believed from *his* reading of the Constitution that Davis could be tried in Pennsylvania or Maryland—two northern states where Confederate armies had fought under the direction of Davis. In those states, a jury would be far more likely to find Davis guilty.

By insisting on Virginia, Speed jeopardized the outcome of the trials, according to Howard. The senator felt the vast majority of southerners hated the fact they had lost and loathed the loyal people in their midst. Given that fact, Howard believed it was "utterly vain to think of obtaining a conviction of those leaders at the hands of a jury made up of such materials."[14] Believing it was impossible to find an impartial jury in the South, Howard predicted "no such conviction, no such trial, will ever be had. Treason will not thus be made odious, but will go without day."

Judge Underwood didn't share Howard's pessimism. Shortly before the May 1866 session of his District Court in Norfolk, Underwood met with President Johnson to discuss the propriety of prosecuting the leaders of the rebellion. Johnson told him he was still very much in favor of trials. As Speed began to prepare the case against Davis in April, Underwood decided he'd bring a new indictment for treason against the Confederate president in May. This was necessary due to Speed's insistence on trying the case in Virginia. The earlier indictment of Davis, drawn up in Washington, DC, in May 1865, would not be actionable.

By this time, Underwood, who was despised by former rebels across Virginia, had become a notorious character in his adopted state.[15] The judge seemed to embrace his role as a loyalist in the midst of traitors—he even kept a signed copy of the Virginia Ordinance of Secession on the wall of his federal courthouse as a reminder of the disloyalty of the state. Shortly after the war,

Underwood had come out strongly in favor of African American citizenship and suffrage. By the spring of 1866, he had emerged as one of the leading advocates for freedmen in the nation, which made him a pariah in the South.

Underwood's grand jury indicted Jefferson Davis for treason on May 10, 1866.[16] The judge had somehow failed to tell the district attorney ahead of time. Chandler then had a mere three hours to produce a document that was quite similar to the indictments of Lee and the others from June 1865. Chief Justice Chase would later note, as we shall see, these hastily produced indictments were seriously flawed. They would eventually need to be redrafted in order to ensure the rebels faced the death penalty as prescribed under the treason statute of 1790. The administration considered treason by the Confederate leadership to be a capital crime.

In his charge to the grand jury, Underwood delivered an especially pugnacious assault on traitors and the Confederacy. He began by telling the grand jurors there was no longer any doubt the government could prosecute Lee and the thirty-six other leaders who had already been indicted for treason a year earlier. It was now "our duty to proceed in the investigation and punishment of some of the crimes which have been committed against our laws."[17] He then told the jurors President Johnson desired that both Jefferson Davis and former Confederate Secretary of War John C. Breckinridge be indicted for treason in Virginia, since the attorney general had ruled that Washington, DC, wasn't the proper location for their trials.

Underwood concluded with an unforgiving attack on antebellum leaders in Virginia. He spoke of the "crimes" of slave masters that were often ignored in polite society:

> The subjection of the women of one complexion to the wild fury of unbridled licentiousness and as a consequence, denying the women of our own complexion the holy rites of marriage or making, in thousands of cases, those rites as much a mockery as a conscious traitor's oath, were proclaimed on every plantation in the bleached faces of the children of the first families, until hardly half our births were of lawful wedlock, and until it would seem that masculine virtue must be nearly extinct in the proud circles of the chivalric aristocracy of the State.

It would have been painful for former slave owners to listen to such a verbal barrage, even if—as in the case of George Washington Parke Custis—there was considerable truth in what he said.

Despite the harsh reaction to his comments, the judge was unbowed.

Indeed, his rhetoric was even more harsh and uncompromising when he addressed the same grand jury at a session of circuit court in Richmond a few weeks later on June 5, 1866.[18] The grand jurors had apparently been threatened by their fellow citizens after the indictment of Davis. Underwood commended them for their bravery and patriotism, adding they shouldn't be surprised by the behavior of the "treasonable and licentious" press of Richmond. He went on to say that the capital of the Confederacy had

> long been the center and seat of the greatest traffic in human beings that has ever disgraced the world—a traffic which has annually employed many hundreds of moral monsters and many millions of capital, subsidizing the press, pulpit and politics of the State, rendering Richmond more infamous among men for its participation in the great crime than all the cities along the coasts of Senegambia, Upper and Lower Guinea, Congo, Loango, Angola or Benguela combined. The wonder rather is, that so many traces of kindness, humanity and Christian civilization should have survived such debasing and brutalizing influences.

These remarks went too far for the *New York Times*, which usually sympathized with abolitionists like Underwood. An editorial wryly mused, "It seems to us that the Judge has displayed his geographical knowledge of the coasts of Africa at the expense of his reputation for a knowledge of the workings of human nature."[19]

Virginians were beside themselves with anger at the judge who became arguably *the* most hated figure in the state throughout the nineteenth century. By this time, Underwood faced death threats and had to travel to and from court with a bodyguard. Unsurprisingly, Lee, who was already the most beloved figure in the state, disliked Underwood, but he mostly kept his criticism to himself. Mary Lee, on the other hand, wrote a friend it was a perfect farce "that such a creature should be allowed to dispense justice."[20] She believed "his meanness and wickedness have affected his brain." The white citizens of Richmond would have enthusiastically agreed with Mary Lee's assessment.

Perhaps Underwood should have been more diplomatic toward his fellow Virginians, especially since he was a federal judge in a state recovering from unimaginable political and economic turmoil. The abolitionist Harriet Beecher Stowe, a good friend of Underwood, felt he was really a polite gentleman who also had extremely strong moral convictions. She told a story of how the young Underwood, upon moving to Virginia, visited a slave auction and "witnessed

with horror the tears, the anguish, the fruitless moans and entreaties of separated mothers, fathers and children, torn asunder by the inter-State slave-
trade."[21] Underwood came back from that visit boiling with rage. From that
point on, Underwood was dedicated to speaking out against the wrongs committed against slaves and freedmen.

★   ★   ★

The Johnson administration hoped the trial of Davis could finally begin
during the June session of the circuit court. Chief Justice Chase remained an
obstacle to moving forward, however.[22] Initially, he had thought the president's Proclamation of Peace in April 1866 had cleared the way for him to
preside over the trial. Since the end of the war, Chase had believed members
of the Supreme Court should not appear in circuit court as long as civil courts
were under military supervision. With peace declared, Chase felt martial law
was finally at an end and the writ of *habeas corpus* had been restored—the
privilege of *habeas corpus*, which determines if the state's detention of a prisoner
is lawful, had been suspended by Congress in 1863.

Throughout April and May, however, Chase noticed that military commissions were still being utilized by the administration. After some thought,
he changed his mind, deciding he wouldn't be able to appear in circuit court
under those circumstances. He met with the president and requested he deliver
a new statement saying, "military authority was abrogated, and the *habeas corpus*
restored in all cases within the jurisdiction of the courts of the United States."[23]
Johnson respectfully told Chase that such a declaration was unnecessary,
though he eventually put the matter to rest by issuing a new and final proclamation declaring peace across the entire United States in August 1866.

That same summer, yet another problem arose that would prevent the
chief justice from presiding at the trial of Davis. Congress passed an act on
July 23, 1866, that altered seven of the circuit courts without providing new
assignments of Supreme Court justices. Chase viewed this action by Congress
as a suspension of the authority of Supreme Court justices to sit in circuit
court. The new allotment would not be carried out by Congress until March
2, 1867. Judge Chase, therefore, was effectively unable to preside over the trial
of Jefferson Davis until March 1867—almost two years after Davis had been
apprehended and jailed. The administration, of course, refused to go forward
with the trial, unless Chase presided. This gave many observers the mistaken
impression President Johnson was unwilling or unable to mount an effective
prosecution of the Confederate president. The Radicals in Congress were

especially exasperated by the endless delays. The House Judiciary Committee would even begin an investigation into this matter in 1867. The Radicals truly believed Johnson had reneged on his pledge to punish traitors. In reality, it was Chase who initially stood in the way of treason trials.

★   ★   ★

Historians have wondered if the chief justice had an ulterior motive for delaying the Davis trial. Could it be possible that Chase, who hoped to someday run again for president, was avoiding taking up such a divisive task? Johnson seemed to think so. The president had a poor opinion of Chase, considering him, "Cowardly and aspiring, shirking and presumptuous, forward and evasive . . . an ambitious politician; possessed of mental resources yet afraid to use them, irresolute as well as ambitious; intriguing, selfish, cold, grasping, and unreliable when he fancies his personal advancement is concerned."[24]

Chase defended himself at the time from those who thought his ambition got in the way of his obligations. He said, "I neither seek nor shun the responsibility of trying anybody."[25] He merely insisted the executive and the judiciary branches be perceived as equal partners. Yes, he was meticulous in his interpretation of the Constitution, but he believed it was his duty to be so as chief justice. Chase also argued the administration could have, if it had desired a speedier trial, gone forward with Judge Underwood presiding alone. Under those circumstances, it would be a "quasi-military" court, but no question could be made of the "regularity of the trial." The administration, of course, did not want to proceed unless Chase was on the bench. Not only would Chase provide credibility to the proceedings, but most cabinet members thought Underwood was too much of a partisan to manage the case by himself.

The chief justice indirectly delayed the case in one other way that would have long-lasting consequences for American jurisprudence. After seeing the indictment of Davis that was delivered in May 1866, he noticed it may have been improperly drafted. The government obviously wanted to try Davis under the Treason Act of 1790, which prescribed the penalty of death for this serious crime. Yet, because the charges in the indictment mentioned violations committed in 1864, Chase believed the Confiscation Act of 1862 may have been the most applicable statute in this case. Under that wartime measure, treason was punishable by a fine not exceeding $10,000 or imprisonment not exceeding ten years, or both. If the government wanted to try Davis under the Treason Act of 1790, then it would have to redraft the indictment so there wouldn't be any confusion. The indictments of Lee and the others from June

1865 would also need to be rewritten eventually, since they had documented crimes committed in 1865, after the Act of 1862 had been passed.[26]

A grand jury handed down a new indictment of Jefferson Davis in March 1868.[27] In this extremely long document, which had been prepared based on the testimony of Robert E. Lee and former Confederate Secretary of War James Seddon, the prosecution stated Davis had committed treason "contrary to the form of the statute respecting the crime of treason, approved on the thirteenth day of April, in the year one thousand seven hundred and ninety." There would be no ambiguity on the question of whether or not Davis faced the death penalty for his crimes. A recent scholar has noted that this indictment of 1868 was remarkable for another reason, too. In the past, American indictments relied on language from fourteenth-century England. This indictment, however, used modern language. Going forward, it would serve as a model for the future, having "initiated a process that would make all previous American treason indictments appear medieval and obsolete."[28]

Lee had been called to Richmond in late November 1867 to provide testimony for the new indictment. The Constitution requires two witnesses for a treason conviction and it was decided Lee would be one of them. Lee spent ten hours at the courthouse on November 26, but wasn't summoned by the grand jury that day. He was eventually called to testify on the following day. The jurors questioned the general for approximately two hours, asking him about military activities that were well known to all Americans. When a prosecutor attempted to elicit testimony placing most of the blame on Davis, Lee told the grand jury, "I am responsible for what I did and I cannot now recall any important movement I made which I would not have made had I acted entirely on my own responsibility."[29] After his testimony was concluded, Lee noticed a black juror had fallen fast asleep—he later joked to Jefferson Davis that if "[I] had had any vanity as an orator, it would have received a rude check."[30] Lee would be expected to be present in court during the upcoming trial.

★   ★   ★

Many Americans, in the spring of 1866, began to doubt President Johnson's commitment to treason trials for the leading rebels. Everyone knew, of course, that Johnson had been the most hawkish figure of all during the war and in the immediate aftermath of the Lincoln assassination. Shortly after the fall of Richmond, Unionists would remember, Johnson had delivered a speech that was merciless toward the leading rebels. When the crowd suggested Jefferson Davis should be hanged, Johnson agreed, declaring Davis should be hanged twenty times higher than Haman.

In subsequent months, however, Johnson's attitude appeared to change. During the summer and fall of 1865, the president became more conciliatory toward southerners—so much so, in fact, that his administration couldn't keep up with the increased demand for pardons. Was Johnson's vow to make treason odious merely one of political expediency that had been easily jettisoned when circumstances changed?

This type of criticism truly bothered Johnson. He could be particularly defensive when it was raised by political opponents at public events. The evidence suggests Johnson had good reason to be upset by the belief he had broken his promise. The charge simply wasn't true.

When the House Judiciary Committee inquired into why Jefferson Davis, Robert E. Lee, and the other Confederate leaders hadn't been tried by 1867, it called an impressive list of Washington, DC, luminaries to appear before the Committee. Grant, Stanton, Seward, Chase, as well as Underwood, Chandler, and many others made the trip to Capitol Hill to testify. Perhaps one of the most unambiguous findings was that Andrew Johnson had been *the* most eager member of his cabinet for prosecuting rebels. The notion that Johnson was somehow soft on the Confederate States leadership was not supported by any of the testimony. It is true he wanted to forgive rank-and-file southerners and was eager for the former Confederate states to rejoin the Union. He also felt pardoned rebels should be able to return to public office across the South. This latter view put him in opposition to Thaddeus Stevens, Charles Sumner, and the other Radicals in Congress.

Critics of Johnson had little sympathy for the commander in chief in the spring of 1866. It had been a year since Appomattox, yet only the Lincoln conspirators and the wretched Captain Wirz had been brought to justice. The fact that Davis, in particular, had not been tried was galling to many devout Unionists. Hadn't Johnson suggested in May 1865 there was evidence linking Davis to the "atrocious murder of the late President, Abraham Lincoln"?[31] In May 1866, Francis Lieber actually provided circumstantial evidence to the House Judiciary Committee purporting to show "Jefferson Davis entertained propositions to assassinate Abraham Lincoln and the most prominent men of the North."[32] Some opponents of Johnson wondered how a monster like Davis could remain unpunished. A few Radicals in Congress even whispered darkly that perhaps Johnson had something to do with the assassination. Was that why he hesitated in prosecuting the Confederate president?

It's now clear these rumors were absurd. There is no persuasive evidence suggesting either Andrew Johnson or Jefferson Davis was directly involved in the assassination of Lincoln. Regardless, Johnson was agitated by the rumors and unfair criticism. His anger, alas, got the better of him during an unfortunate series of speeches delivered in late August and early September 1866. This tour of northern and northwestern cities by Johnson was dubbed "the swing round the circle."[33] Everyone perceived it as an unmitigated political disaster.

Johnson's plan was to tour several cities on his way to attend a ceremony honoring the great Democratic statesman Stephen Douglas, who died shortly after the Civil War began. The crowds throughout the trip were boisterous and the undisciplined Johnson thought he could talk off the cuff just as he did when he campaigned in small towns across Tennessee. It turned out to be an unwise decision to speak extemporaneously.

During a speech in Cleveland, a member of the crowd yelled, "Hang Jeff Davis!"[34] Johnson, showing his defensiveness, responded: "Why don't you hang him? Haven't you got the Court? Haven't you got the Attorney General? Who is your Chief Justice who refused to sit on this trial? I am not the Attorney General. I am no jury." He then asked the crowd why Congress hadn't ordered any of the rebel leaders to be tried. When another crowd member shouted, "Hang Thad Stevens and Wendell Phillips," Johnson replied, "Why not hang them?" At a later speech in St. Louis, the president defended himself from those Radicals who compared him to Judas Iscariot. Tensions got so heated that some folks started shooting. Two members of the audience were actually injured by the gunfire. Of the "swing round the circle" escapade in general, the New York *Independent* declared, "Such a humiliating exhibition has never before been seen, not anything even approaching to it."[35] General Grant called the stump speeches a "national disgrace."[36]

Johnson's remarks about Davis were illuminating. The president believed he had been single-minded in attempting to bring the Confederate leader to justice. Now, it was up to the chief justice and the new attorney general, Henry Stanbery, to ensure a fair trial would be held. Johnson expressed his frustration more formally (and more appropriately) in a letter to Stanbery in October 1866:

> In view of this obstruction, and the consequent delay in the proceeding with the trial of Jefferson Davis under the prosecution for treason, now pending in that court, and there being, so far as the President is informed, no good reason why the civil courts of the United States are not competent to exercise adequate jurisdiction within the district or circuit in which the state of Virginia is

included, I deem it proper to request your opinion as to what further steps, if any should be taken by the executive with a view to a speedy, public, and impartial trial of the accused, according to the constitution and laws of the United States.[37]

Stanbery said there was nothing more the president could do. It would still be several more months before Chase felt it was appropriate for him to preside over the trial.

★   ★   ★

The case against Davis, which had shown glimmers of promise in May 1866, appeared to be in danger just one year later.[38] In the spring of 1867, Johnson's cabinet had legitimate concerns about the two judges who would preside over the trial. Underwood was viewed as too biased, while Chase was considered too unreliable. Meanwhile, the new attorney general, Henry Stanbery, had delegated the case to the lead attorney, William Evarts. Stanbery preferred to argue cases directly before the Supreme Court and didn't wish to become entangled in treason trials. Upon learning this decision, Evarts found himself, after the recent departure from the case of two talented attorneys, insufficiently staffed to manage a trial of such historic and constitutional significance.

After Congress assigned judges to their circuits in March 1867, the trial could finally resume. Chase notified Underwood he would be available for the May 1867 session, but Evarts had to inform the court he wouldn't be ready at that time. A new indictment would be necessary and Evarts had only just learned he'd have to manage the case without the assistance of the attorney general and two of his co-counsels. In light of the endless delays, Underwood grudgingly agreed to set bail for Jefferson Davis at $100,000 during the May session. Horace Greeley—the antislavery editor who was now apparently reversing course and calling for national reconciliation—put up $25,000 of his own money for bail. On May 13, 1867, Jefferson Davis became free on bond, after having served two years in prison. Lee wrote him immediately, "Your release has lifted a load from my heart which I have not words to tell, and my daily prayer to the great Ruler of the world is that he may shield you from all future harm, guard you from all evil, and give you peace which the world can not take away."[39]

All was not yet lost for the prosecution, however. Many northerners, southern Unionists, and freedmen still believed the arch-traitor Davis was

JEFF. D_ HUNG ON A "SOUR APPLE TREE", OR TREASON MADE ODIOUS.

Figure 9.2.   Cartoon on the release of Jefferson Davis. *Source:* **Library of Congress.**

responsible for the deaths of loyal prisoners at Andersonville and Libby prisons. Plus, both Andrew Johnson and his most influential adviser, William Seward, disliked Davis intensely. Evarts focused on strengthening his team later in 1867. He first added a former governor of Virginia, H. H. Wells, who was also an expert criminal attorney. Richard Dana, a prominent Boston lawyer who had assisted the government in the *Prize Cases*—the Supreme Court case that bolstered the government's claim that treason had been committed—also joined the team. By the end of 1867, Attorney General Stanbery told Evarts, "I need not suggest to you that no time should be lost in making full preparations for trial."[40] At around the same time, Evarts wrote cryptically to Dana, "It may be that the trial will take place at the end of November, more likely in May next, as likely as either, not at all."[41] The lead attorney for the prosecution began showing signs of frustration.

Unfortunately for the government, the delays continued. The trial had already been pushed to March 1868, but then the court learned Chase would be once again unavailable. This time, he would be presiding over the impeachment trial of President Andrew Johnson in the US Senate. Chase was finally ready to appear in circuit court on June 3, 1868, but then, it was the lead prosecutor that wouldn't be available. Evarts had been a central member of Johnson's defense team during the impeachment trial and needed time to recuperate from that grueling experience. The Davis trial would be postponed until November 1868—after the election of the next president of the United States. Andrew Johnson had failed to secure the nomination of either party, so he'd be a lame duck by that time. The comedy of errors showed no signs of abating.

★   ★   ★

During the May 1867 session of the circuit court, another element had been introduced into the Davis trial that would prove to be divisive. The first integrated petit jury ever assembled in the South had been entrusted with deciding the case against Jefferson Davis—twelve of the twenty-four jurors were African American.[42] The passage of the Civil Rights Act in 1866 made it possible for African Americans to appear on juries in Virginia, so this was a truly historic moment. Underwood, who all along had been confident he could "pack" a jury, surely believed African American jurors would be more likely than former rebels to deliver guilty verdicts in treason trials. He'd have certainly been right to think so.

The overwhelming majority of white citizens in Richmond were outraged by the mixed jury. According to contemporary reports, locals referred to the African American jurors as "Underwood's nigger jurymen."[43] The *Chicago Tribune* sensed the people of Richmond dreaded the idea of "being subjected to the humiliation of a trial before Judge Underwood, and by a negro jury."[44] Editors at the *New York Times* worried Underwood and his mixed jury would take steps "to procure a conviction which will reflect more lasting disgrace and inflict deeper injury on our whole political system than even an acquittal would involve."[45] Apparently, editors at the *Times*, which one might have thought would be sympathetic to African Americans serving on juries, were wary of the "half and half" jury, as it was known.

If relatively progressive editors were worried about Underwood's jury, one can be certain Andrew Johnson had serious concerns. Sure enough, the president, who frequently expressed racist views of African Americans, was deeply troubled when he heard the news about the mixed jury. We get a glimpse of the president's thinking from a conversation he had with a famous missionary from Maryland in the summer of 1867. The missionary, Paul Bagley, who was trying to get Johnson to drop the case against Davis, provides us with a firsthand account of the president's attitudes toward black jurors.[46] Bagley told Johnson that Judge Underwood said he "could get negroes enough on a jury with a few white men to convict him [Jefferson Davis]." He also notified Johnson that Underwood had told him he'd seize Davis's Mississippi property from him "by fine and would try to have it bid in at half a dollar per acre by his [Davis's] old slaves." Johnson replied, according to Bagley, "It used to be fashionable to try a man before they hanged him." Finally, Bagley reported the president was originally "stout" on matters relating to the trial, but then appeared "moved" by the information about Judge Underwood. The notion of a mixed race jury meting out justice in Virginia almost certainly weakened Johnson's determination to punish traitors like Davis and Lee. His belief in white supremacy trumped his desire to make treason odious.

In any event, the prosecution seemed to have lost its momentum. By the spring and summer of 1868, the president had given up on prosecuting the rebel leaders, though he hesitated to admit that fact publicly. Some historians believe he may have adopted this position because he hoped to become the Democratic nominee for president that year.[47] Ulysses S. Grant would be the candidate for the Republican Party. The Democratic Party supported greater reconciliation between North and South, so dropping charges against Davis and Lee would have been popular with rank-and-file party members. We've also seen that Johnson didn't like the idea of a mixed race jury deciding these cases. Regardless of the actual reasons, the president, in an apparent change of tack, was ready to pardon all Confederates by June 1868. He had to be talked out of that bold gambit by several members of his cabinet. Instead, he issued on July 4, 1868, a general amnesty that excluded only those "under presentment or indictment in any court of the United States having competent jurisdiction upon a charge of treason or other felony."[48] The Davis trial would continue, at least for now. Lee and the other leaders still faced the possibility of treason trials as well.

★   ★   ★

William Evarts became Johnson's attorney general during this time, though he would continue to manage the Davis case. He had done an outstanding job defending the president in the impeachment trial, and as a Republican, he was more likely to be confirmed by a still hostile Congress. Gideon Welles described Evarts as a "remarkably clear-minded man" and a "lawyer of extraordinary ability."[49] Now that he was the nation's top lawyer, Evarts would be in a stronger position for prosecuting Davis.

Yet, Evarts had grown discouraged by the trial by early 1868. So much so, in fact, that he had asked assistant counsel Richard Dana to come up with reasons for dropping the case. The impeachment trial, of course, disrupted everything, so Dana's efforts had to be put aside for a while. Once Evarts became attorney general, Dana reminded him of their pessimism about the case. Evarts then asked Dana to write a letter he could present to the cabinet.

In his brief, Dana laid out a clear and compelling argument for abandoning the case against Davis—and, of course, this same reasoning would apply to Lee and the other Confederate leaders (see appendix B for Dana's entire brief).[50] Dana noted the Constitution clearly defined treason, and the only question to be decided was whether or not secession by a state was a constitutional right. He then immediately answered his own question by stating the Supreme Court, in the *Prize Cases*, had already determined secession and war were treason. It then followed that "the only question of fact submitted to the jury will be whether Jefferson Davis took part in the war." With a slight touch of sarcasm, Dana added, "As it is one of the great facts of history that he was its head, civil and military, why should we desire to make a question of it and refer its decision to a jury, with powers to find in the negative or affirmative to disagree?"

The brief concluded with a discussion of the problems with a jury trial on a case of such monumental importance. It would only take one juror "to defeat the Government and give Jefferson Davis and his favorers a triumph." A negative result, according to Dana, "would be most humiliating to the Government and people of this country, and none the less so from the fact that it would be absurd." Dana believed minor penalties for treason were "beneath the dignity" of the government and the American people no longer desired the death penalty for the Confederate leaders. Taking everything into consideration, Dana declared, "The risk of such absurd and discreditable issues of a great state trial, are assumed for the sake of a verdict which, if obtained, will settle nothing in law or natural practice not now settled, and nothing in fact not now history, while no judgment rendered thereon do we think will be ever executed." In modern terms, he was saying the case offered all downside with very little upside.

In November 1868, right before the circuit court was scheduled to reconvene, Evarts sent Dana's letter to the president and later read it at a cabinet meeting. Evarts recommended a new amnesty, which would include all those Confederate leaders still under indictment. Such a move would "close out the rebellion."[51] Johnson and the cabinet agreed with Evart's recommendation.

Still worried about public opinion, Johnson hesitated before announcing the new amnesty, however. As a result, Evarts tried to postpone the circuit court session in late November. This time, Davis's attorney, O'Conor, refused. He intended to get this case resolved once and for all. Dana and Evarts would be required to continue prosecuting the case.

O'Conor had reason to feel optimistic. He had learned Chief Justice Chase believed the recently passed Fourteenth Amendment should have put an end to the trial. According to Section 3 of the amendment, any Confederate leader who had formerly taken an oath to uphold the Constitution would be prevented from holding any office, civil or military, at the federal or state level. As a result of this punishment, Chase believed any further prosecution would amount to "double jeopardy," which is prohibited under the Constitution.[52]

When the circuit court met between November 30 and December 3, O'Conor laid out the argument that the passage of the Fourteenth Amendment prevented further prosecution of the case. Ironically, Dana, who had written an eloquent letter on why the case should be dropped, had to dutifully provide the counterargument on behalf of the government. It must have been difficult for him to argue for continuing the trial when his heart was no longer in it. On December 5, 1868, Chase told the court that he and Underwood disagreed on the proposition put forward by the defense—Chase in agreement; Underwood opposed. The matter would now be decided by the Supreme Court.

Evarts wished to go no further, believing that Chase, as chief justice, would be able to persuade his fellow members on the Supreme Court of the merits of his view. It would be a humiliating defeat for the government. Evarts suggested to O'Conor that he would enter a *nolle prosequi*—a Latin phrase meaning "will no longer prosecute"—in the case, if the defense team would drop the proposal before the Supreme Court. O'Conor agreed. And then on Christmas Day 1868, Andrew Johnson published a final proclamation granting complete amnesty to all participants in the rebellion including all those under indictment.[53] On February 11, 1869, Evarts entered a *nolle prosequi* for all thirty-nine indictments that had been found against the rebel leaders by the federal court in the state of Virginia.[54] Davis, Robert E. Lee, and the other Confederate leaders would not be prosecuted for treason by the US government. In the words of Evarts, the administration had finally "closed out the rebellion."

★   ★   ★

Johnson's Christmas Day Amnesty provided Robert E. Lee with a full pardon for the offense of treason against the United States. The Fourteenth

Amendment did prevent him, however, from holding state or federal office in the future. As a West Point–trained officer, Lee had taken an oath to uphold the Constitution, so under the amendment he would require a two-thirds vote in Congress if he ever wished to hold federal or local office. At the time of the Christmas Amnesty, Lee would have also been prevented from voting in Virginia under the Underwood Constitution—so named as a result of the prominent role played by John C. Underwood at the Convention that produced the new constitution. The prohibitions on Confederate leaders were soon discarded, however, and Lee would have been allowed to vote when the constitution became operative in early 1870. One additional result of the Amnesty Proclamation was that Lee could now attempt to regain his family estate at Arlington.

Long after Lee's death, in 1898, the final disability under the Fourteenth Amendment was removed for all Confederate leaders who had participated in the rebellion. It was mostly just a symbolic gesture, of course, since very few of the leaders were still alive by that point. A report accompanying the legislation noted that Thaddeus Stevens and Charles Sumner were no longer around "to restrain the hand of clemency in Congress."[55] The war with Spain at the time had led to an increased desire across America for further reconciliation. Congress welcomed the opportunity to forgive the Confederate leadership for all time.

★   ★   ★

Despite Andrew Johnson's best efforts, it's undeniable he failed to make treason odious during his presidency. There would be no convictions and punishments for the crime of treason committed during the Civil War. When Johnson left office, John Brown had been the only American in US history executed for treason.[56]

Johnson deeply regretted this. In a letter to a journalist, written several months before his final Amnesty Proclamation, he said,

> I shall go to my grave with the firm belief that Davis, Cobb, Toombs, and a few others of the arch-conspirators and traitors should have been tried, convicted, and hanged for treason. There was too much precious blood spilled on both sides not to have held the leading traitors responsible. If it was the last act of my life, I'd hang Jeff Davis as an example. I'd show coming generations that, while the rebellion was too popular a revolt to punish many who participated in it, treason should be made odious and arch-traitors should be punished.[57]

Johnson was sincere in his belief. He had desperately wanted to make treason odious, but failed in his attempt to do so.

Johnson blamed Chase for the failure, citing the endless delays of 1865 and 1866. He also faulted Congress. By attempting to impeach him, it had undermined his efforts to bring the *real* traitors to justice. In his farewell speech in March 1869, Johnson declared,

> It will also be recorded as one of the marvels of the times that a party [the Republican Party] claiming for itself a monopoly of consistency and patriotism, and boasting of its unlimited sway, endeavored, by a costly and deliberate trial, to impeach one who defended the Constitution and the Union, not only throughout the war of the rebellion, but during his whole term of office as Chief Magistrate; but, at the same time, could find no warrant or means at their command to bring to trial even the chief of the rebellion. Indeed, the remarkable failures in this case were so often repeated, that for propriety's sake, if for no other reason, it became at last necessary to extend to him an unconditional pardon.[58]

If Johnson had been entirely fair, he, too, would have had to accept some of the blame. His administration's decision to try treason cases where the crimes were actually committed assumed that impartial juries could be found in these places. William Seward, Thaddeus Stevens, and Benjamin Butler—to name just a few legal minds—knew this was wishful thinking. Only military commissions or northern juries were likely to convict Davis, Lee, and the other Confederate leaders of treason.

Perhaps Underwood's idea of a "packed" jury of African Americans and southern Unionists might have worked, but Johnson's racism made such an approach untenable to him. Johnson wanted to punish traitors, while at the same time reinstating the traditional white leadership at all levels of government across the South. It proved to be an impossible circle to square. In the end, his administration offered amnesty, while insisting treason had in fact been committed by the leading rebels. Perhaps treason had not been made odious, yet it's also true America has never had a widespread rebellion since. The Fourteenth Amendment made it clear that citizens now owed their primary allegiance to the federal government not the individual states. It's curious to note that the only official papers Andrew Johnson left behind in the White House after he left office were Robert E. Lee's pardon application and two signed letters from Lee relating to his indictment.[59] Johnson had held on to the pardon, but never personally offered forgiveness.

10

". . . THIS NOBLE MAN DIED 'A PRISONER OF WAR ON PAROLE.'"

General Jubal Early, who had been indicted by the Norfolk grand jury in 1865 along with Lee and the others, was defiant and unbowed when he heard the news about President Johnson's Christmas Day Amnesty Proclamation. Residing in Canada, where he had fled after the war, Early wrote his brother in January 1869,

> The recent proclamation I regard as a final acknowledgment by the United States Government, in all its departments of its inability to hold any of us responsible, under the Constitution and laws as they were, for our resistance to its usurpations; and as it is general in its terms and requires no obligation from any of us, without accepting it as a pardon for offences committed, but regarding it in the light above mentioned, I think I can now return without a compromise of principles, and will do so.[1]

Once back in Virginia, he vowed to oppose "all compromises recognizing in any manner negro equality," telling his brother he'd "prefer political annihilation rather than accede to any compromise of honor."

Jubal Early was *the* prototypical unreconstructed rebel after the South's bitter defeat. Lee affectionately referred to the pugnacious and profane corps commander as his "bad old man." Lee's nephew Fitzhugh joked, "When Early drew his sword in that conflict he threw the scabbard away and was never afterward able to find it."[2] Early, who viewed Andrew Johnson as a "miserable,

171

cowardly renegade," felt the South had been grievously wronged by the war and its aftermath.[3] He also believed Lee's Army of Northern Virginia had never actually been defeated—"it merely wore itself out whipping the enemy."[4] In the decades after the war, Early became the premier defense counsel for Robert E. Lee before the bar of history. One historian described Early as "perhaps the most influential figure in nineteenth-century Civil War writing, North or South."[5]

Though Early thrived on personal confrontation and controversy, he never once had a bad word to say about Lee. He idolized his former boss, even though Lee had to relieve him of his command during the spring of 1865, after a series of setbacks had led to a loss of public confidence in Early's leadership. Lee handled the sensitive matter with kindness and diplomacy, which further endeared him to Early. After the war, Lee and Early corresponded regularly. A note from Lee in 1866 actually inspired Early to write his memoirs. Both generals were committed to writing authoritative histories of the Army of Northern Virginia—in one letter to Lee, Early said, "The most that is left to us is the history of our struggle, and I think that ought to be accurately written. We lost nearly everything but honor, and that should be religiously guarded."[6] In a fatherly way, Lee always encouraged Early in his devotion to the South's cause. Later, Early would become the driving force behind the creation of the Lee cult in the decades after the death of the great soldier.

Unlike his acerbic protégé, Lee did not mention Johnson's Christmas Day Amnesty Proclamation in any of his correspondence. Perhaps he didn't think it would affect his life all that much, one way or another, though he did recognize it improved his odds of regaining Arlington. One can only wonder if he felt a sense of relief when it finally became official he wouldn't face prosecution for the crime of treason. A trial had always remained a possibility from June 1865 until December 1868, though it became considerably less likely with each passing year. Jefferson Davis noted Lee remained in peril as late as 1867 when he had been called to testify before the grand jury in the Davis trial. In a letter to his brother in 1868, Jubal Early mentioned he had been informed by a prominent politician that the treason indictments were still pending.[7] Grant's intervention on Lee's behalf in June 1865 had not in fact quashed his indictment, as we have learned, despite the erroneous belief to the contrary of several observers at the time.

Lee expressed a wide variety of emotions about the indictment while it remained operative. In the summer of 1865, he manfully declared he would stay in Virginia to face any charges brought against him. He had no desire to flee like Jubal Early, John C. Breckinridge, or several of the other Confederate leaders. Indeed, he seemed to go out of his way to broadcast he had no desire to avoid a trial. Lee firmly believed he had done nothing wrong. In fact, like King Lear, he viewed himself as "a man more sinn'd against than sinning." This feeling deeply affected his political outlook over the final years of his life. When some Confederate soldiers offered him a safe haven in the remote countryside of Virginia, which would be protected from the reach of Judge Underwood, Lee replied, "But you would not have your general run away and hide. He must stay and meet his fate."[8]

On another occasion, shortly after the indictments were delivered in June 1865, Lee told a former staff-officer he had made up his mind to "let the authorities take their course. I have no wish to avoid any trial the government may order, and I cannot flee."[9] When a minister angrily denounced the indictment at a gathering, Lee—who was fifty-eight at the time—replied, "Well it matters little what they may do to me; I am old, and have but a short time to live anyway."[10] Later that summer, Lee told his son, "I think however we may expect procrastination in measures of relief, & denunciatory threats etc.—We must be patient & let them take their course."[11]

It's worthwhile reviewing Lee's understanding of his plight after the war. While he didn't wish to appear to be avoiding a treason trial, Lee genuinely believed his parole from Appomattox protected him from prosecution—a view shared by Grant as well, as we have seen. With that in mind, Lee applied for a pardon, presuming that action would also serve as a good example to his fellow rebels. Johnson and his legal advisors disagreed about the protection offered by his parole, however, believing it only protected Lee until 1866 when the war was officially declared over. By that time, Lee seemed resigned to accepting whatever fate might be handed down by the authorities. As a witness in the Davis trial, he saw up close the challenges faced by the government in that case. A successful prosecution of Lee—a beloved southern leader who had apparently been given protection by General Grant—would have been far more difficult. This would not have been lost on Lee, who was a keen observer of events.

By 1869, Lee shared Jubal Early's defiant view of the federal government, though he tended to express it privately and more tactfully. Several months after his indictment was dropped, Lee told an old colleague, in a conversation about his decision to join the Confederacy, "I could have taken no other course save with dishonor, and if it were to be all done over again, I should act in precisely the same way."[12]

★   ★   ★

With his legal status resolved once and for all in December 1868, Lee realized he could now attempt to recover Arlington. Immediately after the war, he had been patiently waiting for his civil rights to be restored before initiating legal proceedings in relation to the estate. In January 1869, just one month after Johnson's Amnesty Proclamation, Lee wrote to the prominent lawyer J. S. Black inquiring about the attorney's earlier offer of assistance with the Arlington case. Lee told Black, who had considerable experience in difficult cases of this sort, that he didn't personally own the estate, though the US government may not have been aware of that fact. Legally, Arlington was held by his wife and would be passed down to their oldest son Custis after her death. Lee said he'd be willing to pursue legal actions on behalf of Mary and Custis, but had no desire to "arouse dark passions, to no good purpose."[13]

Lee had good reason to believe he had been treated unfairly regarding Arlington.[14] During the war, the federal government did have a legal right to seize the property temporarily for defensive purposes. Its strategic location overlooking the nation's capital made it essential that it wouldn't be controlled by the rebels. Taking legal title to the historic 1,100 acre estate, however, based on a meager unpaid tax bill of $92.07 pushed the boundaries of what was acceptable under the law. The fact that no compensation had been provided appeared to violate the Fifth Amendment to the Constitution, which states, "nor shall private property be taken for public use, without just compensation." Both during and after the war, the government's attitude toward the Arlington estate was punitive and unyielding. To federal officials, it somehow seemed morally right that an arch-rebel should lose his property, regardless of the legality of the seizure.

In 1863, the army began settling freedmen on the Arlington estate in a model community that would become famously known as Freedman's Village. In 1864, with Arlington now considered federal property, General Montgomery C. Meigs oversaw the creation of a national cemetery on the Arlington grounds.[15] Pvt. William Christman became the first Union soldier buried on the property on May 13, 1864. The number of grave sites soon grew rapidly after the devastating losses of Grant's Overland Campaign. By the end of June 1864, 2,600 Union soldiers had been buried at Arlington. Meigs believed Lee—Grant's opponent during the deadly spring of 1864—should be prosecuted and punished "by the government which they have betrayed [and] attacked." Turning Arlington into a peaceful resting place for the victims of Lee's treachery would be a fitting punishment for the rebel leader. For Meigs, it was personal—he lost his son during the fighting in the fall of 1864.

Many northerners welcomed the use of Arlington as a cemetery. One newspaper wrote, "How appropriate that Lee's land should be appropriated to two such noble purposes—the free living black man whom Lee would enslave, and the bodies of the dead whom Lee had killed in a wicked cause."[16] The burying of roughly sixteen thousand Union soldiers on the grounds during the war would seriously complicate any efforts by the Lee family to recover Arlington. Meigs allegedly said if they wanted to return to Arlington, they would be sleeping "among ghosts."[17] He also had the foresight to understand it would be politically impossible to disinter the bodies of the brave Union soldiers who were buried on the lawns outside the mansion. Converting Arlington into a national cemetery was one way of punishing Lee for all time.

Unlike her more self-controlled husband, Mary Lee struggled to contain her anger over the government's actions at Arlington. She seethed as she heard of the countless deleterious changes to her property, and wondered why George Washington's precious relics couldn't be returned to the family. Her father, George Washington Parke Custis, had spent a lifetime collecting and preserving relics associated with the preeminent founding father. When a friend asked Mary what she'd do about all the Yankee graves that had been added to the estate, she replied, "My dear, I would smooth them off and plant my flowers."[18] On an earlier occasion, Mary protested that the graves were "planted up to the very door without any regard to common decency."[19]

Arlington's fate was a constant theme in Mary's postwar correspondence —she vowed she would "never rest until it is restored nor will I *ever* relinquish my claim to it."[20] Even Mary's stoical husband let his famous temper flare up occasionally on the subject of the family home, once writing his daughter, "I should have preferred it to have been wiped from the earth, its beautiful hill sunk, and its sacred trees buried, rather than to have been degraded by the presence of those who revel in the ill they do for their own selfish purposes."[21] The immeasurable loss of Arlington was experienced by the Lees as a severe punishment for their decision to side with the Confederacy. The fact that there were "extra-legal" elements to that punishment made it all the harder to accept.

The extremely pious Robert E. Lee also sensed the loss of Arlington may have been a punishment ordained by God. Soon after the estate had been seized by the government, Lee wrote Mary, "I fear we have not been grateful enough for the happiness there within our reach, and our heavenly Father has found it necessary to deprive us of what He has given us."[22] Keenly aware of his own moral failings, Lee stated, "I acknowledge my ingratitude, my trans-gressions, and my unworthiness, and submit with resignation to what he thinks proper to inflict upon me." He also urged his wife to trust in God, believing they both must bear their trials like Christians. A deeply religious man like Lee naturally wondered if God had found fault with his actions. Did Lee wrestle with the possibility he had made the wrong choice in siding with the South, despite his protestations to the contrary? Why else would an all-powerful and all-knowing divinity allow such a devastating defeat?

Neither Robert nor Mary would live to see the return of Arlington. After Mary's death in 1873—three years after the passing of Robert—Custis sued the US government for compensation for the loss of the estate. He eventually won the case in 1882 when the US Supreme Court ultimately determined the government's claim to Arlington was invalid. Custis graciously accepted the government's offer to buy Arlington for $150,000—a considerable sum of money at the time—rather than demanding a return of the property. The Mount Vernon relics were subsequently given back to Custis in 1901, and Arlington became a memorial to Robert E. Lee in 1955. Arlington National Cemetery, with its endless rows of Union dead, remains a national historic landmark today.

★ ★ ★

It was typical of Lee to want to reclaim Arlington without arousing "dark passions." He didn't enjoy engaging in political controversy in public, though it would be inaccurate to view him as apolitical. Indeed, Lee had become radicalized by the war and its aftermath. According to Douglas Southall Freeman, "Lee absorbed the Southern constitutional argument and was convinced by it" as a result of his fighting on behalf of the Confederacy.[23] In early 1861, prior to the war, Lee had declared "secession is nothing but revolution."[24] After 1865, he devoted considerable time and energy to constructing elaborate constitutional arguments defending the legality of secession. In addition to personal correspondence on this issue, he drafted numerous political treatises that were never published. The historian Elizabeth Brown Pryor felt these unfinished pages were "like the smoke from a roiling volcano."[25] Taken as a whole, Lee's political writings after the war represented a very skilled defense of his decision to fight on behalf of the Confederacy. His conviction the war was about states' rights, and not slavery, was the foundation of this defense. That belief would later become a central tenet of the "Lost Cause" tradition.

Lee changed his outlook dramatically on the subject of secession from 1861 to the postwar period. At the height of the secession crisis in early 1861, he concluded there was "no greater calamity for the country than a dissolution of the Union." In a letter to his son Custis on January 23, 1861, Lee argued,

Secession is nothing but revolution. The framers of our Constitution never exhausted so much labor, wisdom, and forbearance in its formation, and surrounded it with so many guards and securities, if it was intended to be broken by every member of the Confederacy at will. It was intended for "perpetual union," so expressed in the preamble, and for the establishment of a government, not a compact, which can only be dissolved by revolution, or the consent of all the people in convention assembled. It is idle to talk of secession. Anarchy would have been established, and not a government, by Washington, Hamilton, Jefferson, Madison, and the other patriots of the Revolution.[26]

Lee did not believe secession was a right granted to the states under the Constitution. In the same letter, he nevertheless concluded,

Still a Union that can be maintained by swords and bayonets, and in which strife and civil war are to take the place of brotherly love and kindness, has no charm for me. I shall mourn for my country and for the welfare and progress of mankind. If the Union is dissolved, and the Government disrupted, I shall return to my native State and share the miseries of my people, and save in defense will draw my sword on none.

So, Lee seemed to be saying that secession was unconstitutional *and* he would abide by Virginia's decision regardless, if it chose to leave the Union. Using Lee's own language, he would become a revolutionary. He'd side with the South, not because it was legal, but rather because that was where his sympathies lay. Such thinking would have been easier to defend if the South had been successful, of course.

His outlook had changed considerably by the close of 1866. At that time, Lee had received a request from Sir John Dalberg Acton (later Lord Acton) for his views on the constitutional issues relating to secession. After consulting a volume on the US Constitution, Lee sent a lengthy reply on December 15, 1866. The "Lord Acton" letter was never published in Lee's lifetime, but it represents the best expression of Lee's postwar view on these subjects.[27] The letter eventually appeared in Lord Acton's *Correspondence* in 1917.

In the letter, Lee had now become far more sympathetic to the idea of secession, though he conceded the result of the war was that the "union of states is inviolable and perpetual under the constitution." Lee believed, however, that Washington and Jefferson denounced "consolidation and centralization of power, as tending to the subversion of State Governments, and to despotism." Such a view seemed to have been embraced by the New England States who advocated secession in 1814, Lee added with a touch of irony. In the end, he determined it was all an unprofitable discussion, "Unprofitable because the judgment of reason has been displaced by the arbitrament of war, waged for the purpose as avowed of maintaining the union of states."

At the heart of the Lord Acton letter, Lee expressed—using all capital letters for emphasis in the original document—a bold statement of his political principles:

> I yet believe that the maintenance of the rights and authority reserved to the state and to the people not only essential to the adjustment and balance of the general system, but the safeguard to the continuance of a free government. I consider it as the chief source of stability to our political system, whereas the consolidation of the states into one vast republic, sure to be aggressive abroad and despotic at home, will be the certain precursor of that ruin which has overwhelmed all those that have preceded it.[28]

By this time, Lee was firmly within the states' rights camp and didn't use words like "revolution" to describe resistance to the centralizing tendencies of the federal government. Concluding his political discourse, he wrote,

> Although the South would have preferred any honourable compromise to the fratricidal war which has taken place, she now accepts in good faith its constitutional results, and receives without reserve the amendment which has already been made to the constitution for the extinction of slavery. That is an event that has been long sought, though in a different way, and by none has it been more earnestly desired than by citizens of Virginia.

The view that Virginians had long sought an end to slavery might seem dubious in light of the available evidence, but it was a central principle in Lee's defense of himself and the South. He first made that point in the interview with Thomas Cook of the *New York Herald* in April 1865, and would consistently reiterate it for the remainder of his life.

The Acton Letter wasn't made public at the time, of course, but Lee had made similar remarks before the Joint Committee for Reconstruction in February 1866, just ten months earlier. On the subject of treason, Lee told Senator Howard that southerners believed their states, in withdrawing from the Union, had carried the individuals of the state along with them. In his own case, he said, "Virginia, in withdrawing herself from the United States, carried me along as a citizen of Virginia, and her laws and her acts were binding on me."[29]

In his testimony before the committee, Lee proudly made no apologies for his role in the war. Going even further, he implied it was the North that would have to earn the trust of the South, if it wished to maintain harmony in the future. It may have been this unyielding attitude that led General Grant to declare, shortly after the hearing, "Lee is behaving badly. He is conducting himself very differently from what I had reason, from what he had said at the time of surrender, to suppose he would."[30] Lee's unwillingness to make public expressions of conciliation bothered Grant, who added, "No man at the South is capable of exercising a tenth part of the influence for good that he is, but instead of using it he is setting an example of forced acquiescence so grudging and pernicious in its effects as to be hardly realized."

While a reluctant Lee had been forced to appear before the Joint Committee on Reconstruction, he uncharacteristically volunteered to enter the political fray during the presidential campaign of 1868, which pitted the Republican Ulysses S. Grant against the Democrat Horatio Seymour. Andrew Johnson had made a bid for the Democratic nomination, but had been unsuccessful. General William Rosecrans, who had fought against Lee during the war, was assisting the Democratic Party and sought a statement from former rebel leaders about the willingness of southerners to cooperate with the government in the future. Lee agreed to Rosecrans's request, while meeting with a large group of former Confederate leaders at White Sulphur Springs, just sixty miles west of Lexington.[31] The statement was drafted by Alexander H. H. Stuart, a young Virginia lawyer, on Lee's behalf. The letter, which became known as the "White Sulphur Manifesto," was dated August 28, 1868, and was signed by thirty-one southern luminaries—Lee, former Vice President Alexander Stephens, and General P. G. T. Beauregard among them. Almost all of the former leaders of the Confederacy supported the Democratic Party at that time.

The manifesto began by declaring the southern people had accepted the results of the war.[32] In good faith, they had abolished slavery and annulled the ordinances of secession. If northerners had been equally conciliatory, then, the signees believed, the "old irritations would have passed away, and the wounds inflicted by the war would have been in a great measure healed." Now, the southern people only wanted a restoration of their rights under the Constitution.

The latter half of the manifesto dealt with southern attitudes toward African Americans. The former rebel leadership reassured northerners that they viewed the freedman with kindness and would "extend to the negroes care and protection." In fact, it was the *North* that was stirring "up the passions of the negroes." Everything would work out fine, if the South could be left alone to manage its own affairs. The signees to the manifesto did not, however, believe the freedmen were quite yet ready for political rights. They opposed any form of suffrage for African Americans.

Lee had raised similar ideas in an interview with the Marquis of Lorne, later ninth Duke of Argyll, back in May 1866. He had said, "The relations between the negroes and the whites were friendly formerly, and would remain so if legislation be not passed in favor of the blacks, in a way that will only do them harm."[33] Underlining the widespread commitment to white supremacy among southerners, Lee added, "The blacks must always here be the weaker; the whites are so much stronger that there is no chance for the black, if the Radical party passes the laws it wants against us."[34] It's quite clear that Lee believed southern freedmen would fare best under the benevolent rule of white southerners, free from the misguided interventions of northern Radicals.

Some of Lee's public statements on racial topics after the war seemed at odds with his private remarks and actions. For example, he frequently declared in public he had favored gradual emancipation before the war, yet in a letter to a Virginia politician in January 1865, as we saw earlier, Lee said he had determined "the relation of master and slave, controlled by humane laws and influenced by Christianity and an enlightened public sentiment, as the best that can exist between the white and black races while intermingled as at present in this country." Having lived in the North for extended periods at different times in his life, Lee knew slavery was unpopular there. His experience managing his father-in-law's slaves had also been an unpleasant ordeal for him. A generous interpretation of his position would be that he disliked the *idea* of slavery, but also couldn't imagine how the races could live together in equality. That's why he told a US congressman that Virginia's "colored population" should leave the state, adding, "I think it would be better for Virginia if she could get rid of them. That is no new opinion with me." This last line, of course, completely contradicts the White Sulphur Manifesto, which predicted "the two races would soon adjust themselves on a basis of mutual kindness and advantage."

It's hard to escape the conclusion Lee meant precisely what he said in January 1865 when he wrote that a benevolent form of slavery was the best means for whites and blacks to live together. Lee believed African Americans were at an inferior stage of development and were not ready to receive the full rights of American citizenship. While managing his father-in-law's estate—we might recall—he put the economic interests of his children above the well-being of roughly two hundred slaves. During the war, he upheld the Confederate policy of denying black Union troops the full protections required for soldiers under the laws of war. After Appomattox, he advised friends and family not to hire freedmen and worked to attract European immigrant labor to Virginia. In 1868, Lee shared his views on the freedmen with his youngest son: "I wish them no evil in the world—on the contrary, will do them every good in my power, and know that they are misled by those to whom they have given their confidence; but our material, social, and political interests are naturally with the whites."[35]

This outlook provides vital context for Lee's conviction that the war was about states' rights and not slavery. Even if we assume this to be true for the sake of argument, it's hard to imagine how *universal* emancipation—as opposed to limited freedom for those slaves who may have been willing to fight for the new nation—would have occurred in the Confederate States of America if it had won the war. And even if universal emancipation did somehow occur, it's quite difficult to imagine freedmen enjoying full civil and political rights in the southern Republic. Addressing the Confederacy's belated and controversial decision in 1865 to allow the arming of slaves in return for their freedom, the historian Bruce Levine argues, "In pushing to enact this measure, they were trying to preserve as much of the Old South as they could."[36]

Despite all of the inconsistencies and contradictions surrounding Lee's views on race, he found it essential to believe the war had been about something nobler than merely preserving the economic self-interest of a slaveholding aristocracy. He was ultra-sensitive to the judgments of history and knew slavery would be considered abhorrent by future generations of Americans. In a letter to a cousin in 1870, Lee wrote, "the reputation of individuals is of minor importance to the opinion which posterity may form of the motives which governed the South in their late struggle for the maintenance of the principles of the Constitution."[37] By reframing the war as being about states' rights, Lee demonstrated a sophisticated understanding of politics and history. His description of himself as apolitical is deceptive.

There are two popular anecdotes about Lee and race after the war well worth considering. One occurred in the spring of 1867 when Lee was allegedly visited by leaders of the Ku Klux Klan. According to Susan Lawrence Davis, who interviewed the leaders and wrote a book titled *Authentic History of the Ku Klux Klan*, the Klansmen told Lee about their work and asked him to join them. As an "unpardoned prisoner," Lee said he couldn't join, but then added, "I would like to assist you in any plan that offers relief. I cannot be with you in person but I will follow you but must be invisible; and my advice is to keep it as you have it, a protective organization."[38] This conversation apparently resulted in the Klan becoming known as the "Invisible Empire" for they would always remember "Lee was their guiding spirit." Even though the story became well known in the South, Lee's most meticulous biographer, Douglas Southall Freeman, couldn't find any supporting documentary evidence for this tale other than Davis's interviews.[39]

The second widely told anecdote involved a simple act by Robert E. Lee at St. Paul's Church in Richmond just two months after the city had been evacuated.[40] According to an account provided several decades after the actual event, the minister of the church was about to administer communion when a tall, well-dressed black man advanced to the communion table.

Apparently, the congregants were startled and "deeply chagrined at this attempt to inaugurate the 'new regime' to offend and humiliate them during their most devoted Church services." It was at this precise moment that Lee— "ignoring the action and the presence of the negro"—arose and walked up to the table "to partake of the communion alongside the black man." An observer reported, "By this action of Gen. Lee the services were conducted as if the negro had not been present. It was a grand exhibition of superiority shown by a true Christian and great soldier under the most trying and offensive circumstances."

A recent, somewhat bowdlerized version of the story appeared in Jay Winik's popular Civil War narrative *April 1865*. Winik presents the story, however, as if Lee was symbolically leading white southerners into a more equal future.[41] That's not quite what happened, according to the original account as it appeared when first published by the *Richmond Times Dispatch* in 1905. As we can see in the direct quotes provided earlier, the communicants actually perceived the episode as an example of Lee standing up to the impudence of a black man. The story of Lee at the communion table may actually have been apocryphal, but we should nevertheless resist the temptation to view it as a milestone in the civil rights movement.[42] The original tale was clearly not intended that way.

★   ★   ★

In the remaining months of Lee's life after the indictments were dropped, his health deteriorated rapidly. It hadn't been all that good to begin with, of course, especially since his heart attack in 1863. By 1865, photographs show him aging rapidly. And throughout much of the postwar period, he talks of not having much longer to live. By early 1869, shortly after the Amnesty Proclamation, he had difficulty walking and was experiencing pain in his chest.[43] At the beginning of 1870, he told his daughter he had trouble walking much farther than the college—a distance of only two hundred yards from his house.

Lee's youngest son reported his father was "constantly in pain and had begun to look upon himself as an invalid" during the last year or so of his life.[44] He was regularly visiting doctors during this time but nothing they prescribed seemed to make him feel any better. In March 1870, after he had developed chest pain at rest—"rest angina" to use the official term—his doctors convinced him to go south for a while with the hope that warmer weather might be beneficial. During the six-week trip to Georgia and Florida, Lee was greeted as a hero by adoring southerners.

In July 1870, perhaps believing he had precious little time for tying up loose ends, Lee met with his lawyers in Alexandria, Virginia, about the Arlington estate. It turned out to be bad news for the Lee family. Because of all the Union soldiers that had been buried there, Lee was informed a bill had been introduced to Congress "to perfect the title of the Government to Arlington and other National Cemeteries."[45] That meant the end to the scant hopes that Lee might recover Arlington during his lifetime.

The last act came during the autumn of 1870, while the dutiful old soldier was carrying out his daily administrative responsibilities at the college. In late September he had a stroke and then fourteen days later, he died quietly at 9:30 a.m. on October 12, 1870. His doctors believed, in the language of the time, he died of "mental and physical fatigue, inducing venous congestion of the brain, which, however, never proceeded so far as apoplexy or paralysis, but gradually caused cerebral exhaustion and death."[46] Modern physicians have determined he suffered from progressive atherosclerosis from 1863 to 1870 and died from the combination of his cardiac illness and a stroke.

It's impossible to know how much Lee's poor health affected his thoughts and actions during the postwar period. Was his desire to retreat to Lexington, Virginia, primarily due to a feeling of physical weakness? We might remember that even in 1865, he had told the trustees he didn't have the energy to teach classes at the college. Was his stoicism in the face of a possible treason trial also influenced by declining health and a sense he didn't have much longer to live? One wonders if a healthier Lee might have been more active in publicly defending himself and promoting his opinions on Reconstruction. At the very least, a healthy Lee may have had the necessary stamina to accomplish his goal of writing a history of the Virginia campaigns. Historians would have been grateful for what would have become an indispensable account of the war.

Years after Lee's death, John William Jones—a chaplain at Washington

College—wrote, "this noble man died 'a prisoner of war on parole'—his application for 'amnesty' was never granted, or even noticed—and the commonest privileges of citizenship, which are accorded to the most ignorant negro were denied this *king of men*."[47] Jones, who compiled essential collections of writings by and about Lee, is not quite right in his assessment. The *true* story of Lee's punishment for his role in the war is far more nuanced than Jones indicated.

The toughest penalty against Lee, of course, was the government's decision in January 1864 to acquire Arlington due to unpaid taxes. This was a huge loss for Lee personally and his family would not be compensated for it during his lifetime. The fact that Arlington remains federal property to this day suggests this was the most meaningful sanction against Lee.

At Appomattox in April 1865, Lee became a prisoner of war on parole. He signed a document at the time promising he would not "serve in the armies of the Confederate States, or in any military capacity whatever against the United States of America, or render said to the enemies of the latter, until properly exchanged."[48] We have seen that the parole only lasted until the war was officially declared over—eventually President Johnson did so in August 1866. Additionally, Lee had been indicted for treason by the Norfolk court in June 1865, and his indictment remained operative until it was dropped in February 1869.

Lee suffered yet another penalty by the government for his role in the war, as a result of the ratification of the Fourteenth Amendment in July 1868. According to Section 3,

> No person shall be a Senator or Representative in Congress or elector of President and Vice President, or hold any office, civil or military, under the United States, or under any state, who, having previously taken an oath, as a member of Congress, or as an officer of the United States . . . shall have engaged in insurrection or rebellion against the same, or given aid or comfort to the enemies thereof.

In addition to being prevented from holding public office, Lee was initially prohibited from voting in his beloved Virginia as a result of the Underwood Constitution, which had been created in 1867 and 1868. Lee's voting rights, along with other former rebels, were restored in July 1869, however. At the time of his death, Lee would have been eligible to vote in Virginia.

On Christmas Day 1868, Johnson proclaimed, "to all and to every person who, directly or indirectly, participated in the late insurrection or rebellion a full pardon and amnesty for the offense of treason against the United States . . .

with restoration of all rights, privileges, and immunities under the Constitution and the laws which have been made in pursuance thereof." So, Lee had in fact been pardoned by Johnson, though it was part of a general amnesty. For political reasons, Johnson never intended to reply individually to Lee's pardon application of 1865. Whether or not Lee's oath had been misplaced was immaterial. Johnson had no desire to personally pardon either Lee or Jefferson Davis. The latter, a bitter foe of Johnson, never intended to apply for one.

Lee's indictment was formerly dropped in February 1869, so at the time of his death, the only legal disability he faced was under the Fourteenth Amendment, though he still had been denied Arlington without compensation. Long after his death, that disability from the Fourteenth Amendment was removed by Congress. Whether this repeal applied posthumously was subject to debate, though it didn't really matter for practical purposes.

When we step back and look at the totality of the government's treatment of Lee, we see that he did suffer substantial economic and political penalties for his role in commanding the armies of the Confederate States of America. Most of them, but not all, had been removed by the time of his death. When you factor in the loss of Arlington, it's fair to say that Lee paid dearly for his decision to side with the South. Northerners and southerners nevertheless tended to view Lee's treatment differently. Many northerners felt Lee had been lucky to escape the hangman's noose, and should have been somewhat more conciliatory toward the government as a result. The vast majority of southerners, on the other hand, believed their hero had been treated harshly by the authorities. It made it difficult for them to restore their allegiance to a government that would act in such a way.

★ ★ ★

Mary Lee did not wait long, after her husband died, to attempt to reclaim her ancestral property. Just weeks after his death, she petitioned Congress with the high hopes they'd carefully examine the facts of the case and decide in her favor. In retrospect, it's understandable she would make the attempt at that time. The outpouring of grief and affection for her husband, in both the South and North, was astonishing. So much so, in fact, that Frederick Douglass noted soon after his death, "We can scarcely take up a newspaper . . . that is not filled with nauseating flatteries of the late Robert E. Lee."[49] Also, it made sense that Mary would wish to leave Lexington now that her husband was gone.

According to her petition, Congress should form a joint committee that would "take the statements of Mrs. Lee in order to identify her property with greater certainty, to discover the extent of her losses, and they shall report all facts necessary to a settlement upon the principles of substantial justice."[50] She also requested the joint committee should report "on what terms a suitable spot for a cemetery can be purchased in the neighborhood, and the probable cost of removing the bodies to the new place of sepulcher." Senator Thomas Clay McCreery, a Democrat from Kentucky, attempted to introduce the proposal on Mrs. Lee's behalf. It's safe to say that neither one of them was prepared for the hostile response in the Senate.[51]

Several senators rose to denounce Lee's treason. Senator Lyman Trumbull, who had been a co-author to the Thirteenth Amendment abolishing slavery, declared, "Lee did more perhaps than any other man to drench the land in blood." Senator Oliver Morton of Indiana, outraged by McCreery's glowing remarks about Lee, replied, "Sir, the enormity of his crimes cannot be concealed by strewing of flowers of rhetoric over his grave." Denouncing Lee further, Nevada Senator James Nye said, "History will record him as a traitor. The testimony of the living today records him as a traitor; and if the countless dead could speak, they would add their testimony to the truth of the charge."

The possibility that Union graves might be disturbed to make way for Mrs. Lee's return to Arlington angered the senators most of all. Senator Morton believed it would be a desecration of the "graves of the patriotic dead" to remove them "in tender consideration of the rights of the widow of the arch-rebel of the most wicked rebellion in history!" Several senators made similar remarks about the sanctity of federal graves on the site. Senator Nye felt it was too soon to even consider such an idea, saying, "we are going too fast in this thing. We are asked to forget the past." If Meigs had believed converting Arlington into a national cemetery would prevent a return of the Lee family, he appeared to be correct in his assumption.

As was often the case in the Senate at that time, Senator Charles Sumner was the most eloquent of all in attacking the petition. He began his remarks by stating, "I am not disposed to speak of General Lee. It is enough to say that he stands high on the catalogue of those who have imbrued their hands in their country's blood. I hand him over to the avenging pen of history." He then told his fellow senators that Stanton had *deliberately* buried the Union dead at Arlington "in perpetual guard over that ground, so that no person of the family of Lee should ever dare to come upon it unless to encounter the ghosts of those patriots." Sumner agreed with Senator Nye who felt the dead at Arlington were as sacred as the Constitution—an interesting comparison given how much Lee tried to frame his decision as permissible according to his reading of the Constitution.

Sumner concluded his oration by quoting Shakespeare's epitaph:

Good Friend! For Jesus' sake forbear
To dig the dust inclosed here.
Blest be the man that spares these stones;
And cursed be he that moves my bones.

Noting these lines had protected Shakespeare's body for over two and a half centuries, Sumner proclaimed, "I write them now over the grave of every one of our patriot dead. May they continue for centuries to come to guard their remains." The hapless Senator McCreery was stunned by the onslaught of his colleagues. The Senate ultimately decided against even the introduction of the resolution by a vote of 54 to 4.

11

". . . YOU GENTLEMEN THAT USE THE PEN SHOULD SEE THAT JUSTICE IS DONE US."

Had he been successful instead of the Hero of the Lost Cause he could not have been more beloved and honored.

—Mrs. Robert E. Lee, 1870

The combative Jubal Early was always especially sensitive to attacks—both real and imagined—on Robert E. Lee and the Confederate cause. In an address before the Southern Historical Society at White Sulphur Springs in 1873, he told his compatriots, "we cannot escape the ordeal of history. Before its bar we must appear, either as criminals—rebels and traitors seeking to throw off the authority of a legitimate government to which we were bound by the ties of allegiance—or as patriots defending our rights and vindicating the true principles of the government founded by our fathers."[1]

Until then, the South's enemies, as Early called them, had been presenting the former rebels as traitors—the government had literally indicted key leaders for treason and the press had accused them of various misdeeds, committed during the war. Using the word "indictment" in a symbolic sense, Early asked, "Shall we permit the indictment to go forth to the world and to posterity without a vindication of our motives and our conduct? Are we willing that our enemies shall be the historians of our cause and our struggle?" After a pause, he answered his own question, "No! a thousand times no!"[2]

The subject of history was of critical importance to the old Confederates of the Southern Historical Society. In the White Sulphur Springs address, Early urged his listeners to remain steadfast in the ongoing rhetorical wars:

> The men who by their deeds caused so many of the battlefields of the South to blaze with a glory unsurpassed in the annals of the world, cannot be so recreant to the principles for which they fought, the traditions of the past, and the memory of their own comrades "dead upon the field of honor," as to abandon the tribunal of history to those before whose immense numbers and physical power alone they were finally compelled to yield from mere exhaustion.[3]

Robert E. Lee was foremost among the men who had performed great deeds, and Jubal Early spent the remainder of his life defending and promoting the memory of the beloved Confederate general, in lecture halls and the leading journals of the day.

Early, who was described by a contemporary as "the fearless guardian of the fame of Lee," and his fellow Lee admirers controlled the tremendously influential Southern Historical Society, an organization devoted to vindicating the truth about the Civil War.[4] The society published the *Southern Historical Society Papers*, which included essential documents and debates on all of the central topics of the war.[5] Lee in particular received exhaustive and hagiographical treatment in issue after issue. In 1877, for example, roughly 90 percent of the fifty articles published were about Lee and the Army of Northern Virginia. By the early twentieth century, a leading academic journal said of the society's papers, "no library, public or private, which pretends to historic fullness, can afford to be without these volumes."[6]

Lee had already played an active role, both privately and publicly, in laying out his own defense during the last five years of his life. He had argued the war wasn't about slavery, but rather states' rights. He had also emphasized the relatively small size of his army in relation to the endless resources possessed by his opponents. Finally, he had insisted the South be restored to its proper place within the Union with the various southern states being allowed to run their affairs as they saw fit. Lee's arguments would become central tenets in the Lost Cause tradition that was later advanced even further after his death by such former lieutenants as General Jubal Early and Colonels Walter Taylor, Charles Marshall, and Charles Venable.[7]

In the battle over the memory of both Lee and the Confederate cause, this group would achieve extraordinary success. Indeed, one modern historian believed they had been so successful that, "In the popular mind, the Lost Cause represents the national memory of the Civil War; it has been substituted for the history of the war."[8] Recent data provides support for this view. In 2011, a poll from the Pew Research Center found 48 percent of Americans believed states' rights was the main cause of the Civil War compared with just 38 percent who felt slavery was the main cause. A McClatchy-Marist Poll from August 2015 reported that 41 percent of all Americans did not believe "slavery led the nation into civil war." The Lost Cause outlook still has a powerful hold on the American memory.[9]

In one respect, the Lost Cause was an elaborate defense by former rebels against a broad indictment of their actions handed down by northerners soon after the war. In another sense, the Lost Cause tradition represented a longing for an idealized prewar South that was prosperous and governed by orderly relations between master and slave. The word "lost" therefore had two meanings. It referred to defeat on the battlefield *and* an antebellum culture that had disappeared forever. The fact that slavery was increasingly unpopular in the North, and much of the rest of the world, made it necessary to downplay the role of slavery as a factor in the war, even though it was central to the prewar society that was so highly valued. The Lost Cause tradition required a highly selective memory on the part of its adherents.

★   ★   ★

The journalist and Virginian Edward Pollard, who wrote for the Richmond *Examiner* during the war, was the first defender of the Confederacy to adopt the term "Lost Cause."[10] He developed the idea in two highly influential books: *The Lost Cause* (1866) and *The Lost Cause Regained* (1868). Pollard believed the actual word "slavery" was an odious term that had been used by northerners to further their own centralizing agenda. In reality, slavery in the South had been a mild system of servitude, according to Pollard, that "elevated the African, and was in the interest of human improvement."[11] Such a benign system made the southern slave "the most striking type in the world of cheerfulness and contentment."

Pollard accepted that slavery had been defeated, though he also believed the South still possessed the upper hand in the ongoing war of ideas. For him, the war had decided many things, but it did not "decide negro equality; it did not decide negro suffrage; it did not decide State rights."[12] His position—which is shockingly racist to modern Americans—was that the "South's goal should be in the securing the supremacy of the white man," while keeping the African American "in a condition where his political influence is as indifferent as when he was a slave."[13] Success in this goal, Pollard argued, would result in the "lost cause regained." Ultimately, his extremely troubling worldview was dependent on viewing African Americans as inferior. It then followed, he posited, that "slavery was justified & denying African Americans political rights in the future is necessary."

Jubal Early's thinking on racial matters was quite similar to Pollard's. In Early's *A Memoir of the Last Year of Independence in the Confederate States of America*, published in 1867, he argued that slavery had been used during the war "as a catch word to arouse the passions of a fanatical mob." Unfortunately for the South, the civilized world opposed its independence due to the slavery question. Early felt this was unfortunate, since he believed "the war was not made on our part for slavery."

Like Pollard, Early saw slavery in the prewar South as beneficial, writing, "The condition of domestic slavery, as it existed in the South, had not only resulted in a great improvement in the moral and physical condition of the negro race, but had furnished a class of laborers as happy and contented as any in the world, if not more so."[14] He also argued that slavery had been the best way to manage the four million African Americans living in the South: "Reason, common sense, true humanity to the black, as well as the safety of the white race, required that the inferior race should be kept in a state of subordination." Unlike Pollard, Early did not gracefully accept emancipation, believing the former slaves were now free to "starve, to die, and to relapse into barbarism."

Pollard and Early, perhaps *the* two most important propagandists on behalf of the Lost Cause, believed slavery was a benevolent institution that uplifted African Americans, while creating vast wealth for the South and the rest of America. Lee expressed a similar, if less enthusiastic view, when he said—as we have seen previously—during the closing months of the war, "the relation of master and slave, controlled by humane laws and influenced by Christianity and an enlightened public sentiment," was probably the best that could exist between the white and black races. Ironically, despite the central role that slavery played in antebellum southern society, all three denied it was the primary factor in causing the war. Pollard and Lee would have agreed with Early, who said, "the struggle made by the people of the South was not for the institution of slavery, but for the inestimable right of self-government, against the domination of a fanatical faction at the North; and slavery was the mere occasion of the development of the antagonism between the two sections."[15]

Such a view begins to resemble the proverbial Scholastic debates enjoyed by medieval theologians. Behind the intellectual contortions, believers in the Lost Cause looked back longingly at a world that had been dependent on chattel slavery, while also recognizing that slavery would never be accepted as a legitimate reason for having fought such a destructive, demoralizing war. So, despite overwhelming evidence to the contrary, the Lost Cause adherents chose to simply deny that slavery had been a cause of the war, a view that became, in the words of the historian Robert F. Durden, the "cardinal element of the Southern apologia."[16]

The notion that the war wasn't fought over slavery requires so many qualifications as to be an almost meaningless thing to believe. In his "Second Inaugural Address," Lincoln was astute in describing the cause of the war:

> One-eighth of the whole population were colored slaves, not distributed generally over the Union, but localized in the southern part of it. These slaves constituted a peculiar and powerful interest. All knew that this interest was somehow the cause of the war. To strengthen, perpetuate, and extend this interest was the object for which the insurgents would rend the Union even by war, while the Government claimed no right to do more than to restrict the territorial enlargement of it.[17]

Shortly before the war began, the Confederate Vice President Alexander Stephens also made it clear for all time that the war was about slavery: "The new constitution has put at rest, forever, all the agitating questions relating to our peculiar institution African slavery as it exists among us. . . . Our foundations are laid, its cornerstone rests, upon the great truth that the negro is not equal to the white man; that slavery, subordination to the superior race is his natural and normal condition."[18] An editor in Georgia in 1862 was even more succinct: "Negro slavery is the South, and the South is negro slavery."[19]

Additionally, slavery was the central theme in the "Declaration of Causes" proclaimed by Mississippi, Georgia, South Carolina, and Texas after those states seceded.[20] The authors of the Mississippi declaration wrote, "That blow has been long aimed at the institution, and was at the point of reaching its consummation. There was no choice left us but submission to the mandates of abolition, or a dissolution of the Union, whose principles had been subverted to work out our ruin." Many more examples can be provided, of course, but that isn't really necessary. As the historian Charles Dew has shown, "slavery and race were absolutely critical elements in the coming of the war." Dew adds, "defenders of the Lost Cause need only read the speeches and letters of the secession commissioners to learn what was really driving the Deep South to the brink of war in 1860–61."[21]

The proponents of the Lost Cause were more interested in success than accuracy. And their case would be much stronger if they focused on defending states' rights and celebrating the greatness of Robert E. Lee. It made no sense at all to emphasize the role played by slavery in bringing about secession, especially after it had been abolished by the Thirteenth Amendment. Despite all of the various contradictions, the Lost Cause, with Lee as its supreme figurehead, was built upon a foundation of white supremacy. Lee himself embraced that idea, too, though he would have been uncomfortable being deified by the movement.

★   ★   ★

Glorifying the memory of Robert E. Lee proved to be a more straightforward task for his acolytes than denying slavery's role in bringing on the war. Upon hearing the news of Lee's death, Jubal Early remarked, "the loss is a public one, and there are millions of hearts now torn with anguish at the news that has been flashed over the wires to all corners of the civilized world."[22] Shortly after the funeral, Early addressed the veterans of the Army of Northern Virginia, noting in amazement that "such a man went down to his grave a disenfranchised citizen by the edict of his contemporaries—which infamous edict, the fiat of an inexorable despotism, has been forced to be recorded upon the statute book of his native State."[23] In truth, Lee was no longer disenfranchised at the time of his death, but Early was clearly outraged by the North's apparent lack of respect for his chief. He urged his fellow soldiers to erect "an enduring monument to him that will be a standing protest, for all time to come, against the judgment pronounced against him."

It would take a while, but Early eventually achieved his dream of erecting a monument to Lee in Richmond on May 29, 1890, twenty years after his death.[24] On that beautiful spring day, beginning at 6:00 a.m. in the former Confederate capital, roughly 150,000 people gathered for the unveiling of the colossal monument that had been designed by the Frenchmen, Antonio Mercie. Among the honored guests were two of Lee's daughters, Mildred and Mary, and two of his sons, Rooney and Robert Jr. Lee's nephew Fitzhugh, who had recently been governor of Virginia, was the Chief Marshall of the ceremonies. Gen. Joseph Johnston and Jubal Early also played formal roles at the event.

The featured speaker for the dedication ceremony was Colonel Archer Anderson, an executive at Tredegar Iron Works in Richmond. He began his lengthy speech by acknowledging how remarkable it was that the South could

Figure 11.1. Unveiling of the Lee Monument, Richmond 1890. *Source:* E. Benjamin Andrews, *History of the United States*, vol. 5 (New York: Charles Scribner's Sons, 1912).

now enthusiastically honor its military chief, twenty five years after Appomattox.[25] Despite all of the bloodshed and bitterness, the South hadn't been forced to "renounce any glorious memory." Rather, it was "free to heap honors upon their trusted leaders, living or dead." This was something that all Americans should be proud of, he felt.

Anderson's remarks revealed that the Lee cult was in full flower in 1890. At one point, he gushed, "Lee was the purest and best man of action whose career history has recorded." That was high praise indeed in a city that also had monuments to such founding fathers as George Washington and Chief Justice John Marshall. Anderson also declared that no one, even Lee's critics, had ever "discovered one single deviation from the narrow path of rectitude and honor." He even concluded his remarks stating that "it pleased Almighty God to bestow upon these Southern States a man so formed to reflect His attributes of power, majesty, and goodness!" Apparently God had given the South the perfect man, perhaps as a consolation for not granting it victory. It may seem odd that God would reward the South with one hand, while denying it triumph on the battlefield with the other. Regardless, the South had been truly blessed to have had Lee as its leader. Almost everyone in attendance would have agreed with Anderson on that point.

After the main speech, General Johnston pulled the cord that revealed the statue. The *Richmond Dispatch* described what happened next: "The men went wild. Veterans shouted and cried and hugged each other. . . . The women and children waved handkerchiefs, parasols, and fans. The artillery thundered; the musketry followed, volley upon volley."[26] Richmond officially had its Lee monument. Its total height was a mammoth sixty-one feet, two inches. Upon seeing the monument for the first time, a Confederate veteran remarked that he experienced "all the old-time emotions, and his heart told him, 'That's Marse Robert.'" The excitement of the day was so intense that one young boy climbed the Washington Monument in Richmond's Capitol Square—a climb of seventy-five feet—and placed a Confederate flag in the "hands of the Father of his country."

After the ceremony, a reporter for the *New York Times* said of Lee, "his memory is, therefore, a possession of the American people." The *Times* reporter also noted that four or five "old colored men" were in attendance that day. At one point, Jubal Early said to a colleague, "I want to introduce you to two reputable colored gentlemen of Virginia—Benjamin and Pleasant Saunders—two of my old slaves."[27] Benjamin and Pleasant said to the man, according to the reporter, "We is Mars' Jubal's niggers. We is, and we done come over two hundred miles to pay our specs to him." Jubal Early then added, "These are respectable darkies; none of your scalawag niggers." One sees in this anecdote that Early longed for the social relations that existed before the war. The quoted material is also a commentary on the era—the *Times* seemed to give little thought to reporting the story in this way.

Evidence suggests that most of Richmond's African American community opposed the Lee monument. Black members of Richmond's city council voted against funds for both the Lee cornerstone ceremony in 1887 and the 1890 unveiling event.[28] After witnessing the 1890 ceremony, John Mitchell Jr.—an African American editor for the black newspaper *Richmond Planet*—wrote, "This glorification of States Rights Doctrine—the right of secession and the honoring of men who represented that cause fosters in this Republic the spirit of Rebellion and will ultimately result in handing down to generations unborn a legacy of treason and blood."[29]

Outside of the South, the response to the monument was mixed. Some mainstream newspapers like the *New York Times* and the *New York Herald* were mostly supportive. There was also considerable criticism, however, in various newspapers and public forums across the North and West. One withering critique was delivered by Republican Senator John Ingalls of Kansas, in a Memorial Day address at Gettysburg the day after the ceremony in Richmond.[30]

Even though it had been twenty years since the general's death, Ingalls returned to some familiar criticisms. Lee had violated his oath to the Constitution and had committed treason. Ingalls was incredulous that Lee was being celebrated in Richmond on the day before Memorial Day, despite having committed these infamous crimes:

> And yet, by a great object lesson in treason, in disloyalty, in perjury, in violation of faith, of public and private honor, upon the very day that has been for a quarter of a century almost made sacred by the common concurrence of the loyal and patriotic people of the Republic for the consecration of the graves of the Union dead, those who profess to have accepted the results of the war in good faith who profess that they had furled the flag of treason and rebellion forever, who profess that they came back under the Constitution and laws of the United States with honor and patriotism, choose this occasion of all other anniversaries in the 365 days in the year, with every augmentation of insolence which they should copy, a Confederate flag is placed in the hand—the bronze hand—of the statue of Washington!

Cries of shame apparently burst out from the audience after hearing about the Confederate flag being placed in Washington's bronze hand. To many northerners, that appeared to be a particularly provocative act.

Throughout his speech, Ingalls expressed outrage at how *successful* the Lost Cause tradition had become in reframing how the war would be remembered. He was mystified that the South, twenty-five years after the end of the struggle, was apparently teaching its children that only God knew whether the North or the South was right. He responded angrily by recalling, "Millions of human beings were held in slavery, cruel, monstrous, inconceivable in its conditions of humiliation, dishonor and degradation; unending and unrequited toil, helpless ignorance, nameless and unspeakable, families separated at the auction-block and women and children tortured with the lash." Despite this horror, eleven states tried to secede from the Union in order to make "this system of slavery the corner-stone of another social and political fabric." Ingalls was adamant: one side was right and the other was wrong. As a result of the Union's victory, it was now true that "the sun rises upon no master, and sets upon no slave."

While Ingalls believed the North's cause was morally superior, he also appreciated that southerners might want to memorialize their dead and pay out pensions to Confederate veterans. He even believed it was acceptable if they wanted to eulogize the Lost Cause "and carry the stars and bars if they prefer it to the star-bangled banner of the nation." What Ingalls would not accept, however, was the assertion that "Lincoln and Davis, that Grant and Lee, that Logan and Jackson [were] equally entitled to the respect and the reverence of mankind and that God only knows exactly which was right." Such beliefs, according to Ingalls, were "blasphemy," deserving of "rebuke and condemnation."

★　★　★

The editor John Mitchell was also struck by the moral ambiguity of the unveiling ceremony. In an editorial for his newspaper, he wrote, "The honoring of the Confederacy was indulged in while everyone in that joyous throng stood ready to declare to you that the South was right and the North was wrong. 'Not beaten but overpowered,' they would say."[31] Perplexed by the display of Confederate emblems, Mitchell wondered what all of this could possibly mean.

John Mitchell's parents had been house slaves. After graduating from Richmond Normal and High School in 1881, Mitchell began his career as a teacher. Later, he became the editor of the *Richmond Planet*, a black weekly founded in 1883. Known as the "fighting editor," he also served on the Richmond City Council from Jackson Ward, a mostly black neighborhood. In defending his council vote against funds for the Lee ceremony, he had said that those who bore the "clinking chains of slavery" should not be expected to vote for such an event.[32]

Figure 11.2. John Mitchell Jr., editor of the *Richmond Planet. Source:* The Library of Virginia.

In his editorial, Mitchell wondered what Americans were teaching rising generations in the South by placing "Lee on equality with Washington." He believed this devotion to the Lost Cause showed an improper appreciation of the Union. All of the South's frequent displays on behalf of its former leaders had gone too far, according to Mitchell. It was doing the South no good, while actually causing "much harm." In another observation in his newspaper, shortly after the Lee monument ceremony, Mitchell offered an African American perspective on Civil War memory: "The Negro was in the Northern processions on Decoration Day and in the Southern ones, if only to carry buckets of ice-water. He put up the Lee monument, and should the time come, will be there to take it down. He's black and sometimes greasy, but who could do without the Negro."[33]

Unfortunately for Mitchell and fellow African Americans, things would get much worse in the South before they would get better. The historian David Blight has noted that "the unveiling of the Lee monument came just before the final substantive national debate the country would have in the nineteenth century over the black man's right to vote and the responsibilities of the government to protect that right."[34] Alas, over the next two decades, African Americans would become disenfranchised in each of the former Confederate states including Virginia. "High atop his monument in Richmond," writes Blight, "Lee represented many of the inspirations Southerners now took from their heritage: a sense of pride and soldierly honor, an end to defeatism, and a new sense of racial mastery."[35]

★   ★   ★

The renowned English historian George Macaulay Trevelyan once quipped that social history was "history with the politics left out." Similarly, the hagiographic treatment of Lee in the decades after the war was southern history with the African American experience left out. Within this tradition, Lee's role in upholding a social system based on chattel slavery was reframed as a noble defense of a Constitution he loved. Hardly mentioned at all was his reactionary opposition to the essential task of transforming freedmen into citizens after the war. Overall, the heroic Lee tradition portrayed him as an opponent of slavery before the war and a lead actor in bringing about sectional reconciliation afterward. The centrality of the idea of white supremacy to his actions and worldview were effectively erased from the historical record by his disciples. The beatified Lee required purity, unsullied by the fierce racial debates of his time. As a result of the Lost Cost mythmaking, however, posterity has "lost" a more accurate appraisal of the man.

The famous novelist Henry James noticed this absence of the African American experience when he visited Richmond in 1905 for a travel book he was writing. Upon arriving in the city, he felt it "had grown lurid, fuliginous, vividly tragic."[36] As he wandered around the town that had sent roughly 350,000 slaves downriver in the decades before the Civil War, he became conscious that something essential was *missing*. It was only after standing in front of the Lee monument lost in thought that he eventually figured out the riddle.

James admired the "equestrian statue of the Southern hero" and felt it was a monument of considerable artistic merit.[37] The surrounding neighborhood, however, was desolate: "somehow empty in spite of being ugly, and yet expressive in spite of being empty." It was only upon turning his back on the monument and the surrounding area that James was able to solve "the riddle of the historic poverty of Richmond."[38]

For James, Richmond's problem was that it had "worshipped false gods." He then concluded, "As I looked back, before leaving it, at Lee's stranded, bereft image, which time and fortune have so cheated of half the significance, and so, I think of half the dignity, of great memorials, I recognized something more than the melancholy of a lost cause. The whole infelicity speaks of a cause that could never have been gained."[39] Fighting to uphold a slave-based social system—a project described by James as "extravagant, fantastic, and today pathetic in its folly"—wasn't just a lost cause, it was an unwinnable cause. Going further, one might say it was unwinnable because it was a *bad* cause that violated the essence of our founding principles. Only by restoring the black experience to the narrative does that become clear to all Americans.

APPENDIX A

A correspondent of the *New York Herald*, writing from Richmond, gives the following account of an interview with General Lee:

"Richmond, Virginia, April 21, 1865," In order if possible to get some clear light for the solution of the new complications growing out of the murder of President Lincoln, I yesterday sought and obtained an interview with that distinguished soldier and leader of the rebel armies, General Robert E. Lee, and was permitted to draw out his views on the very important questions suggested. It is proper to say that my reception was everything that could be expected from a gentleman who has always been considered a type of the once famous chivalry, and, I had almost said, nobility of Virginia. Pen and ink sketches of General Lee have been so numerously made of late by newspaper writers that any attempt at this time by me in that direction would be a work of supererogation. I may simply say that the firm step, the clear voice, the bright, beaming countenance, the quick intelligence, the upright form, and the active manner of the General very strongly belie the portraitures of him which are so common. All the vigour and animation and ability of ripe manhood are prominently conspicuous in his bearing. His venerable white hair and beard simply inspire respect for the mature ideas and deliberate expressions that come from this conspicuous rebel leader, but in nowise convey an impression of decay or old age. It was certainly embarrassing to me, on introducing the object of my visit, to say that I intended to lay his political views before the public, as his military career had already been. His reply, "I am a paroled prisoner," at once appealed to my sympathy. A frank, generous man, how far may I properly question him without touching upon his views of honour in reference to his parole? But when he added, "I have never been a politician, and know but little of political leaders; I am a soldier," I felt easier. I assured him that I had no desire to offend his sensibility, or tempt him to violate any presumable obligation under his parole; but that, being prominently identified with the rebellion, his views on the questions arising out of that rebellion would be of great interest at the present moment, and doubtless of great importance and influence in the settlement of the troubles agitating the country, and with this view only I called upon him. He replied that the prominence he held was unsought by himself and distasteful to him. That he preferred retirement and seclusion. But was ready to make any sacrifice or perform any honourable act that would tend to the restoration of peace and tranquillity to the country. It will not be possible to relate the extended conversation that ensued with any approach to exactness, no notes having been taken, and it will not, therefore, be attempted; but I will confine myself to a record of the views expressed by General Lee on several prominent topics, as I understood him to express himself. The General's attention was directed to his written and spoken determination to draw his sword in defence only of his native State, and the inquiry was raised as to what he considered the defence of Virginia, and what degree of deliberation he had given to that expression. He stated that, as a firm and honest believer in the doctrine of State rights, he had considered his allegiance due primarily to the State in which he was born and where he had always resided. And, although he was not an advocate of secession at the outset, when Virginia seceded he honestly believed it his duty to abide her fortune. He opposed secession to the last, foreseeing the ruin it was sure to entail. But when the State withdrew from the Union he had no resource, in his view of honour and patriotism, but to abide her fortunes. He went with her, intending to remain merely a private citizen. When he resigned his commission in the United States' army he had no intention of taking up arms in any other service, and least of all in a service antagonistic to the United States. His State, however, called for him, and entertaining the fixed principles he did of State sovereignty, he had no alternative but to accept the service to which he was called. When he made use of the declarations that have been so extensively quoted of late he had accepted only a commission from Virginia. Subsequently, when Virginia attached herself to the Southern Confederacy, the same political impressions impelled him to follow her, and when he accepted service under the Rebel Government he did so on the principle that he was defending his native State. And yet, by the act of accepting such service he was bound in honour to serve in any part of the Confederacy where he might be called, without reference to State lines; and the reconciliation with his former avowal, if any were necessary, was found in the fact that Virginia, standing or falling with the other Southern States, in defending them all he was defending the one to which he considered his allegiance primarily due. As to the effect of his surrender, he was free to say it was a severe blow to the South, but not a crushing blow. It was of military, not political, significance. I asked, "Was not that surrender a virtual surrender of the doctrine of State rights?" "By no means," the General replied. "When the South shall be wholly subdued there will then undeniably be a surrender of that doctrine. But the surrender of a single army is simply a military necessity. The army of Northern Virginia was surrendered because further resistance on its part would only entail a useless sacrifice of life. But that army was merely a part of the force of the South. When the South shall be forced to surrender all its forces, and returns to the Union, it indisputably, by that act, surrenders its favourite doctrine of secession. That principle will then be settled by military power." On this question of State sovereignty the General contends that there exists a legitimate casus belli. In the convention that formed the organic law of the land the question of defining the relative powers of the States and their relation to the general Government was raised, but after much discussion was dropped and left unsettled. It has remained so unsettled until the present time. The war is destined to set it at rest. It is unfortunate that it was not settled at the outset; but, as it was not settled then, and had to be settled at some time, the war raised on this issue cannot be considered treason. If the South is forced to submission in this contest, it of course can only be looked upon as the triumph of Federal power over State rights, and the forced annihilation of the latter. With reference to the war in the abstract, the General declared it as his honest belief that peace was practicable two years ago, and has been practicable from that time to the present day whenever the general Government should see fit to seek it, giving any reasonable chance for the country to escape the consequences which the exasperated North seemed determined to impose. The South has, during all this time, been ready and anxious for peace. They have been looking for some word or expression of compromise or conciliation from the North upon which they might base a return to the Union. They were not prepared, nor are they yet, to come and beg for terms; but were ready to accept any fair and honourable terms, their own political views being considered. The question of slavery did not lie in the way at all. The best men of the South have long been anxious to do away with this institution, and were quite willing to-day to see it abolished. They consider slavery forever dead. But with them, in relation to this subject, the question has ever been, "What will you do with the freed people?" That is the serious question to-day, and one that cannot be winked at. It must be met practically and treated intelligently. The negroes must be disposed of, and if their disposition can be marked out the matter of freeing them is at once settled. But unless some humane course is adopted, based on wisdom and Christian principles, you do a gross wrong and injustice to the whole negro race in setting them free. And it is only this consideration that has led the wisdom, intelligence, and Christianity of the South to support and defend the institution up to this time. The conversation then turned into other channels, and finally touched upon the prospects of peace. And here a very noticeable form of expression was used by the General. In speaking of the probable course of the Administration towards the South, the General remarked that "if we do" so and so. I immediately called his attention to the expression, and sought an explanation of the sense in which he used the pronoun "we," but obtained none other than a marked repetition of it. It was noticeable throughout the entire interview that in no single instance did he speak of the Southern Confederacy, nor of the Yankees, nor the Rebels. He frequently alluded to the country, and expressed most earnestly his solicitude for its restoration to peace and tranquillity, cautiously avoiding any expression that would imply the possibility of its disintegration. Throughout all the conversation he manifested an earnest desire that such counsels should prevail and such policies be pursued as would conduce to an immediate peace, implying in his remarks that peace was now at our option. But he was particular to say that should arbitrary or vindictive or revengeful policies be adopted the end was not yet. There yet remained a great deal of vitality and strength in the South. There were undeveloped resources and hitherto unavailable sources of strength which harsh measures on our part would call into action; and that the South could protract the struggle for an indefinite period. We might, it was true, destroy all that remained of the country east of the Mississippi river by a lavish expenditure of men and means; but then we would be required to fight on the other side of the river, and, after subduing them there, we would be compelled to follow them into Mexico, and thus the struggle would be prolonged until the whole country would be impoverished and ruined; and this we would be compelled to do if extermination, confiscation, and general annihilation and destruction are to be our policy. For if a people are to be destroyed they will sell their lives as dearly as possible. The assassination of the President was then spoken of. The General considered this event in itself one of the most deplorable that could have occurred. As a crime it was unexampled and beyond execration. It was a crime that no good man could approve from any conceivable motive. Undoubtedly the effort would be made to fasten the responsibility of it upon the South; but, from his intimate acquaintance with the leading men of the South, he was confident there was not one of them who would sanction or approve it. The scheme was wholly unknown in the South before its execution, and would never have received the slightest encouragement had it been known, but, on the contrary, the most severe execration. I called the General's attention, at this point, to a notice that had been printed in the Northern papers, purporting to have been taken from a paper published in the interior of the South, proposing for the sum of 1,000,000 dollars to undertake the assassination of the President and his Cabinet. The General affirmed that he had never seen nor heard of such a proposition, nor did he believe that it had ever been printed in the South, though if it had, it had been permitted merely as the whim of some crazy person that could possibly amount to nothing. Such a crime was an anomaly in the history of our country, and we had yet before its perpetration to learn that it was possible of either earnest conception or actual execution. It was a most singular and remarkable expression to escape the lips of such a man as General Lee that "the South was never more than half in earnest in this war." I cannot attempt to translate this remark or elucidate it. Its utterance conveyed to me the impression that the South was most heartily sick of the war, and anxious to get back into the Union and to peace. The General added that they went off after political leaders in a moment of passion and under the excitement of fancied wrongs, honestly believing that they were entering a struggle for an inalienable right and a fundamental principle of their political creed. A man should not be judged harshly for contending for that which he honestly believes to be right. Such was the position of the vast majority of the Southern people now. And now that they are defeated they consider that they have lost everything that is worth contending for in the Government. They have sacrificed home, friends, property, health, all on this issue. Men do not make such sacrifices for nothing. They have made the sacrifice from honest convictions, and now that they have lost in the issue they feel that they have no interests left in this country. It is the opinion of General Lee that unless moderation and liberality be exercised towards them the country will lose its best people. Already, he says, they are seeking to expatriate themselves, and numerous schemes are started to go to Mexico, to Brazil, to Canada, to France, or elsewhere. He is called upon frequently to discountenance and suppress such undertakings. The country needs these young men. They are its bone and sinew, its intelligence and enterprise, its hope for the future; and wisdom demands that no effort be spared to keep them in the country and pacify them. It was a most noticeable feature of the conversation that General Lee, strange as it may appear, talked throughout as a citizen of the United States. He seemed to plant himself on the national platform, and take his observations from that standpoint. He talked calmly, deliberately, earnestly, but with no show of interest other or different from what might be expected from an honest believer in his peculiar opinions. The conversation, which had been greatly protracted, so much so that I became uneasy for fear of trespassing on time that I had no right to claim, terminated with some allusions to the terms of peace. Here there was, perhaps naturally and properly, more reticence than on any other topic. But it was plain from what transpired that the only question in the way of immediate peace was the treatment to be accorded the vanquished. Everything else, by implication, seems to be surrendered. Slavery, State rights, the doctrine of secession, and whatever else of political policy may be involved in the strife is abandoned, the only barrier to an immediate and universal suspension of hostilities and return to the Union being the treatment the national authorities may promise those who have been resisting its power and paramount authority. It is proper to say that this was not so stated by General Lee, but is simply an inference from the conversation that took place on that topic. On the contrary, the General seemed very cautious in regard to terms. In order to get at his views, if possible, I suggested the conservative sentiment of the North, which proposed a general amnesty, to all soldiers and military officers, but that the political leaders of the South be held to a strict accountability. "Would, that be just?" he asked. "What has Mr. Davis done more than any other Southerner that he should be punished? It is true that he has occupied a prominent position as the agent of a whole people, but that has made him no more nor less a rebel than the rest. His acts were the acts of the whole people, and the acts of the whole people were his acts. He was not accountable for the commencement of the struggle. On the contrary, he was one of the last to give his adherence to the secession movement, having strenuously opposed it from the outset and portrayed its ruinous consequences in his speeches and by his writings. Why, therefore, should he suffer more than others?" Of course, it was not my province to discuss those questions, and as this illustration disclosed the bent of the General's mind it was all that I desired to know. In taking leave of the General I took occasion to say that he was greatly respected by a very large body of good men at the North, and that as a soldier he was universally admired, and that it was earnestly hoped that he would yet lead an army of United States' troops in the enforcement of the Monroe doctrine. He thanked me for the expression of Northern sentiment toward himself, but as for more fighting he felt that he was getting too old, his only desire now being to be permitted to retire to private life and end his days in seclusion. It was, I thought, an evidence of painful sadness at heart that prompted the added expression that he would have been pleased had his life been taken in any of the numerous battle fields of which he had fought during this war. While talking on the subject of abolition of slavery, I remarked that it had lately been charged in some of the newspapers of the North that the Custis slaves, some 200 in number, who had been left in General Lee's custody for emancipation, had not been emancipated. The General said this was a mistake. As executor of the will, he was required to emancipate these slaves at a certain time. That time had not arrived when the war broke out. It did arrive one or two years afterwards. At that time he could not get to the courts of the county in which Arlington is located to take out the emancipation papers as prescribed by law. But he did take out papers from the Supreme Court of the State in this city, liberating them all, and they are so recorded in the records of the court. He sent word of their freedom to the negroes of Arlington, and the necessary papers were sent to those at the White House, and to all others that could be reached, and they were all thus liberated, together with a number who were either the General's or Mrs. Lee's private property.

APPENDIX B

Letter from Richard Dana[1]

Boston, August 24, 1868
    The Honorable
        William M. Evarts,
            Attorney General,
                Sir,

           While preparing with yourself, before you assumed your present post, to perform the honorable duty the President had assigned to us, of conducting the trial of Jefferson Davis, you know how much my mind was moved, from the first, by doubts of the expediency of trying him at all. The reasons which prevented my presenting those doubts no longer exist, and they have so ripened into conviction that I feel it my duty to lay them before you in form as you now hold a post of official responsibility for the proceeding.

After the most serious reflection, I cannot see any good reason why the Government should make a question of whether the late civil war was treason and whether Jefferson Davis took any part in it, and submit those questions to the decision of a petit jury of the vicinage of Richmond at nisi prius.

As the Constitution in terms settles the fact that our republic is a state against which treason may be committed, the only constitutional question attending the late war was whether a levying of war against the United States which would otherwise be treason is relieved of that character by the fact that it took the form of secession from the Union by state authority. In other words, the legal issue was, whether secession by a state is a constitutional right, making an act legal and obligatory upon the nation which would otherwise have been treason.

This issue I suppose to have been settled by the action of every department of the Government, by the action of the people itself, and by those events which are definitive in the affairs of men.

The Supreme Court in the Prize Courts (2 Black's Ref) held, by happily a unanimous opinion that acts of the States, whether secession ordinances, or in whatever form cast, could not be brought into the cases, as justifications for the war, and had no legal effect on the character of the war, or on the political status of territory or persons or property, and that the line of enemy's territory was a question fact depending upon the line of bayonets of an actual war. The rule in the Prize Courts has been steadily followed in the Supreme Court since, and in the Circuit Courts, without an intimation of a doubt. That the lawmaking and executive departments have treated this secession and war as treason is matter of history, as well as is the action of the people in the highest sanction of war.

It cannot be doubted that the Circuit Court at the trial will instruct the jury in conformity with these decisions, that the late attempt to establish and sustain by war by independent empire within the United States was treason. The only question of fact submitted to the jury will be whether Jefferson Davis took part in the war. As it is one of the great facts of history that he was its head, civil and military, why should we desire to make a question of it and refer its decision to a jury, with powers to find in the negative or affirmative or to disagree? It is not an appropriate question for the decision of a jury, certainly it is not a fact which a Government should, without great cause, give a jury a chance to ignore.

We know that these indictments are to be tried in what was for five years enemy's territory, which is not yet restored to the exercise of all its political functions, and where the fires are not extinct. We know that it only requires one discontent juror to defeat the Government and give Jefferson Davis and his favorers a triumph. Now, is not such a result one which we must include in our calculation of possibilities? Whatever modes may be legally adopted to draw a jury, or to purge it, and whatever the influence of the court or of counsel, we know that a favorer of treason may get upon the jury. But that is not necessary. A fear of personal violence or social ostracism may be enough to induce one man to withhold his ascent from the verdict, especially as he need not come forward personally, nor give a reason, even in the jury room.

The possible result would be most humiliating to the Government and people of this country, and none the less so from the fact that it would be absurd. The Government would be stopped in the judicial course because it could neither assume nor judicially determine that Jefferson Davis took part in the late civil war. Such a result would also bring into doubt the adequacy of our penal system to deal with such cases as this.

If it were important to secure a verdict as a means of punishing the defendant, the question would present itself differently. But it would be beneath the dignity of the Government and of the issue, to inflict upon him a minor punishment, and, as to a sentence of death, I am sure that, after this lapse of time, and after all that has occurred in the interval, the people of the United States would not desire to see it enforced.

In fine, after the fullest consideration, it seems to me that, by pursuing the trial, the Government can get only a reaffirmation by a Circuit Court at nici prius of a rule of public law settled for this country in every way in which such a matter can be settled, only giving to a jury drawn from the region of the rebellion a chance to disregard the law when announced. It gives that jury a like opportunity to ignore the fact that Jefferson Davis took any part in the late civil war. And one man upon the jury can secure the results. The risk of such absurd and discreditable issues of a great state trial, are assumed for the sake of a verdict which, if obtained, will settle nothing in law or natural practice not now settled, and nothing in fact not now history, while no judgment rendered thereon do we think will be ever executed.

Besides these reasons, and perhaps because of them, I think the public interest in the trial has ceased among the most earnest and loyal citizens.

If your views and those of the President should be in favor of proceeding with the trial, I am confident that I can do my duty as counsel to the utmost of my ability and with all zeal. For my doubts are not what the verdict ought to be. On the contrary, I should feel all the more strongly, if the trial is begun, the importance of victory to the Government, and the necessity of putting forth all power and using all lawful means to secure it. Still, I feel it my duty to say that if the President should judge otherwise, my position in the case is at his disposal.

Very respectfully
Your ob't. ser't.
(signed) Richard H. Dana, Jr.

NOTES

INTRODUCTION

1. Woodrow Wilson, *Robert E. Lee: An Interpretation* (Chapel Hill: University of North Carolina Press, 1924), 21–22. Wilson's address of January 19, 1909, originally appeared in *The North Carolina Record*, May 1909.

2. Douglas Southall Freeman, *R. E. Lee: A Biography*, vol. 4 (New York: Charles Scribner's Sons, 1934), 494.

3. H. W. Crocker, *Robert E. Lee on Leadership* (New York: Three Rivers Press, 2000), 4.

4. *Philadelphia Inquirer*, June 8, 1865.

5. "Ford's Remarks upon Signing a Bill Restoring Rights of Citizenship to General Robert E. Lee," August 5, 1975, *Ford Library and Museum*, https://fordlibrarymuseum.gov/library/speeches/750473.htm.

6. "Career and Character of General T. J. Jackson," *Proceedings of the Southern Historical Society Convention*, vol. 25 (Richmond: Published by the Society, 1897), 109.

7. "Citizenship Is Voted for Robert E. Lee," *New York Times*, July 23, 1975.

8. Elmer Oris Parker, "Why Was Lee Not Pardoned?" *Prologue* 2 (Winter 1970): 181–84.

9. Parker, "Why Was Lee Not Pardoned?" 181.

10. Harry Byrd, "Statement on Senate Floor," February 21, 1974, *Ford Library and Museum*, https://www.fordlibrarymuseum.gov/library/document/0055/1669056.pdf.

11. "Debate on Restoring Lee's Citizenship," July 22, 1975, *Congressional Record*, vol. 121, part 19, 23945.

12. "Debate on Restoring Lee's Citizenship," 23941–42.

13. *Bradford Reporter*, October 26, 1865.

14. LeRoy Graf, ed., "Remarks on the Fall of Richmond," *Andrew Johnson Papers*, vol. 7 (Knoxville: University of Tennessee Press, 1986), 543–46.

15. "The Paroled Rebel Soldiers and the General Amnesty," *New York Times*, June 4, 1865.

16. *Ohio Farmer* quoted in Cayce Myers, "Southern Traitor or American Hero," *Journalism History* 41, no. 4 (Winter 2016): 215.

17. *Cleveland Morning Leader*, May 16, 1865.

18. *New York Daily Tribune*, March 26, 1866.

19. *Report of the Joint Committee on Reconstruction* (Washington, DC: Government Printing Office, 1866), 133.

20. "Indictment of R. E. Lee Is Found; Box Yields Long-Sought Paper," *New York Times*, January 8, 1937; *New York Herald*, June 13, 1865; *Baltimore Sun*, June 20, 1865; *New Orleans Tribune*, June 25, 1865.

21. Bradley T. Johnson, *Reports of Cases Decided by Chief Justice Chase* (New York: Diossy, 1876), 7.

22. Freeman, *R. E. Lee*, vol. 4, note 38, 202.

23. David Blight, *Race and Reunion* (Cambridge, MA: Belknap Press, 2001), 1.

24. "Address of Jubal Early," *Proceedings of the Southern Historical Society Convention*, August 14, 1873 (Baltimore: Turnbull Brothers, 1873), 27.

25. Thomas Connelly, *The Marble Man* (Baton Rouge: Louisiana State University Press, 1977), 51.

26. Frederick Douglass, "Address at the Graves of the Unknown Dead," May 30, 1871, *Frederick Douglass Papers*, Library of Congress.

27. "Bombast," *New National Era*, November 10, 1870.

28. Ta-Nehisi Coates, *Between the World and Me* (New York: Random House, 2015), 102.

29. Wynton Marsalis, "Why New Orleans Should Take Down Robert E. Lee's Statue," *Times-Picayune*, December 15, 2015.

30. Henry James, *The American Scene* (London: Chapman and Hall, 1907), 370.

31. James, *The American Scene*, 394.

32. James, *The American Scene*, 371.

CHAPTER 1

1. Elizabeth Varon, *Appomattox: Victory, Defeat, and Freedom at the End of the Civil War* (New York: Oxford University Press, 2014), 9 and 261, note 5. Varon's account of Lee and Grant at Appomattox is invaluable. See also Caroline Janney, *Remembering the Civil War: Reunion and the Limits of Reconciliation* (Chapel Hill: University of North Carolina Press, 2013), 40–73.

2. Robert E. Lee to John C. Breckinridge, March 9, 1865, *U.S. War Department, The War of the Rebellion: Official Record of the Union and Confederate Armies*, ser. I, vol. 46, pt. 2, p. 1295; James Longstreet, *From Manassas to Appomattox: Memoirs of the Civil War in America* (New York: J.B. Lippincott, 1896), 620.

3. Varon, *Appomattox*, 8–9; R. E. Lee to Jefferson Davis, April 12, 1865, *DeButts-Ely collection of Lee family papers, 1749–1914*, Library of Congress.

4. J. William Jones, ed., *Personal Reminiscences, Anecdotes, and Letters of Gen. Robert E. Lee* (New York: D. Appleton, 1867), 297.

5. Jones, *Personal Reminiscences*, 297.

6. Jones, *Personal Reminiscences*, 297.

7. Robert E. Lee to Jefferson Davis, April 20, 1865, *DeButts-Ely collection*.

8. Varon, *Appomattox*, 42.

9. *OR*, 46, (3), 619, 641, 665–66. Preceding page numbers are provided for the complete correspondence between Lee and Grant at Appomattox.

10. Ulysses S. Grant, *Personal Memoirs of U. S. Grant* (New York: Da Capo Press, 1982), 550.

11. Grant, *Personal Memoirs*, 551.

12. Grant to Lee, *OR*, 46 (3), 619.

13. Grant to Lee, *OR*, 46 (3), 642.

14. Grant to Lee, *OR*, 46 (3), 642.

15. Brooks Simpson, *Let Us Have Peace* (Chapel Hill: University of North Carolina Press, 1997), 82; Varon, *Appomattox*, 60–61; John Russell Young, *Around the World with General Grant* (New York: Subscription Book Department, 1879), 445.

16. "Correspondence between Lee and Grant," *New York Times*, March 21, 1865; Lee and Grant correspondence, *OR*, 46 (2), 824–26.

17. Stanton quoted in Brooks Simpson, *Ulysses S. Grant: Triumph over Adversity* (Minneapolis, MN: Houghton Mifflin, 2000), 411; Stanton to Grant, *OR*, 47 (3), 285.

18. "Grant's Terms to Lee," *New York Times*, April 26, 1865.

19. Charles Marshall, *Appomattox: An Address* (Baltimore: Guggenheimer, Weil, 1894), 13.

20. J. William Jones, ed., *Life and Letters of Robert E. Lee: Soldier and Man* (New York: Neale Publishing, 1906), 369.

21. Jones, *Life and Letters*, 369.

22. Emory Thomas, *Robert E. Lee: A Biography* (New York: W.W. Norton, 1997), passim; Freeman, *R. E. Lee*, vol. 4, passim.

23. Fitzhugh Lee, *Robert E. Lee* (New York: D. Appleton, 1894), 42.

24. Frederick Maurice, ed., *Lee's Aid-de-Camp* (Lincoln: University of Nebraska Press, 2000), 173.

25. Lee to unnamed relative quoted in *Confederate Veteran*, January 1917, vol. 25, 308.

26. Jones, *Life and Letters*, 380.

27. Jones, *Life and Letters*, 380.

28. Grant, *Personal Memoirs*, 552–53.

29. Andrew Johnson, *Proclamation 157—Declaring That Peace, Order, Tranquility, and Civil Authority Now Exists in and throughout the Whole of the United States of America*, August 20, 1866, http://www.presidency.ucsb.edu/ws/?id=71992/.

30. *Surrender at Appomattox: First-hand Accounts of Robert E. Lee's Surrender to Ulysses S. Grant* (Wetware Media, 2011), passim; Charles Marshall, *Appomattox*, passim; Varon, *Appomattox*, 51–62.

31. Grant to Lee, *OR* 46 (3), 665.

32. Bruce Catton, *U. S. Grant and the American Military Tradition* (New York: Open Road, 2013). Kindle edition.

33. Varon, *Appomattox*, 62.

34. Varon, *Appomattox*, 62; John Y. Simon, ed., *The Papers of Ulysses S. Grant*, January 1–September 30, 1867, vol. 15 (Carbondale: Southern Illinois Press, 1967), 214.

35. Simpson, *Let Us Have Peace*, 87.

36. Admiral Porter, *Incidents and Anecdotes of the Civil War* (New York: D. Appleton, 1886), 314.

37. Simpson, *Let Us Have Peace*, 78.

38. John Fabian Witt, *Lincoln's Code: The Laws of War in American History* (New York: Free Press, 2012), 286–87.

39. E. P. Alexander, "Lee at Appomattox," *Century Magazine*, vol. 63, 930.

40. Grant to Stanton, *OR* 46 (3), 663.

41. Varon, *Appomattox*, 68–74; Maurice, *Lee's Aide-de-Camp*, 278; Freeman, *R. E. Lee*, vol. 4, 154.

42. Freeman, *R. E. Lee*, vol. 4, 159–63.

43. "Recounting the Dead," *New York Times*, September 30, 2011; "Civil War Casualties," *Civil War Trust*, https://www.civilwar.org/learn/articles/civil-war-casualties.

44. Freeman, *R. E. Lee*, vol. 4, 163; Elizabeth Brown Pryor, *Reading the Man: A Portrait of Robert E. Lee through His Private Letters* (New York: Penguin, 2008), 429.

45. "Still Taking Pictures (Mathew Brady)," *The World*, April 12, 1891, 26. Brady provides us with the correct day for the sitting: "the day but one after he arrived in Richmond." Many accounts get this date wrong.

46. Roy Meredith, *Mr. Lincoln's Camera Man, Mathew B. Brady* (New York: Dover, 1974), 109.

47. Robert Wilson, *Mathew Brady: Portraits of a Nation* (New York: Bloomsbury, 2014), 190–92.

48. Wilson, *Mathew Brady*, 192.

49. Freeman, *R. E. Lee*, vol. 4, 193.

50. Charles Bracelen Flood, *Lee: The Last Years* (Boston: Houghton Mifflin, 1981), 44.

51. Wilson, *Mathew Brady*, 191.

52. Lee's reaction to Lincoln's death: "Interview with Lee," *New York Herald*, April 29, 1865; *Philadelphia Inquirer*, April 19, 1865.

53. Michael Gorman, "Lee the 'Devil' Discovered at Image of War Seminar," *Center for Civil War Photography* 3, no. 1 (February 2006): 1–3.

54. Gorman, "Lee the 'Devil,'" 1–3.

55. *The Providence Journal* piece published in *Bangor Daily Whig & Courier*, May 1, 1865; Varon, *Appomattox*, 185–86.

56. "Interview with Lee," *New York Herald*, April 29, 1865; Varon, *Appomattox*, 186–89. Elizabeth Varon provides an excellent discussion of this important interview.

57. "Jeff Davis to the Rebel Congress," *New York Times*, January 19, 1863.

58. Henry Cleveland, ed., *Alexander H. Stephens, in Public and Private: With Letters and Speeches, Before, During, and Since the War* (Philadelphia, 1886), 717–29.

59. Lee quoted in Brown Pryor, *Reading the Man*, 433.

CHAPTER 2

1. George Alfred Townsend, *The Life, Crime, and Capture of John Wilkes Booth* (New York: Dick & Fitzgerald, 1865), 5.

2. Michael Kauffman, *American Brutus: John Wilkes Booth and the Lincoln Conspiracies* (New York: Random House, 2004), passim; Townsend, *Life, Crime, and Capture*, passim.

3. Hans Trefousse, *Andrew Johnson: A Biography* (New York: W.W. Norton, 1989), 193–95.

4. John Rhodehamel and Louise Taper, ed., *"Right or Wrong, God Judge Me" The Writings of John Wilkes Booth* (Urbana: University of Illinois Press, 2000), 146.

5. Gideon Welles, *Diary of Gideon Welles*, vol. 2 (Boston: Houghton Mifflin, 1911), 286.

6. Trefousse, *Andrew Johnson*, 194.

7. Graf, "Remarks on the Fall of Richmond," *Johnson Papers* 7 (1986): 543–44.

8. James Blaine, *Twenty Years of Congress*, vol. 2 (Norwich: Henry Bill Publishing, 1884), 8.

9. Edward Neill, *Reminiscences of the Last Year of President Lincoln's Life* (St. Paul, MN: Pioneer Press, 1885), 16–17.

10. William Marvel, *Lincoln's Autocrat: The Life of Edwin Stanton* (Chapel Hill: University of North Carolina Press, 2015), 370. Accounts differ as to what Stanton actually said at the time.

11. "Funeral of Abraham Lincoln," *New York Times*, April 20, 1865.

12. Marvel, *Lincoln's Autocrat*, 368–70; Stanton to Charles Francis Adams, April 15, 1865, *Edwin Stanton Papers*, Library of Congress.

13. Simpson, *Let Us Have Peace*, 91–93.

14. Welles, *Diary*, vol. 2, 289; "The Succession," *New York Times*, April 16, 1865.

15. Jacob Schuckers, *The Life of Salmon Portland Chase* (New York: D. Appleton, 1874), 518–19.

16. "The New President," *New York Times*, April 16, 1865.

17. Trefousse, *Andrew Johnson*, 188–92. Trefousse's account appears to be the most balanced.

18. Biographical sketch of Johnson: Trefousse, *Andrew Johnson*, passim; Annette Gordon-Reed, *Andrew Johnson* (New York: Time Books, 2011), passim; Eric McKitrick, *Andrew Johnson and Reconstruction* (New York: Oxford University Press, 1960), passim.

19. Trefousse, *Andrew Johnson*, 85.

20. Trefousse, *Andrew Johnson*, 44.

21. Douglass quoted in Gordon-Reed, *Johnson*, 2.

22. Trefousse, *Andrew Johnson*, 58.

23. Trefousse, *Andrew Johnson*, 236.

24. Gordon-Reed, *Johnson*, 3.

25. Frank Moore, ed., *Speeches of Andrew Johnson* (Boston: Little, Brown, 1865), 77–176.

26. Moore, *Speeches of Andrew Johnson*, 176–290.

27. Marvell, *Stanton*, 371.

28. Earl of Clarendon, *The History of the Rebellion and Civil Wars in England*, vol. 1 (Oxford: Clarendon Press, 1826), 292.

29. Welles, *Diary*, vol. 2, 290–91.

30. John Nicolay, *Abraham Lincoln—Condensed* (New York: The Century Co. 1919), 532.

31. Marvel, *Stanton*, 369.

32. Welles, *Diary*, vol. 2, 290–91.

33. Wade quoted in Trefousse, *Andrew Johnson*, 197; George W. Julian, *Political Recollections, 1840–1872* (Chicago: Jansen, McClurg, 1883), 257.

34. Trefousse, *Andrew Johnson*, 197–98.

35. Julian, *Recollections*, 243–44.

36. "George W. Julian Journal—The Assassination of Lincoln," *Indiana Magazine of History* 11, no. 4 (1915), 324–27.

37. Chandler quoted in Martha Hodes, *Mourning Lincoln* (New Haven, CT: Yale University Press, 2015), 91.

38. Hodes, *Mourning Lincoln*, 109–14.

39. "Our National Loss," *New York Times*, April 17, 1865.

40. Ralph Waldo Emerson, "Abraham Lincoln," http://www.bartleby.com/90/11 15.html.

41. Herman Melville, "The Martyr," https://www.poetryfoundation.org/poems/55 909/the-martyr-56d237ee35044.

42. Alonzo Quint, *Three Sermons Preached in the North Congregational Church, New Bedford, Mass* (New Bedford, MA: Mercury Job Press, 1865), 45.

43. Quint, *Three Sermons Preached*, 33.

44. Quint, *Three Sermons Preached*, 37.

45. Quint, *Three Sermons Preached*, 43.

46. Flood, *The Last Years*, 58; Myrta Lockett Avary, *Dixie after the War* (New York: Doubleday, 1906), 89.

47. Blaine, *Twenty Years of Congress*, vol. 2, 14–15.

48. See *Andrew Johnson papers, 1783–1947*, Library of Congress.

49. Linskill to Johnson, *Johnson Papers*, June 7, 1865.

50. Martha Hodes makes this point brilliantly in *Mourning Lincoln*. See also Drew Gilpin Faust, *This Republic of Suffering: Death and the American Civil War* (New York: Random House, 2008).

51. Gilpin Faust, *Republic of Suffering*, xii.

52. Walt Whitman, *When Lilacs Last in the Dooryard Bloom'd*, https://www.poetryfoun dation.org/poems/45480/when-lilacs-last-in-the-dooryard-bloomd.

53. Daniel Mark Epstein, *Lincoln and Whitman* (New York: Random House, 2004), passim.

54. LeRoy Graf, *The Papers of Andrew Johnson*, vol. 7, has many of the speeches to the various delegations.

55. Graf, *Johnson Papers*, vol. 7, 610–15.

56. "Restoration of the Stars and Stripes," *New York Times*, April 18, 1865.

57. Frank Freidel, *Francis Lieber: Nineteenth Century Liberal* (Baton Rouge: Louisiana State Press, 1947), 358; See also Witt, *Lincoln's Code* on Lieber.

58. Stanton to Holt, *Edwin McMasters Stanton Papers*, Library of Congress, May 2, 1865; Holt reply included in *Stanton Papers*.

59. "Rewards for the Arrest of Jefferson Davis and Others," *American Presidency Project*, May 2, 1865, http://www.presidency.ucsb.edu/ws/?pid=72356.

60. Ellis Paxson Oberholtzer, *A History of the United States*, vol. 1 (New York: Macmillan, 1917), 10–16; William Blair, *Why Didn't the North Hang Some Rebels? The Postwar Debate over Punishment for Treason* (Milwaukee, WI: Marquette University Press, 2004), 8–9.

61. Wendell Phillips, "The Lesson of President Lincoln's Death," April 23, 1865, 15, https://archive.org/details/universalsuffrag00beec.

62. Phillips, "The Lesson of President Lincoln's Death."

63. *New York Tribune*, May 1, 1865.

64. *Cleveland Morning Leader*, May 16, 1865.

65. *Ohio Farmer* piece quoted in Cayce Myers, "Southern Traitor or American Hero," *Journalism History* 41, no. 4 (Winter 2016): 215. This article provides an excellent sampling of newspaper accounts.

66. "The Rebel Chiefs," *Harper's Weekly*, May 13, 1865, 290.

67. "The Death of Slavery," *The Liberator*, May 5, 1865.

68. *New York Times*, April 30, 1865.

69. "The Paroled Rebel Soldiers," *New York Times*, June 4, 1865.

70. *Raftsman's Journal*, August 16, 1865.

CHAPTER 3

1. John Savage, ed., *The Life and Public Services of Andrew Johnson* (New York: Edward and Jenkins, 1865), 346–49.

2. John C. Underwood Papers, *Library of Congress*; Patricia Hickin, "John C. Underwood and the Antislavery Movement in Virginia, 1847–1860," *Virginia Magazine of History and Biography* 73 (1965), 156–68; Richard Lowe, *Republicans and Reconstruction in Virginia, 1856–70* (Charlottesville: University Press of Virginia, 1991), 34–35; "John C. Underwood," *Encyclopedia Virginia*, https://www.encyclopediavirginia.org/Underwood_John_C_1809-1873#start_entry.

3. *Petersburg Index*, May 10, 1866.

4. John Niven, *Salmon P. Chase: A Biography* (New York: Oxford University Press, 1995), 434.

5. *Underwood Papers*, Library of Congress.

6. Underwood to Andrew Johnson, April 21, 1865, *U.S. District Court, Virginia Box*, National Archives and Records Administration, College Park, Maryland.

7. James Randall, *Constitutional Problems Under Lincoln* (New York: D. Appleton, 1926), 98.

8. Underwood to Salmon Chase, April 28, 1865, *NARA*, College Park, Maryland.

9. Bradley T. Johnson, *Reports of Cases Decided by Chief Justice Chase*, 5–7.

10. Johnson, *Reports of Cases*, 6.

11. Johnson, *Reports of Cases*, 6.

12. Johnson, *Reports of Cases*, 6.

13. legislation.gov.uk, http://www.legislation.gov.uk/aep/Edw3Stat5/25/2/section/II; Jonathan White, "The Trial of Jefferson Davis," in *Constitutionalism in the Approach and Aftermath of the Civil War*, ed. Paul D. Moreno and Jonathan O'Neill (New York: Fordham University Press, 2013).

14 "Treason Act: The Facts," *The Guardian*, October 17, 2014.

15. Bruce Lenman, *The Jacobite Risings in Britain, 1689–1746* (London. Eyre Methuen, 1980), 272.

16. White, "The Trial of Jefferson Davis," 113–32; William Blair, *With Malice toward Some* (Chapel Hill: University of North Carolina Press, 2014), 1–66.

17. R. Kent Newmyer, *The Treason Trial of Aaron Burr* (New York: Cambridge University Press, 2012), passim.

18. Newmyer, *The Treason Trial of Aaron Burr*, 62.

19. Allan MacGruder, *John Marshall* (Boston: Houghton Mifflin, 1885), 228.

20. Newmyer, *The Treason Trial of Aaron Burr*, 63.

21. Newmyer, *The Treason Trial of Aaron Burr*, 63.

22. 67 U.S. 635, Supreme Court, Cornell University Law School, https://www.law.cornell.edu/supremecourt/text/67/635.

23. Benjamin Butler to Andrew Johnson, Graf, *Johnson Papers*, 634–37.

24 Testimony of James Speed, *Impeachment Investigation: Testimony Taken before the Judiciary Committee of the House of Representatives* (Washington, DC: Government Printing Office, 1867), 798–99.

25. Johnson quoted in Graf, "Remarks on the Fall of Richmond," *Johnson Papers*, 543–44.

26. Letter from Francis Pierpont to Stanton, May 14, 1865, *Francis H. Pierpont Government Executive Papers, 1861–1865*, The Library of Virginia, Richmond, Virginia.

27. "Indictment of Davis," *New York Times*, May 27, 1865; White, "The Trial of Jefferson Davis," 113–32.

28. *Philadelphia Inquirer*, June 8, 1865.

29. "Behind the Closed Door of the Grand Jury," *New York Times*, February 6, 1949.

30. *Philadelphia Inquirer*, June 8, 1865.

31. "Indictment of R. E. Lee Is Found; Box Yields Long-Sought Paper," *New York Times*, January 8, 1937; *New York Herald*, June 13, 1865; *Baltimore Sun*, June 20, 1865; *New Orleans Tribune*, June 25, 1865. List of individuals with ranks compiled by author.

32. *Richmond Commercial Bulletin*, June 15, 1865; "Letter to the Editor," *Richmond Commercial Bulletin*, July 6, 1865.

33. Johnson, *Cases Decided by Chase*, 7.

34. Testimony of Underwood, *Impeachment Investigation*, 578–79.

35. US Circuit Court (5th Circuit), Court Records, 1790–1882. Federal Records collection. Library of Virginia. Richmond.

36. *New York Herald*, June 13, 1865; *New York Times*, June 12, 1865.

37. For numerous accounts of Underwood at the time: Underwood Papers, Library of Congress.

CHAPTER 4

1. Freeman, *R. E. Lee*, vol. 4, 521–24.

2. George Meade, *The Life and Letters of George Gordon Meade*, vol. 2 (New York: Charles Scribner's Sons, 1913), 278–79.

3. Captain Robert E. Lee, ed., *Recollections and Letters of Robert E. Lee* (New York: Dover Publications, 2007), 168.

4. Lee, *Recollections and Letters*, 168.

5. *Report of the Joint Committee on Reconstruction*, 136.

6. Freeman, *R. E. Lee*, vol. 4, 198–200.

7. Captain Lee, *Recollections of Lee*, 166.

8. Freeman, *R. E. Lee*, vol. 4, 200–203.

9. Letter from Lee to Captain Tatnall quoted in Captain Lee, *Recollections of Lee*, 163.

10. Brown Pryor, *Reading the Man*, 310–11; See also Anthony Gaughan, *The Last Battle of the Civil War* (Baton Rouge: Louisiana State University Press, 2011).

11. Jonathan T. Dorris, *Pardon and Amnesty under Lincoln and Johnson* (Chapel Hill: University of North Carolina Press, 1953), 95–135.

12. "President Johnson's Amnesty Proclamation," May 29, 1865, Library of Congress; Text of Proclamation also in *New York Times*, May 30, 1865.

13. James Speed, June 7, 1865, *The Reports of Committees of the House of Representatives* (Washington, DC: Government Printing Office, 1866), 1086.

14. Welles, *Diary* (2), 301–307.

15. Testimony of Grant, *Impeachment Investigation*, 827.

16. Underwood to Johnson, May 17, 1865, Graf, *Johnson Papers* (7), 85.

17. Underwood to Johnson, 387.

18. Freeman, *R. E. Lee*, vol. 4, 203.

19. Adam Badeau, *Grant in Peace from Appomattox to Mount McGregor* (Hartford, CT: S.S. Scranton, 1887), 25.

20. Badeau, *Grant in Peace*, 25.

21. J. William Jones, *Personal Reminiscences of Lee*, 201.

22. Jones, *Personal Reminiscences of Lee*, 201.

23. Simon, *Papers of Grant* (15), 210–13.

24. Simon, *Papers of Grant* (15), 150.

25. Lee & Grant correspondence, *OR*, 46 (2), 824–26.

26. Stanton to Grant, *OR*, 47 (3), 285.

27. Lee and Grant correspondence, *OR*, 46 (2), 825–26.

28. James Speed quoted in *Official Opinions of the Attorneys General*, vol. 11 (Washington, DC: W.H. & O.H. Morrison, 1869), 205–206.

29. N. P. Chipman, *The Tragedy of Andersonville* (San Francisco: Blair-Murdoch, 1911), 41.

30. Simon, *Papers of Grant* (17), 210–14.

31. Simon, *Papers of Grant* (15), 204.

32. Grant quoted in Badeau, *Grant in Peace*, 31.

33. Simon, *Papers of Grant* (15), 204.

34. Simpson, *Let Us Have Peace*, 109.

35. Simpson, *Let Us Have Peace*, 109.

36. Speed to L. H. Chandler, June 20, 1865. *Attorney General's papers*, NARA, College Park, Maryland.

37. Testimony of Grant, *Impeachment Investigation*, 825–45. Grant gave a similar account in an interview with the *New York Herald*, July 24, 1878.

38. Badeau, *Grant in Peace*, 25–26.

39. Speed to L. H. Chandler, June 20, 1865. *Attorney General's papers*, NARA, College Park, MD. A copy of this letter that was dated incorrectly was later circulated widely. The transcription provided is from the original letter at the National Archives.

40. J. H. Ashton to Fielding Edwards, June 13, 1865. *Attorney General's papers*, NARA, College Park, Maryland.

41. Adam Badeau, *Military History of Ulysses S. Grant*, vol. 3 (New York: D. Appleton, 1867), 2.

42. Hamlin Garland, *Ulysses S. Grant: His Life and Character* (New York: Doubleday & McClure, 1898), 332–33.

43. "Lincoln's Terms of Peace," *The Sun*, May 24, 1885.

44. *New York Herald*, July 24, 1885.

45. *Joseph S. Fowler Papers*, Library of Congress.

CHAPTER 5

1. Lee to W. H. Taylor quoted in Walter Herron Taylor, *Four Years with General Lee* (New York: D. Appleton, 1878), 155.

2. Captain Lee, *Recollections of Lee*, 177–78.

3. Captain Lee, *Recollections of Lee*, 174.

4. Captain Lee, *Recollections of Lee*, 171.

5. Jones, *Life and Letters*, 202.

6. Jones, *Life and Letters*, 205–206.

7. Dorris, *Pardon and Amnesty*, 141–44.

8. Dorris, *Pardon and Amnesty*, 141.

9. Dorris, *Pardon and Amnesty*, 141.

10. Welles, *Diary* (2), 358.

11. Welles, *Diary* (2), 358.

12. "End of the Assassins," *New York Times*, July 8, 1865.

13. "End of the Assassins."

14. David Miller DeWitt, *The Assassination of Abraham Lincoln and Its Expiation* (New York: Macmillan, 1909), 286.

15. Trefousse, *Johnson*, 223.

16. Captain Lee, *Recollections of Lee*, 172.

17. James Longstreet, *From Manassas to Appomattox* (Philadelphia: J.B. Lippincott, 1896), 633–34.

18. Simon, *Papers of Grant* (15), 401–402.

19. Longstreet, *Manassas to Appomattox*, 634.

20. J. William Jones, *Personal Reminiscences of Lee*, 80–132.

21. Jones, *Personal Reminiscences*, 83–84.

22. Jones, *Personal Reminiscences*, 83–84.

23. Flood, *The Last Years*, 88.

24. *Massachusetts Historical Society*, vol. 46 (Boston, 1913): 145–48.

25. Flood, *The Last Years*, 88.

26. City Missionary Association, *General Robert E. Lee, The Christian Soldier* (Philadelphia: Claxton, Remsen & Haffelfinger, 1873), 181–82.

27. J. William Jones, *Personal Reminiscences of Lee*, 83–84.

28. Lee's Oath and records kept by Davidson at NARA, Special Collections, College Park, Maryland.

29. *Official Opinions of the Attorneys General*, vol. 11, 228.

30. J. William Jones, *Personal Reminiscences of Lee*, 207–08.

31. This is a line from a poem by Alexander Pope that Lee was especially fond of.

32. Johnson to Chase in Bradley T. Johnson, *Cases Decided by Chief Justice Chase*, 9.

CHAPTER 6

1. James Williamson, *Prison Life in the Old Capitol* (West Orange, NJ, 1911), 132–53; "Execution of Wirz," *New York Times*, November 11, 1865.

2. "History of Andersonville Prison," *Andersonville National Historic Site*, National Park Service, https://www.nps.gov/ande/learn/historyculture/camp_sumter_history.htm; General N. P. Chipman, *The Tragedy of Andersonville* (San Francisco: Blair-Murdoch, 1911), 51–110. For a comprehensive account, see *Trial of Henry Wirz*, United States 40th Congress, 2nd Session. 1867–1868. *House Executive Document No. 23*, December 7, 1867, Library of Congress.

3. Henry Wirz, *Andersonville National Historic Site*, National Park Service, https://www.nps.gov/people/henry-wirz.htm.

4. "The Rebel Assassins," *New York Times*, August 22, 1865.

5. Witt, *Lincoln's Code*, 299; Chipman, *Tragedy of Andersonville*, 28–30.

6. *Trial of Henry Wirz*, Library of Congress.

7. Chipman, *Tragedy of Andersonville*, 258–59.

8. "Trial of Captain Wirz," *New York Times*, September 21, 1865.

9. Holt in Chipman, *Tragedy of Andersonville*, 429–35.

10. Chipman, *Tragedy of Andersonville*, 435.

11. Marvell, *Stanton*, 387–90.

12. "The Reconstruction Question," *New York Times*, July 30, 1865.

13. George Washington Julian, "The Punishment of the Rebel Leaders," *Speeches on Political Questions* (New York: Hurd and Houghton, 1872), 328–29.

14. Russell Conwell, *The Life and Public Services of James G. Blaine* (Boston: B.B. Russell, 1884), 272.

15. Chipman, *Tragedy of Andersonville*, 35; *New York Times*, October 19, 1865.

16. Williamson, *Prison Life*, 139–42.

17. Chipman, *Tragedy of Andersonville*, 24; See also 19–26 for Chipman's criticisms of Davis.

18. Captain Lee, *Recollections of Lee*, 230–34.

19. *Report of the Joint Committee on Reconstruction*, 135.

20. *Report of the Joint Committee on Reconstruction*, 135.

21. "Jeff Davis to the Rebel Congress," *New York Times*, January 19, 1863.

22. *OR*, ser. 2, vol. 8, 800–801. Sections 4, 5, and 7 of the act are provided here.

23. *New York Times*, August 3, 1863; see also Witt, *Lincoln's Code*, 258–63.

24. "Remember Fort Pillow!," *New York Times*, April 11, 2014.

25. "The Fort Pillow Massacre," *New York Times*, May 6, 1864.

26. "Confusion and Courage at Olustee," *New York Times*, February 20, 2014.

27. John David Smith, ed., *Black Soldiers in Blue* (Chapel Hill: University of North Carolina Press, 2002), 60–61.

28. *OR*, ser. 2, vol. 4, 954.

29. *OR*, ser. 2, vol. 6, 194; see also Howard Westwood, "Captive Black Union Soldiers in Charleston *What to Do?*," Gregory J. W. Urwin, ed., *Black Flag over Dixie* (Carbondale: Southern Illinois University Press, 2004), 38–42.

30. Graf, *Johnson Papers* (9), 377.

31. Thomas J. Ward, *Black Soldiers in Confederate Prisons*, http://www.history.army.mil/html/bookshelves/resmat/civil_war/articles/article_from_AH78w.pdf.

32. Ward, *Black Soldiers*.

33. *OR*, ser. 2, vol. 7, 909.

34. *OR*, ser. 2, vol. 7, 914.

35. *OR*, ser. 2, vol. 7, 914.

36. *Report of the Joint Committee on Reconstruction*, 135.

37. *OR*, ser. 2, vol. 7, 1010–12.

38. *OR*, ser. 2, vol. 7, 606–607.

39. *OR*, ser. 2, vol. 6, 226.

40. *OR*, ser. 2, vol. 7, 691.

41. A. C. Roach, *The Prisoner of War* (Indianapolis, IN: Railroad City Publishers, 1865), 4.

42. Roach, *The Prisoner of War*, 4.

43. See Witt, *Lincoln's Code*, 320, on this important topic.

44. Witt, *Lincoln's Code*, 320.

45. "General Orders No. 100: The Lieber Code," *The Avalon Project*, Yale University, http://avalon.law.yale.edu/19th_century/lieber.asp.

46. *OR*, ser. 2, vol. 7, 33.

CHAPTER 7

1. Julian, "Dangers and Duties of the Hour," *Speeches*, 263.

2. Julian, "Dangers and Duties of the Hour," 263.

3. Julian, "Dangers and Duties of the Hour," 265.

4. Julian, "Dangers and Duties of the Hour," 266–67.

5. Julian, "Dangers and Duties of the Hour," 267–68.

6. Julian, "Dangers and Duties of the Hour," 268.

7. Julian, "Dangers and Duties of the Hour," 290.

8. Julian, *Recollections*, 268.

9. *Cincinnati Gazette* account in *The Daily Journal*, December 4, 1865.

10. *The Daily Journal*, December 4, 1865.

11. Trefousse, *Johnson*, 220; Eric McKitrick, *Andrew Johnson and Reconstruction* (New York: Oxford University Press, 1960), 92.

12. Whitelaw Reid, *After the War: A Southern Tour* (New York: Moore, Wilstach & Baldwin, 1866), 296.

13. Reid, *After the War*, 298.

14. Reid, *After the War*, 300.

15. Testimony of John Minor Botts, *Report of the Joint Committee on Reconstruction*, 114–23; See also Richard Lowe, *Republicans and Reconstruction in Virginia* (Charlottesville: University of Virginia Press, 1991), 52–60.

16. See Richard Lowe, "Testimony from the Old Dominion before the Joint Committee on Reconstruction," *The Virginia Magazine of History and Biography*, vol. 104, no. 3 (Summer 1996): 373–98.

17. Blaine, *Twenty Years of Congress* (2), 70.

18. *The Works of Charles Sumner*, vol. 7 (Boston: Lee and Shepard, 1873), 77.

19. Graf, *Johnson Papers* (6), note 4, 339.

20. David Herbert Donald, *Charles Sumner and the Rights of Man* (New York: Knopf, 1970), 221.

21. Donald, *Charles Sumner*, 221.

22. Donald, *Charles Sumner*, 229.

23. Trefousse, *Johnson*, 237.

24. *New York Times*, June 19, 1865.

25. "Anecdotes of Andrew Johnson," *The Century Magazine* 85 (November 1912): 440.

26. Trefousse, *Johnson*, 180; see also Fawn Brodie, *Thaddeus Stevens: Scourge of the South* (New York: Norton, 1966).

27. McKitrick, *Andrew Johnson*, note 19, 260.

28. *New York Times*, September 10, 1865.

29. *New York Times*, September 10, 1865.

30. Reid, *After the War*, 429.

31. *Report of the Joint Committee on Reconstruction*, III–VI.

32. Alfred Conkling, *The Life and Letters of Roscoe Conkling* (New York: Charles Webster, 1889), 271.

33. Trefousse, *Johnson*, 238.

34. "First Annual Message," December 4, 1865, http://www.presidency.ucsb.edu/ws/?pid=29506.

35. *OR*, ser. 2, vol. 8, 844–55.

36. Testimony of Speed, *Impeachment Investigation*, 799.

37. Testimony of Speed, *Impeachment Investigation*, 809–10.

38. *Report of the Joint Committee on Reconstruction*, 6–10.

39. *Report of the Joint Committee on Reconstruction*, 129–36.

40. Brown Pryor, *Reading the Man*, 45.

41. Herman Melville, "Lee in the Capitol," http://www.online-literature.com/melville/3769/.

42. Earl Maltz, "Radical Politics and Constitutional Theory," *Michigan Historical Review* 32 (Spring 2006): 20.

43. Lowe, "Testimony from the Old Dominion before the Joint Committee on Reconstruction," 387.

44. Lowe, "Testimony from the Old Dominion," 386.

45. Thomas, *Robert E. Lee*, 383.

46. Freeman, *R. E. Lee*, vol. 4, 256.

47. Freeman, *R. E. Lee*, vol. 4, 257.

CHAPTER 8

1. Robert E. Lee to Amanda Parks, March 9, 1866, *DeButts-Ely collection*.

2. *New York Daily Tribune*, March 26, 1866.

3. *New York Daily Tribune*, June 24, 1859; see also, *Carroll County Democrat*, June 2, 1859, for an early account of the capture of the slaves.

4. Varon, *Appomattox*, 233.

5. *The Independent*, April 5, 1866.

6. Lee to George Fox, April 13, 1866, *DeButts-Ely collection*.

7. Mary Custis Lee to W. G. Webster, February 17, 1858, *Mary Lee Papers*, Library of Virginia.

8. Jones, *Life and Letters*, 82–84.

9. *Report of the Joint Committee on Reconstruction*, 136.

10. Freeman, *R. E. Lee*, vol. 1, 390.

11. Brown Pryor, *Reading the Man*, 270.

12. *Carroll County Democrat*, June 2, 1859; *New York Daily Tribune*, June 24, 1859.

13. "The Erotic South," *Liberator*, October 8, 1858.

14. *New York Daily Tribune*, June 28, 1859.

15. *Raftsman's Journal*, May 27, 1863.

16. *Courier & Gazette*, June 15, 1863; for an excellent discussion of this quote, see "Research Exercise: Rumor at Arlington," *Crossroads*, June 24, 2011, https://cwcrossroads .wordpress.com/2011/06/14/research-exercise-rumor-at-arlington/.

17. "Why the Lee Quote Is Still Valid," Interpreting the Civil War, June 16, 2011, http://www.civilwarconnect.com/2011/06/html.

18. *National Anti-Slavery Standard*, August 1, 1865.

19. Lee to G. W. Custis in J. William Jones, *Life and Letters*, 100–102.

20. Robert Vaughn, "Notes on the United States Since the War," *British Quarterly Review* 42 (July and October 1865): 469.

21. Lee to E. J. Quirk, March 1, 1866, *DeButts-Ely collection*.

22. *The Independent*, June 4, 1868.

23. A complete copy in Karl Decker and Angus McSween, *Historic Arlington* (Washington, DC: Decker and McSween Publishing, 1892), 80–81.

24. *EXR George Washington Parke Custis v. Mary Ann Randolph Lee*, etc, Chancery Court Records, Arlington County, Case no. 1859–017, Accession 43749, Box 88, Library of Virginia; Joe Ryan, "General Lee: Slave Whipper?," *American Civil War*, http://joeryancivil war.com/Civil-War-Subjects/General Lee-Slaves/General-Lee-Slave-Whipper.html; Murray H. Nelligan, "Old Arlington," PhD Dissertation, Columbia University, 1954, 407–10.

25. "The Slaves of Mr. Custis," *Boston Traveller*, December 24, 1857.

26. *New York Times*, January 8, 1858.

27. Decker and McSween, *Historic Arlington*, 80–81.

28. Note of Argument for Appellant, *Custis's Exr. v. Lee and Others*, Supreme Court of Appeals of Virginia, Alexandria Library.

29. Emory Thomas, *Robert E. Lee*, 176.

30. George Washington Parke Custis to William Winston, *Papers of George Washington*, Reel #4, Mount Vernon.

31. Thomas, *Robert E. Lee*, 177.

32. *EXR George Washington Parke Custis v. Mary Ann Randolph Lee*, etc, Chancery Court Records, Arlington County, Case no. 1859–017, Accession 43749, Box 88, Library of Virginia.

33. *EXR George Washington Parke Custis v. Mary Ann Randolph Lee*.

34. *EXR George Washington Parke Custis v. Mary Ann Randolph Lee*; see also Jonathan Horn, *The Man Who Would Not Be Washington: Robert E. Lee's Civil War* (New York: Scribner, 2015), 168.

35. Note of Argument for Appellant, *Custis's Exr. v. Lee and Others*, Supreme Court of Appeals of Virginia, Alexandria Library.

36. Horn, *The Man Who Would Not Be Washington*, 168–69.

37. Horn, *The Man Who Would Not Be Washington*, 169; see also Lee to G. W. C. Lee, January 4, 1862, in Clifford Dowdey, ed., *The Wartime Papers of R. E. Lee* (Boston: Little, Brown, 1961), 100–101.

38. Lee to G. W. C. Lee, January 19, 1862, in *The Wartime Papers*, 104–06.

39. Deed of Manumission, December 29, 1862, Museum of the Confederacy, http://www.moc.org/sites/default/files/PDFs/manumission_document.pdf.

40. Lee to Seddon, January 10, 1863, in *The Wartime Papers*, 388–90.

41. Thomas, *Robert E. Lee*, 56.

42. *DeButts-Ely Collection of Lee Family Papers, 1749–1914*, Library of Congress.

43. Joseph Robert, "Lee the Farmer," *Journal of Southern History* 3 (November 1937): 422–40.

44. Lee to W. O. Winston, July 12, 1858, The Gilder Lehrman Institution of American History. Custis-Lee family papers.

45. Robert, "Lee the Farmer," *Journal of Southern History*, 422–40.

46. Thomas, *Robert E. Lee*, 72.

47. Robert, "Lee the Farmer," *Journal of Southern History*, 422–40.

48. Jones, *Life and Letters*, 90–91.

49. Thomas, *Robert E. Lee*, 174.

50. George Washington Parke Custis to William Winston, *Papers of George Washington*, Reel #4, Mount Vernon.

51. Jones, *Life and Letters*, 82–84.

52. Lee to Andrew Hunter, January 11, 1865 in *OR*, series 4, vol. 3, 1012–13.

53. "An Interview with Gen. Robert E. Lee," *Century Magazine*, May 1885, 166.

CHAPTER 9

1. Johnson would issue another proclamation declaring the war at an end in all southern states including Texas on August 20, 1866.

2. Captain Lee, *Recollections of Lee*, 220–21.

3. William Cooper, *Jefferson Davis, American* (New York: Alfred Knopf, 2000), 533, 558–59.

4. Lee to Varina Davis, February 23, 1866, *DeButts-Ely collection*.

5. Cooper, *Jefferson Davis*, 536–67.

6. Speed letter, January 6, 1866, *Impeachment Investigation*, 422–23.

7. For the cabinet's view, see Speed's testimony, *Impeachment Investigation*, 791–813.

8. Witt, *Lincoln's Code*, 317–24.

9. Testimony of Underwood: *Report of the Joint Committee on Reconstruction*, 10.

10. Chase to Greeley, June 25, 1866, in Robert Warden, *An Account of the Private Life and Public Services of Salmon Portland Chase* (Cincinnati: Wilstach, Baldwin), 662–63.

11. Schuckers, *The Life of Salmon Portland Chase*, 52.

12. Speed letter, January 6, 1866, *Impeachment Investigation*, 422–23; see also Roy Nichols, "United States vs. Jefferson Davis, 1865–1869," *American Historical Review* 31, no. 2 (January 1926): 267–68.

13. Freidel, *Francis Lieber*, 374.

14. Senator Howard, *The Congressional Globe*, First Session, 39th Congress (1866), 569.

15. "John C. Underwood," *Encyclopedia Virginia*, https://www.encyclopediavirginia
.org/Underwood_John_C_1809-1873#start_entry.

16. "Jefferson Davis Indicted," *New York Times*, May 12, 1866.

17. "Jefferson Davis Indicted."

18. "Trial of Jeff. Davis," *Baltimore Sun*, June 6, 1866.

19. "Judge Underwood's Charge," *New York Times*, June 9, 1866.

20. Freeman, *R. E. Lee*, vol. 4, note 12, 336.

21. H. B. Stowe, "The Death of Another Veteran, With Reminiscences of the Conflict," *Christian Union* 9 (January 7, 1874): 1.

22. Nichols, "United States vs. Jefferson Davis, 1865–1869," 267–71; Bradley T. Johnson, *Cases Decided by Chief Justice Chase*, 9–42.

23. Testimony of Chase, *Impeachment Investigation*, 544–45.

24. Welles, *Diary* (2), 366.

25. John Niven, ed., *The Salmon P. Chase Papers, Correspondence, 1865–1873*, vol. 5 (Kent, OH: Kent State University Press, 1998), 183–84; Testimony of Chase, *Impeachment Investigation*, 544–49; White, "The Trial of Jefferson Davis," 128.

26. Chase to Jacob Schuckers, May 15, 1866, in Niven, *The Salmon P. Chase Papers*, 183–84; Testimony of Lucius Chandler, *Impeachment Investigation*, 96.

27. White, "The Trial of Jefferson Davis," 127–30.

28. White, "The Trial of Jefferson Davis," 127–30.

29. Emory Thomas, *Robert E. Lee*, 387.

30. John Warwick Daniel, *Life and Reminscences of Jefferson Davis* (Baltimore: R.H. Woodward, 1890), 412.

31. *New York Times*, May 4, 1865.

32. Carl Lokke, "The Captured Confederate Records under Francis Lieber," *The American Archivist*, no. 4 (October 1946): 311.

33. David Dewitt, *The Impeachment and Trial of Andrew Johnson* (New York: Macmillan, 1903), 114–23.

34. Dewitt, *The Impeachment*, 116.

35. Trefousse, *Johnson*, 266.

36. William McFeely, *Grant* (New York: W.W. Norton, 1982), 252.

37. Paul Bergeron, ed., *Johnson Papers* (11), 316.

38. For an excellent narrative of the Davis case, see Nichols, "United States vs. Jefferson Davis, 1865–1869."

39. J. William Jones, *Personal Reminiscences of Lee*, 258–59.

40. Nichols, "United States vs. Jefferson Davis, 1865–1869," 275.

41. Nichols, "United States vs. Jefferson Davis, 1865–1869," 276.

42. *Chicago Tribune*, May 23, 1867; "The First Integrated Jury Impaneled in the United States," *Negro History Bulletin* 33 (October 1, 1970): 134.

43. *Chicago Tribune*, May 23, 1867.

44. *Chicago Tribune*, May 23, 1867.

45. *New York Times*, October 28, 1867.

46. See Dunbar Rowland, ed., *Jefferson Davis Constitutionalist*, vol. 7 (Jackson: Mississippi Department of Archives and History, 1923), 126–29.

47. Trefousse, *Johnson*, 337.

48. Andrew Johnson, "Proclamation 170," *The American Presidency Project*, http://www
.presidency.ucsb.edu/ws/?pid=72270.

49. Welles, *Diary* (3), 409.

50. Dana to Evarts, August 24, 1868, *Andrew Johnson papers, 1783–1947*, Library of Congress; Richard Henry Dana, "The Reasons for Not Prosecuting Jefferson Davis," *Proceedings of the Massachusetts Historical Society* 64, 205–08.

51. Nichols, "United States vs. Jefferson Davis, 1865–1869," 282.
52. Nichols, "United States vs. Jefferson Davis, 1865–1869," 282.
53. "The Christmas Pardon," *Chicago Tribune*, January 1, 1869.
54. *New York Times*, February 14, 1869.
55. Dorris, *Pardon and Amnesty*, 389.
56. Blair, *With Malice toward Some*, 13.
57. "Anecdotes of Andrew Johnson," *Century Magazine*, 440.
58. *New York Times*, March 4, 1869.
59. *The Boston Globe*, May 15, 1872.

CHAPTER 10

1. "What Jubal Early Thinks of the Amnesty Proclamation," *New York Times*, January 17, 1869.
2. Millard Bushong, *Old Jube: A Biography of General Jubal A. Early* (Boyce, VA: Carr Publishing, 1955), 289.
3. Bushong, *Old Jube*, 289.
4. Bushong, *Old Jube*, 297.
5. Connelly, *The Marble Man*, 51.
6. Gary Gallagher, "Jubal Early, the Lost Cause, and Civil War History," in *The Myth of the Lost Cause and Civil War History*, ed. Gary Gallagher and Alan Nolan (Bloomington: Indiana University Press, 2010), 39.
7. Jubal Early to Sam Early, September 6, 1868, *Jubal Anderson Early Papers, 1829–1930*, Library of Congress.
8. Freeman, *R. E. Lee*, vol. 4, 192.
9. Lee to W. H. Taylor quoted in Walter Herron Taylor, *Four Years with General Lee*, 155.
10. Freeman, *R. E. Lee*, vol. 4, 206.
11. Lee to Fitzhugh Lee in Captain Lee, *Recollections of Lee*, 177–78.
12. J. William Jones, *Personal Reminiscences of Lee*, 142.
13. Freeman, *R. E. Lee*, vol. 4, 388.
14. For an excellent summary of the legal issues relating to Arlington, see Anthony Gaughan, *The Last Battle of the Civil War* (Baton Rouge: Louisiana State University Press, 2011), 1–11.
15. Brown Pryor, *Reading the Man*, 311–16.
16. Quoted in Robert O'Harrow, *The Quartermaster: Montgomery C. Meigs, Lincoln's General, Master Builder* (New York: Simon & Schuster, 2016), 207.
17. Brown Pryor, *Reading the Man*, 313.
18. Connelly, *The Marble Man*, 35.
19. Brown Pryor, *Reading the Man*, 313.
20. Brown Pryor, *Reading the Man*, 446.
21. Jones, *Life and Letters*, 156.
22. Captain Lee, *Recollections of Lee*, 32.
23. Freeman, *R. E. Lee*, vol. 4, 303.
24. Freeman, *R. E. Lee*, vol. 1, 421.
25. Brown Pryor, *Reading the Man*, 450.
26. Freeman, *R. E. Lee*, vol. 1, 421.
27. Freeman, *R. E. Lee*, vol. 4, 302–06; John Neville Figgis, ed., *Selections from the Correspondence of the First Lord Acton*, vol. 1 (London: Longmans, Green, 1917), 302–05.

28. *Robert E. Lee Papers*, Washington and Lee University.

29. *Report of the Joint Committee on Reconstruction*, 133.

30. "An Hour with General Grant," *New York Times*, May 24, 1866; Varon, *Appomattox*, 238–39.

31. *New York Times*, September 5, 1868; Flood, *The Last Years*, 195–98; Brown Pryor, *Reading the Man*, 451–54.

32. *New York Times*, September 5, 1868.

33. Duke of Argyll, *Passages from the Past*, vol. 1 (London: Hutchinson), 166.

34. Duke of Argyll, *Passages from the Past*, 166.

35. Captain Lee, *Recollections of Lee*, 306.

36. Bruce Levine quoted in David Blight, "Desperate Measures," *Washington Post*, March 5, 2006.

37. Michael Fellman, *The Making of Robert E. Lee* (Baltimore: Johns Hopkins University Press, 2000), 280.

38. Susan Lawrence Davis, *Authentic History: Ku Klux Klan, 1865–1877* (New York: Susan Lawrence Davis, 1924), 81, 204.

39. See note 70 in Freeman, *R. E. Lee*, vol. 4, 317.

40. "Negro Communed at St. Paul's Church," *The Times-Dispatch*, April 16, 1905.

41. Jay Winik, *April 1865* (New York: Harper Perennial, 2001), 362–63.

42. Andy Hall, "Fantasizing Lee as a Civil Rights Pioneer," *The Civil War Monitor*, http://www.civilwarmonitor.com/front-line/fantasizing-lee-as-a-civil-rights-pioneer.

43. Captain Lee, *Recollections of Lee*, 381–83.

44. Captain Lee, *Recollections of Lee*, 380.

45. Captain Lee, *Recollections of Lee*, 396.

46. Freeman, *R. E. Lee*, vol. 4, 521–25.

47. Jones, *Personal Reminiscences of Lee*, 213.

48. *New York Times*, April 18, 1865.

49. "Bombast," *New National Era*, November 10, 1870.

50. Senator McCreery, *The Congressional Globe*, First Session, 41st Congress, 3rd Session (1870), 73.

51. See *The Congressional Globe*, First Session, 41st Congress, 3rd Session (1870), 73–82.

CHAPTER 11

1. "Address of Jubal Early," *Proceedings of the Southern Historical Society Convention*, August 14, 1873, 27.

2. "Address of Jubal Early," 27.

3. "Address of Jubal Early," 27.

4. Connelly, *The Marble Man*, 51.

5. Connelly, *The Marble Man*, 72–78.

6. Connelly, *The Marble Man*, 72.

7. Connelly, *The Marble Man*, 47–48.

8. Alan Nolan, "The Anatomy of a Myth," in *The Myth of the Lost Cause and Civil War History*, 12.

9. "What Caused the Civil War?" *Pew Research Center*, http://www.pewresearch.org/fact-tank/2011/05/18/what-caused-the-civil-war/; *Washington Post*, August 6, 2015.

10. According to James Cobb, the term "Lost Cause" was appropriated from Sir Walter Scott's description of the Scottish struggle for independence, *New York Times*, August 22, 2017.

11. Edward Pollard, *The Lost Cause* (New York: E.B. Treat, 1867), 49.

12. Pollard, *The Lost Cause*, 752.

13. Edward Pollard, *The Lost Cause Regained* (New York: G.W. Carleton, 1868), 14.

14. "Preface to Early's Memoir," in *New York Times*, January 7, 1867.

15. "Preface to Early's Memoir."

16. Alan Nolan, *Lee Considered* (Chapel Hill: University of North Carolina Press, 1991), 164.

17. Abraham Lincoln, "Second Inaugural," *The Atlantic Online*, https://www.theatlantic.com/past/docs/issues/99sep/9909lincaddress.htm.

18. Alexander Stephens, "Corner Stone Speech," TeachingAmericanHistory.org, http://teachingamericanhistory.org/library/document/cornerstone-speech/.

19. Drew Gilpin Faust, *The Creation of Confederate Nationalism* (Baton Rouge: Louisiana State University Press, 1989), 60.

20. "The Declaration of Causes of Seceding States," *Civil War Trust*, https://www.civilwar.org/learn/primary-sources/declaration-causes-seceding-states.

21. Charles Dew, *Apostles of Disunion: Southern Secession Commissioners and the Causes of the Civil War* (Charlottesville: University of Virginia Press, 2001), 81.

22. Gary Gallagher, *Lee and His Generals in War and Memory* (Baton Rouge: Louisiana State University Press, 1998), 224.

23. *Proceedings of the Southern Historical Society Convention*, vol. 17, 190.

24. *Proceedings of the Southern Historical Society Convention*, vol. 17, 262–335; "The Lee Statue Unveiled," *New York Times*, May 30, 1890; see also *Richmond Dispatch*, May 29 and 30, 1890.

25. Archer Anderson, "Robert E. Lee, An Address," *Lee Monument Association* (Richmond, VA: Wm. Ellis Jones, 1890).

26. *Richmond Dispatch*, May 30, 1890.

27. *New York Times*, May 30, 1890.

28. Sarah Shields, Richard Guy Williams, and Robert Winthrop, *Richmond's Monument Avenue* (Chapel Hill: University of North Carolina Press, 2001), 49.

29. "What It Means," *Richmond Planet*, May 31, 1870.

30. "The Feeling in Dixie," *Richmond Planet*, June 7, 1890.

31. "What It Means," *Richmond Planet*, May 31, 1870.

32. Blight, *Race and Reunion*, 260.

33. *Richmond Planet*, June 7, 1890.

34. Blight, *Race and Reunion*, 271.

35. Blight, *Race and Reunion*, 272.

36. Henry James, *The American Scene*, 369.

37. Henry James, *The American Scene*, 393.

38. Henry James, *The American Scene*, 394.

39. Henry James, *The American Scene*, 394.

APPENDIX B

1. Dana to Evarts, August 24, 1868, *Andrew Johnson Papers, 1783–1947*, Library of Congress.

SELECTED BIBLIOGRAPHY

MANUSCRIPTS

Library of Congress

Zachariah Chandler Papers
Salmon P. Chase Papers
Lydia Maria Francis Child Correspondence
Custis-Lee Family Papers
DeButts-Ely collection of Lee Family Papers
Frederick Douglass Papers
Jubal Anderson Early Papers
Joseph Smith Fowler Papers
Joshua R. Giddings and George Washington Julian Papers
Ulysses S. Grant Papers
Joseph Holt Papers
Andrew Johnson Papers
Edwin McMasters Stanton Papers
John C. Underwood Papers

Library of Virginia

Case files of applications for presidential pardons from former Virginia Confederates
Robert E. Lee Papers in the collections of Duke University
Executive papers of Governor Francis H. Pierpont
Walter Herron Taylor Papers
John C. Underwood Papers from The Huntington Library Collection
US Circuit Court (Fifth Circuit). Court records, 1790–1882.

National Archives and Records Administration, Washington DC, and College Park, Maryland

General Records of the Department of Justice (RG 60)
Attorney General Papers: Letters Sent; Letters Received
General Records of the Department of State (RG 59)
Records of the Adjutant General's Office, 1780s–1917 (RG 94)
War Department Collection of Confederate Records (RG 109)
Amnesty Papers

Virginia Historical Society

Robert Edward Lee Papers

Washington and Lee University, Lexington, Virginia

Robert E. Lee Papers

PERIODICALS

Alexandria (Va.) Gazette
Baltimore Sun
Century Magazine
Chicago Tribune
Cleveland Morning Leader
Congressional Record
Harper's Weekly
The Independent
The Liberator
The Nation
National Anti-Slavery Standard
New National Era
New York Herald
New York Times
New York Tribune
Philadelphia Inquirer
Raftsman's Journal
Richmond Dispatch
Richmond Planet
Southern Historical Society Papers

Printed Primary Sources

Blaine, James. *Twenty Years of Congress*, 2 vols. Norwich: Henry Bill Publishing, 1884.

Craven, Avery, ed. *"To Markie": The Letters of Robert E. Lee to Martha Custis Williams.* Cambridge, MA: Harvard University Press, 1933.

Dowdey, Clifford, and Louis H. Manarin, eds. *The Wartime Papers of R. E. Lee.* Boston: Little, Brown, 1961.

Graf, LeRoy, ed. *Andrew Johnson Papers*, vol. 7. Knoxville: University of Tennessee Press, 1986.

Grant, Ulysses S. *Personal Memoirs of U. S. Grant.* New York: Da Capo Press, 1982.

Johnson, Bradley. *Reports of Cases Decided by Chief Justice Chase.* New York: Diossy, 1876.

Jones, J. William, ed. *Life and Letters of Robert E. Lee: Soldier and Man.* New York: Neale Publishing, 1906.

———, ed. *Personal Reminiscences, Anecdotes, and Letters of Gen. Robert E. Lee.* New York: D. Appleton, 1867.

Julian, George W. *Political Recollections, 1840–1872.* Chicago: Jansen, McClurg, 1883.

———. *Speeches on Political Questions.* New York: Hurd and Houghton, 1872.

Lee, Fitzhugh. *General Lee.* New York: D. Appleton, 1895.

Longstreet, James. *From Manassas to Appomattox: Memoirs of the Civil War in America.* New York: J.B. Lippincott, 1896.

Marshall, Charles. *Appomattox: An Address.* Baltimore: Guggenheimer, Weil & Co., 1894.

Meade, George. *The Life and Letters of George Gordon Meade*, vol. 2. New York: Charles Scribner's Sons, 1913.

Niven, John, ed. *The Salmon P. Chase Papers, Correspondence, 1865–1873*, vol. 5. Kent, OH: Kent State University Press, 1998.

Official Opinions of the Attorneys General, vol. 11. Washington, DC: W.H. & O.H. Morrison, 1869.

Porter, David D. *Incidents and Anecdotes of the Civil War.* New York: D. Appleton, 1886.

Preston, Walter Creigh. *Lee: West Point and Lexington.* Yellow Springs, OH: Antioch Press, 1934.

Quint, Alonzo. *Three Sermons Preached in the North Congregational Church, New Bedford, Mass.* New Bedford, MA: Mercury Job Press, 1865.

Reid, Whitelaw. *After the War: A Southern Tour.* New York: Moore, Wilstach & Baldwin, 1866.

Roach, A. C. *The Prisoner of War.* Indianapolis, IN: Railroad City Publishers, 1865.

Simon, John Y., ed. *The Papers of Ulysses S. Grant*, vol. 15. Carbondale: Southern Illinois Press, 1967.

Townsend, George Alfred. *The Life, Crime, and Capture of John Wilkes Booth.* New York: Dick & Fitzgerald, 1865.

U.S. Congress. *Impeachment Investigation: Testimony Taken before the Judiciary Committee of the House of Representatives.* Washington, DC: Government Printing Office, 1867.

————. *Report of the Reconstruction Committee.* 39th Cong., 1st sess., 1865–1866. Washington, DC: Government Printing Office, 1866.

U.S. War Department. *War of the Rebellion, A Compilation of the Official Records of the Union and Confederate Armies,* 127 vols. Washington, DC: Government Printing Office, 1880–1901.

Welles, Gideon. *Diary of Gideon Welles,* 3 vols. Boston: Houghton Mifflin, 1911.

Williamson, James. *Prison Life in the Old Capitol.* New Jersey: 1911.

SECONDARY WORKS

Avary, Myrta Lockett. *Dixie after the War.* New York: Doubleday, 1906.

Badeau, Adam. *Grant in Peace from Appomattox to Mount McGregor.* Hartford: S.S. Scranton, 1887.

————. *Military History of Ulysses S. Grant,* vol. 3. New York: D. Appleton and Co., 1867.

Blair, William. *With Malice toward Some: Treason and Loyalty in the Civil War Era.* Chapel Hill: University of North Carolina Press, 2014.

Blight, David. *Race and Reunion.* Cambridge, MA: Belknap Press, 2001.

Bushong, Millard. *Old Jube: A Biography of General Jubal A. Early.* Boyce, VA: Carr Publishing, 1955.

Catton, Bruce. *U. S. Grant and the American Military Tradition.* New York: Open Road, 2013.

Chipman, N. P. *The Tragedy of Andersonville.* San Francisco: Blair-Murdoch, 1911.

Connelly, Thomas. *Marble Man: Robert E. Lee and His Image in American Society.* Baton Rouge: Louisiana State University Press, 1977.

Cooper, William. *Jefferson Davis, American.* New York: Alfred Knopf, 2000.

Crenshaw, Ollinger. *General Lee's College.* New York: Random House, 1969.

Davis, Susan Lawrence. *Authentic History: Ku Klux Klan, 1865–1877.* New York: Susan Lawrence Davis, 1924.

Decker, Karl, and Angus McSween. *Historic Arlington.* Washington, DC: Decker & McSween, 1892.

DeWitt, David Miller. *The Assassination of Abraham Lincoln and Its Expiation.* New York: Macmillan, 1909.

————. *The Impeachment and Trial of Andrew Johnson.* New York: Macmillan, 1903.

Dorris, Jonathan Truman. *Pardon and Amnesty under Lincoln and Johnson.* Chapel Hill: University of North Carolina Press, 1953.

Du Bois, W. E. B. *Black Reconstruction in America, 1860–1880.* New York: Free Press, 1992.

Epstein, Daniel Mark. *Lincoln and Whitman.* New York: Random House, 2004.

Faust, Drew Gilpin. *This Republic of Suffering.* New York: Vintage, 2009.

Fellman, Michael. *The Making of Robert E. Lee.* New York: Random House, 2000.

Flood, Charles Bracelen. *Lee: The Last Years.* Boston: Houghton Mifflin, 1998.

Foner, Eric. *Reconstruction: America's Unfinished Revolution, 1863–1877*. New York: Harper and Row, 1988.

Freeman, Douglass Southall. *R. E. Lee*, 4 vols. New York: Charles Scribner's Sons, 1934–1937.

Freidel, Frank. *Francis Lieber: Nineteenth Century Liberal*. Baton Rouge: Louisiana State Press, 1947.

Gallagher, Gary, and Nolan, Alan, eds. *The Myth of the Lost Cause and Civil War History*. Bloomington: Indiana University Press, 2010.

Garland, Hamlin. *Ulysses S. Grant: His Life and Character*. New York: Doubleday & McClure, 1898.

Gaughan, Anthony. *The Last Battle of the Civil War*. Baton Rouge: Louisiana State Press, 2011.

Gordon-Reed, Annette. *Andrew Johnson*. New York: Time Books, 2011.

Hodes, Martha. *Mourning Lincoln*. New Haven, CT: Yale University Press, 2016.

Janney, Caroline. *Remembering the Civil War: Reunion and the Limits of Reconciliation*. Chapel Hill: University of North Carolina Press, 2013.

Kauffman, Michael. *American Brutus: John Wilkes Booth and the Lincoln Conspiracies*. New York: Random House, 2004.

Lenman, Bruce. *The Jacobite Risings in Britain, 1689–1746*. London: Eyre Methuen, 1980.

Lowe, Richard. *Republicans and Reconstruction in Virginia, 1856–1870*. Charlottesville: University Press of Virginia, 1991.

Marvel, William. *Lincoln's Autocrat: The Life of Edwin Stanton*. Chapel Hill: University of North Carolina Press, 2015.

Maurice, Frederick, ed. *Lee's Aid-de Camp*. Lincoln: University of Nebraska Press, 2000.

McFeely, William. *Grant: A Biography*. New York: W.W. Norton, 1981.

McKitrick, Eric. *Andrew Johnson and Reconstruction*. Chicago: University of Chicago Press, 1860.

Melville, Herman. *The Battle-Pieces of Herman Melville*. Edited by Hennig Cohen. New York: Thomas Yoseloff, 1963.

Meredith, Roy. *Mr. Lincoln's Camera Man, Mathew B. Brady*. New York: Dover, 1974.

Moreno, Paul D., and O'Neill, Jonathan, eds. *Constitutionalism in the Approach and Aftermath of the Civil War*. New York: Fordham University Press, 2013.

Neill, Edward. *Reminiscences of the Last Year of President Lincoln's Life*. St. Paul, MN: Pioneer Press, 1885.

Nelligan, Murray. "Old Arlington." PhD dissertation, Columbia University, 1954.

Newmyer, R. Kent. *The Treason Trial of Aaron Burr*. New York: Cambridge University Press, 2012.

Nivan, John. *Salmon P. Chase: A Biography*. New York: Oxford University Press, 1995.

Nolan, Alan. *Lee Considered*. Chapel Hill: University of North Carolina Press, 1991.

O'Harrow, Robert. *The Quartermaster: Montgomery C. Meigs, Lincoln's General, Master Builder*. New York: Simon & Schuster, 2016.

Pollard, Edward. *The Lost Cause*. New York: E.B. Treat., 1867.

————. *The Lost Cause Regained*. New York: G.W. Carleton, 1868.

Pryor, Elizabeth Brown. *Reading the Man: A Portrait of Robert E. Lee through His Private Letters*. New York: Penguin, 2007.

Riley, Franklin, ed. *General Lee after Appomattox*. New York: Macmillan, 1922.

Sanborne, Margaret. *Robert E. Lee: The Complete Man, 1861–1870*. Philadelphia: J.B. Lippincott, 1967.

Schuckers, Jacob. *The Life of Salmon Portland Chase*. New York: D. Appleton, 1874.

Simpson, Brooks. *Let Us Have Peace*. Chapel Hill: University of North Carolina Press, 1997.

————. *Ulysses S. Grant: Triumph over Adversity*. Minneapolis, MN: Houghton Mifflin, 2000.

Thomas, Emory. *Robert E. Lee*. New York: W.W. Norton, 1995.

Trefousse, Hans. *Andrew Johnson*. New York: W.W. Norton, 1989.

————. *The Radical Republicans*. New York: Knopf, 1968.

Varon, Elizabeth. *Appomattox: Victory, Defeat, and Freedom at the End of the Civil War*. New York: Oxford University Press, 2014.

Wilson, Robert. *Mathew Brady: Portraits of a Nation*. New York: Bloomsbury, 2014.

Wilson, Woodrow. *Robert E. Lee: An Interpretation*. Chapel Hill: University of North Carolina Press, 1924.

Winik, Jay. *April 1866*. New York: Harper Perennial, 2006.

Witt, John Fabian. *Lincoln's Code: The Laws of War in American History*. New York: Simon & Schuster, 2012.

Young, John Russell. *Around the World with General Grant*. New York: Subscription Book Department, 1879.

INDEX

ABOUT THE AUTHOR

John Reeves has been a teacher, editor, and writer for over twenty-five years. The Civil War, in particular, has been his passion since he first read Bruce Catton's *The American Heritage Picture History of the Civil War* as an elementary school student in the 1960s. Recently, John's articles on Robert E. Lee have been featured in the *Washington Post* and on the History News Network.

Earlier in his career, he taught European and American history at various colleges in Chicago, the Bronx, and London. He graduated Phi Beta Kappa with a bachelor's in economics from Syracuse University in 1984. Later, he received a master's in European history from the University of Massachusetts at Amherst and pursued a PhD in history at the University of Illinois at Chicago. His dissertation was on Britain's role in Persia in the late nineteenth and early twentieth centuries.

Throughout his career, Reeves has tried to make history lively and accessible for ordinary readers and students. Over the years, he has taught European and American history at Lehman College, Bronx Community College, and Southbank University in London. His next book is on the Battle of the Wilderness. He lives in Washington, DC, with his wife and two children.